RUSSIAN YOUTH

In the generation that has passed, what have we learned about the rule of law, legality, legal reasoning, and deviance in Russia? And what about the general subject of legal socialization—how young people learn about rules, norms, and laws; what their attitudes about rules and laws are; and, if and whether this knowledge and these attitudes shape their behavior? The second edition of *Russian Youth* asks and answers these questions.

James O. Finckenauer is a Professorial Fellow in the Division of Global Affairs at Rutgers University, USA. He previously served the School of Criminal Justice from 1974 to 2011 as an Associate Professor, Professor I, and Professor II. He also served as President of the NJ Council of Educational Institutions for Law Enforcement, the Academy of Criminal Justice Sciences, and the International Association for the Study of Organized Crime. He was a visiting professor in Australia, China, Germany, Japan, and Russia, and studied or lectured in Europe, Asia, the former Soviet Union, Latin America, and the Middle East. From 1998 to 2002, he was Director of the International Center at the National Institute of Justice of the U.S. Department of Justice, while on academic leave; and in 2007 he was a Fulbright Senior Specialist in Hong Kong.

RUSSIAN YOUTH

Law, Deviance, and
the Pursuit of Freedom

Second Edition

James O. Finckenauer

NEW YORK AND LONDON

Second edition published 2018
by Routledge
711 Third Avenue, New York, NY 10017

and by Routledge
2 Park Square, Milton Park, Abingdon, Oxon, OX14 4RN

Routledge is an imprint of the Taylor & Francis Group, an informa business

© 2018 Taylor & Francis

The right of James O. Finckenauer to be identified as author of this work has been asserted by him in accordance with sections 77 and 78 of the Copyright, Designs and Patents Act 1988.

All rights reserved. No part of this book may be reprinted or reproduced or utilised in any form or by any electronic, mechanical, or other means, now known or hereafter invented, including photocopying and recording, or in any information storage or retrieval system, without permission in writing from the publishers.

Trademark notice: Product or corporate names may be trademarks or registered trademarks, and are used only for identification and explanation without intent to infringe.

First edition published by Transaction Publishers 1995

Library of Congress Cataloging-in-Publication Data
A catalog record for this book has been requested

ISBN: 978-1-138-55891-5 (hbk)
ISBN: 978-1-138-55897-7 (pbk)
ISBN: 978-1-315-12118-5 (ebk)

Typeset in Bembo
by Keystroke, Neville Lodge, Tettenhall, Wolverhampton

CONTENTS

List of Tables	*vii*
Foreword	*ix*
Preface	*xiii*

Introduction to the Second Edition	1
1 Legal Socialization in Disparate Legal Contexts	14
2 Foundations for the Study of Legal Socialization	32
3 Law and Law Reform	48
4 Crime, Delinquency, and Youth Problems	67
5 Corruption, the Shadow Economy, and Organized Crime: An Unsavory Context for Learning Legality	86
6 The Joys and Sorrows of Cross-Cultural Research	101
7 A Soviet and an American View of the Law	111
8 Law and Deviance through the Eyes of Russian Youth	141

vi Contents

9 Three Perspectives: American, Soviet, and Russian   166

10 Voices of a New Russia   180

Appendix   *190*
Bibliography   *197*
Index   *209*

TABLES

2.1	Dimensions of Legal Consciousness	45
5.1	Colored Markets in the USSR	91
7.1	Guilt About Breaking the Teacher's Rules by Country, Sex, and Delinquency Status, with Age	121
7.2	Correlation Matrix of Attitudes: United States	127
7.3	Correlation Matrix of Attitudes: Soviet Union	128
7.4	The Teacher as an Authority Figure by Country, Sex, and Delinquency Status, with Age	129
7.5	The Parent as an Authority Figure by Country, Sex, and Delinquency Status, with Age	130
7.6a	Peers as Authority Figures by Country, Sex, and Delinquency Status, with Age	131
7.6b	Deviant Peers as Authority Figures by Country, Sex, and Delinquency Status, with Age	132
7.7	Law Fairness by Country, Sex, and Delinquency Status, with Age	133
7.8	Law Efficacy by Country, Sex, and Delinquency Status, with Age	135
7.9	Law Operatives by Country, Sex, and Delinquency Status, with Age	135
7.10	Moral Validity of Law by Country, Sex, and Delinquency Status, with Age	137
7.11	Wrongfulness of Behaviors by Country, Sex, and Delinquency Status, with Age	137
7.12	Own Law-Abidingness by Country, Sex, and Delinquency Status, with Age	138

viii Tables

8.1	Attitudinal Correlates of Legal Reasoning (LDL)	147
8.2	Legal Developmental Level by Delinquency Status and Sex, with Age and Knowledge of the Law	149
8.3	Status Correlates of Legal Reasoning (LDL)	150
8.4	Delinquency Index by Age, KOL, LDL, OLABIDE, MORALV, Sex, and LFAIR	153
8.5	Moral Validity by Sex and Delinquency Status, with KOL, Age, and LDL	156
8.6	Law Fairness by Sex and Delinquency Status, with KOL, Age, and LDL	157
8.7	Law Efficacy by Sex and Delinquency Status, with KOL, Age, and LDL	157
8.8	Law Operatives by Sex and Delinquency Status, with KOL, Age, and LDL	158
8.9	Wrongfulness of Behaviors by Sex and Delinquency Status, with KOL, Age, and LDL	159
8.10	Own Law-Abidingness by Sex and Delinquency Status, with KOL, Age, and LDL	160
8.11	Peers by Sex and Delinquency Status, with KOL, Age, and LDL	161
8.12	Teachers by Sex and Delinquency Status, with KOL, Age, and LDL	162
8.13	Status Correlates of Delinquent Behavior	162
8.14	Delinquency Index by LDL, Age, KOL, and Status/KOL	162
8.15	Delinquency Index by Sex, KOL, LDL, and Age	163
8.16	Predicting Seriousness of Delinquency	163
9.1	Comparative Legal Socialization Levels	169
9.2	American, Soviet, and Russian Attitudinal Correlates of Moral Validity	172
9.3	Normative Views of Deviance by Delinquency Level and Sex, with Age	178
A.1	Reliability/Validity of ILVI	192

FOREWORD

Russia before the revolution enjoyed lively scholarly debates on crime and justice. Among the early criminologists of a sociological bent, A. F. Koni, M. P. Tchoubinsky, and M. N. Gernet stood out, as Boris Brasol—then recently exiled from Russia—informed his American audience in his remarkable work *The Elements of Crime (Psycho-Social Interpretation)* (Brasol, 1927: 3). Brasol himself was one of these pioneers, although his influence in Russia came too late, and in America perhaps too early (see Mueller, 1969: 91–2, 135). The revolution did not change Russians' interest in matters criminological.

During Lenin's years at the helm of the Soviet ship of state, criminology was a vibrant intellectual pursuit (Connor, 1972: 23–34). With Stalin's accession to power, this situation changed drastically. Criminology was replaced by party doctrine. Crime statistics became state secrets and empirical research became impossible, even if it had been allowed. Only after Stalin's death can we speak of an empirical science of criminology in the Soviet Union. Scientists at the Criminal Law Section of the All-Union Scientific Research Institute of Criminalistics (1957), the Scientific Research Institute of the Militia (1958), the All-Union Institute for the Study of the Causes and Elaboration of Measures of Prevention of Crime of the USSR Procuracy (1963), and, above all, the Institute of State and Law of the USSR Academy of Sciences (which traces its origins to 1922) began publishing research papers and critiquing each other. But throughout the 1960s, Soviet criminologists worked in relative isolation. Few of them visited the United States or other Western countries, and few American criminologists worked with Soviet counterparts. Yet, already in 1957, Soviet scholars participated in the work of the International Association of Penal Law, attending the congress of that association in Athens. From that point on, Soviet criminologists contributed actively to international criminological developments, especially the activities of

x Foreword

the United Nations. This international outreach reflected the confidence that Soviet scholars were gaining through the development of their discipline, and their impact on policymaking within the Soviet Union. Many distinguished scholars share the credit for the development of modern Soviet criminology, and perhaps this credit should go to them collectively since they worked largely in unison or contact with each other. But one name stands out as having earned particular merit for leadership in the re-establishment of criminology, that of academician Vladimir Nikolayevich Kudriavtsev.

Characteristically, he personally eschews such credit, claiming no honors for any of his numerous highly regarded and policy-setting publications (see Kudriavtsev, 1972, 1976, 1981, 1983, 1984). Having had the pleasure of working with a colleague as cracklingly bright and witty as Kudriavtsev during my years at the United Nations, in 1983 I proposed to him—during a criminological meeting in Milan, Italy—that he and his researchers join our team at Rutgers University for exploration of issues of common criminological interest. He readily agreed. In 1985, thanks to the support of the International Research and Exchanges Board (IREX), our Rutgers team sojourned to the Soviet Union for one of a series of conferences, in which we first focused on problems of urban crime. The Soviet team also visited Rutgers twice. The focus then shifted to exploring the question of how youngsters internalize society's values, and how such socialization impacts on juvenile delinquency. At this point, Professor James O. Finckenauer proposed, and we agreed, to undertake a joint empirical research project—the very first American–Soviet empirical research in this field. Under team leaders Finckenauer and Alexander Maksimovich Yakovlev, with the meritorious contribution of June Louin Tapp, all obstacles were overcome. The results are now before us. The book by Dr. Finckenauer, which builds upon the work by him and his colleagues, speaks for itself on what it proves from the criminological perspective.

Here I simply wish to point to what it proves from the perspective of international cooperation: criminology has become a global science, as it partakes of the globalization of all aspects of life. Cooperation among scholars cross-culturally is necessary and possible. Our cooperation with our Soviet colleagues dates to the period of the post-Khrushchev, pre-Gorbachev second Cold War. Yet even then we reached out, recognized each other as fellow human beings and fellow scientists, perhaps even as ambassadors of good will, for our example in the scientific sphere soon was emulated in the political sphere.

Democratization started in the waning days of the USSR and with it came ever-greater opportunities for our Soviet colleagues to engage in empirical research in their own country, as well as internationally with colleagues all over the world. But aside from these lofty achievements, there are some of immediate and practical impact. It is no accident that rule-of-law concepts, including such guarantees as the right to counsel in all criminal cases, the right to have one's conviction reviewed by the highest courts in the land and, indeed, to test the constitutional basis of statutory law, were introduced into the USSR *corpus juris*. These reforms that

Foreword **xi**

remain in Russian law were proposed, drafted, and fought through by our Soviet teammates, who had studied and witnessed their operational significance while working with us in the United States. Academician Kudriavtsev became vice president, first of the USSR Academy of Sciences, and then of the Russian Academy; and Professor Yakovlev became a member of the former Soviet Congress of People's Deputies. In their positions of leadership, they used every opportunity to promote the new rule-of-law concept. Whatever the final outcome of the latest Russian revolution, these reforms will ultimately find expression in the thoughts and behavior patterns of children and youth.

The learning experience has not been purely one-way. The American teammates have learned a lot about what it is that made for a low-crime society, alas one that has witnessed a rise in crime during the period of transition to democracy. Above all, they have gained tremendous respect for their Soviet, and now Russian colleagues who brazenly undertook the task of fundamental reform in the face of overwhelming odds, resistance, skepticism, or even derision from some quarters. May the spirit of cooperation persist; may we be able to count on each other for support, for the benefit of our own societies and all other societies on this earth.

G. O. W. Mueller
Professor of Criminal Justice
Chief (Ret.) UN Crime Prevention and
Criminal Justice Branch

References

Brasol, B. (1927) *The Elements of Crime (Psycho-Social Interpretation)*. New York: Oxford University Press, with introductions by J. H. Wigmore and W. A. White.

Connor, W. D. (1972) *Deviance in Soviet Society*, New York: Columbia University Press.

Kudriavtsev, V. N. (1972) *Obshchaia teoriia kvalifikatsii prestuplenii* (General Theory of Qualification of Crime) Moscow: Iurid.

Kudriavtsev, V. N. (1976) *Prichiny pravonarushenii* (Causes of Lawbreaking). Moscow: Nauka.

Kudriavtsev, V. N. (1981) *Mekhanizm prestupnogo povedeniia* (Mechanism of Criminal Behavior). Moscow: Nauka.

Kudriavtsev, V. N. (1983) *Mezhdunarodnoe sotrudnichesivo v borbe s ugolovnoi prestupnostiu* (International Collaboration in the Fight against Crime). Moscow: Mezhdunarodnye otnosheniia.

Kudriavtsev, V. N. (1984) *Problemy sovershenstvovaniia ugolovnogo zakona* (Problems of Perfecting Criminal Law). Moscow: AN USSR.

Mueller, G. O. W. (1969) *Crime, Law and the Scholars*, London: Heinemann; Seattle: University of Washington Press; Cambridge Studies in Criminology, Vol. 25.

PREFACE

This book is the culmination of two research initiatives pursued serially over a five-year period. It is also the end of what has been a very tortuous road at times during those five years. The first of the two studies around which the book is built was truly an original in collaborative empirical research involving the United States and what was then the Soviet Union. That study had the somewhat ponderous title, "Legal Knowledge, Values, and Behavior of American and Soviet Delinquent and Non-Delinquent Youth: A Cross-Cultural Study of Legal Socialization." The research, which grew out of an American–Soviet conference dealing with the subject of legal knowledge and values clarification, was conducted between the fall of 1987 and the spring of 1990. At the time the project was initiated, there seemed to be some very good and compelling reasons for undertaking such an effort. There had been no joint studies on this subject involving our two countries. There had been no studies specifically of legal socialization—the learning of values and norms concerning rules and laws, and their enforcement—in the USSR. Further, there had been no studies anywhere that examined the complex relationship of legal socialization and deviant behavior, specifically juvenile delinquency.

Difficulties and delays in the attempt to publish our first results ran into the disintegration of the Soviet Union itself at the end of 1991. This momentous event made it imperative that the subject be re-examined. Although some thought had earlier been given to the idea that the first effort was really a sort of pilot study, there were no assurances at that time that it was ever going to go any further. Certainly no one even imagined that the USSR was going to disappear, and that the conditions for a kind of natural experiment were going to arise. But that, of course, is exactly what happened. The impetus for further work under the circumstances thus became much greater than would have otherwise been

xiv Preface

the case. The second study, carried out in the fall of 1992, profited greatly from the trials and errors of the initial project. In the first chapter of what follows, I attempt to make the case for the importance of legal environment, of legal context, in shaping the process known as legal socialization. If one embraces my argument, and the further assumption that the U.S. and the USSR provided a dramatic contrast in their sociolegal and political systems, then it follows that an examination of the differential effects of those disparate systems on our respective youth is merited. My sources throughout include personal observations, discussions, and interviews (both formal and informal) during seven visits to the former Soviet Union between 1985 and 1992—a period that includes both the Gorbachev and post-Soviet eras. Other sources are discussions with Russian émigrés and persons who used to define themselves as Sovietologists, the American and Russian media, and both popular and scholarly literature.

After laying out what is generally known about legal socialization in Chapter 2, in Chapters 3, 4, and 5 I develop the various pieces of the particular legal context that existed in Soviet Russia. The relevant contextual pieces that are analyzed and described include the history of law and its enforcement, crime and delinquency, and the special problems of corruption, of organized crime, and of the domination of the Soviet legal system by a "partocracy" of the Communist Party.

The remaining chapters detail the evolution and execution of both phases of the legal socialization research project, lay out and interpret the data, and draw conclusions and implications. The latter are practical as well as theoretical.

I want first and foremost to acknowledge here the contributions of my principal co-investigators in the first research: the late June Louin Tapp, professor of child psychology and adjunct professor of law at the University of Minnesota; and, Aleksandr M. Yakovlev, former head of the section on the theory and sociology of criminal law, Institute of State and Law, Soviet (now Russian) Academy of Sciences. Yakovlev was also an elected member of the Congress of People's Deputies of the USSR from 1989 to 1991. The other first and foremost person for acknowledgment is my friend and colleague, Aleksandr S. Nikiforov, a senior researcher at the Institute of State and Law, who worked on the first project, but who was critical in arranging and implementing the 1992 study. He, more than anyone, made the second-phase research possible. I also want to thank him for a rigorous review of the book manuscript.

We were aided considerably in the first study by a number of graduate students: Gina Annunziato, Julie Davis, Marnie Hiester, Katherine Hutchinson, John Ogawa, and Mathew Sanchez (University of Minnesota); and Mary Brewster, Laura Nelson-Green, and Lola Omole (Rutgers University). On the Soviet side, participants included Leo Ivanov and Viktor Kogan (Institute of State and Law); and Clara Pervushina, chief of the Moscow Juvenile Receiving and Distribution Center, who arranged for surveys in that facility.

Assistance in the second phase came from Yuri Kozlov and Ninel Kuznetsova of Moscow State University; Valentina A. Nikiforova (a senior teacher at two

Moscow schools); and Tamara A. Matveeva, Violetta V. Abramkina, and Michael B. Neverov (Moscow school principals). A number of graduate students of the Rutgers University School of Criminal Justice worked on the 1992 data analyses, and I thank them all. Special thanks are extended to Chris Maxwell, who not only was able to convert my sometimes vague directions and requests into quantitative analyses, but who literally preserved the integrity of research findings.

Thanks for their support and encouragement should also go to the members of the original American and Soviet delegations, and to their heads, Gerhard O. W. Mueller and Vladimir N. Kudriavtsev. For their willingness to participate as subjects of the study, I heartily thank the agency, institutional, and school representatives, and especially the young people in both our countries, who provided us with the essential information.

A number of persons reviewed and commented on the manuscript during its development. I want to especially thank Peter Solomon, Louise Shelley, Elizabeth Lissenberg, and Peter Juviler; and also Carol Stephens and Leila Litvinova. Finally, I am grateful for the financial and other support from the International Research & Exchanges Board, the University of Minnesota, Rutgers University, and the former Soviet Academy of Sciences, Institute of State and Law. Without it research would not have been possible.

INTRODUCTION TO
THE SECOND EDITION

> The true value of this work, it is firmly believed, rests in its "firstness," and in its heuristic effects. Thus, the ultimate conclusions and implications are yet to be drawn.

It was with these words that I concluded my book *Russian Youth: Law, Deviance, and the Pursuit of Freedom* in 1995. So, here we are now, some 20-plus years hence. What can be said—what can I say—about any further and "ultimate" conclusions and implications? In the generation that has passed, what have we learned about the rule of law, legality, legal reasoning, and deviance in Russia? And what about the general subject of legal socialization—how young people learn about rules, norms, and laws; what their attitudes about rules and laws are; and, if and whether this knowledge and these attitudes shape their behavior? These were all areas that were the subjects of *Russian Youth*.

Before venturing into what can now be said about these various topics—which is a fair amount—let me mention at the outset what I cannot say. *Russian Youth* was built around two empirical studies—surveys of youth—conducted first in the period 1987–1990, and then subsequently in 1992. Both American and Russian young persons were included in these surveys. Having completed the first admittedly somewhat problem-plagued study, as explained in the book, a very fortuitous event occurred—the Soviet Union collapsed and disappeared! A country of 15 linked republics, the Union of Soviet Socialist Republics (USSR), the largest of which was Russia itself, fairly suddenly broke up into multiple independent countries at the end of 1991. This created the remarkable opportunity for a pre- and post-natural experiment. We could compare the attitudes and behaviors of Russian youth with their Soviet Russian predecessors. We did just

2 Introduction

that—and those results, compared with our American youth, were at the heart of *Russian Youth*!

That particular empirical research has not been replicated. Thus, I cannot say with exactitude how the attitudes and behaviors of today's Russian youth (as those were precisely measured in our surveys) would compare to those of the young people of 1987 and 1992. But what I can do is tap into some contemporary surveys of people in Russia that pose questions, not identical to but comparable to many of the questions we asked in 1987 and 1992. For example, relatively recently, Russian youth have been asked about their trust in such legal entities as the public prosecutor's office, the courts, and other state as well as social institutions. Their answers would obviously have a bearing on their perceptions of the legitimacy of these institutions, and those perceptions in turn can influence both attitudes and behavior. On the broader issue of law and legal developments in Russia generally, a great deal is known. Therefore, we can paint a quite thorough picture of the legal and political environment that has evolved in Russia since 1991; this is an environment that has to have had a bearing on the moral and legal development of the current generation of Russians.

Part of the context for understanding what has happened over the past 25 years requires not only assessing these larger legal and political developments, but also revisiting studies into the general topic of legal socialization to see what more we have learned during this quarter-century about that subject as well. And that is where we will begin.

Legal Socialization Update

As described in the Preface to *Russian Youth*, our aforementioned earlier studies were themselves the products of a cooperative research exchange between the Rutgers University School of Criminal Justice and the Institute of State and Law of the Soviet Academy of Sciences. It was jointly agreed that assessing the state of legal knowledge of young persons in our two countries, their attitudes about rules and laws, their sense of obligation toward law-abidingness, and most importantly, any relationship between their knowledge and attitudes on the one hand, and their likelihood of engaging in some form of deviant behavior on the other, would constitute a very pertinent as well as feasible comparative research endeavor for our two teams.

The state of legal socialization knowledge and research at that time was pretty much limited to a cognitive developmental approach that theorized and demonstrated that as people mature they develop increasingly more complex abilities to reason about laws, legal institutions, and legal authorities (see, for example, Cohn and White, 1990). Building upon the moral development work of scholars such as Lawrence Kohlberg, June Louin Tapp and her colleagues had demonstrated that children and youth pass through different developmental levels regarding laws and rules as they mature. Higher-order legal reasoning was shown, largely via paper and pencil tests dealing with abstract and hypothetical situations, to be positively correlated with the maturation process. The focus was on moral and legal reasoning.

What had received much less attention at that time was whether and how real-world external influences affected this legal development. In other words, little was known about the effects of actual experiences with rules and laws on legal socialization. And basically nothing was known about the relation of legal developmental levels and actual behavior. One of the goals of the original U.S./Russian research was to move toward filling these gaps.

Several important developments have taken place in research on legal socialization in the intervening years since the early 1990s. Among these is the research of scholars such as Fagan, Piquero, and Tyler as well as that of Cohn, Trinkner, et al. Another development is the evolution of the idea of a culture of lawfulness that arose out of the work of Roy Godson and his colleagues.

Building upon the research of Tom Tyler with its focus on what he called procedural justice (Tyler, 2006), Jeff Fagan and Alex Piquero, along with Tyler, have investigated the influence of procedural justice on the legal development of children and youth. In his earlier research, Tyler had found that how people interact with legal authorities, such as the police, is very important in shaping their perceptions of the fairness and legitimacy of the legal system. The police tend to be the primary representatives of the legal system for most people, because it is the police with whom they are most likely to interact. Dealings with other authorities, such as prosecutors, judges, and corrections officials, tend to be rarer. Tyler found that people are generally much more willing to accept even a punitive outcome, such as being issued a traffic ticket or even being arrested, if they view the process that produced that outcome as being a just one. And by "just" is meant whether, for example, they have been given an opportunity to be heard and their explanations and even excuses have been taken into account. In common parlance, this is what is meant by "having your day in court"!

Even more importantly—beyond an acceptance of the justice of an immediate outcome, Tyler and others have found—is the creation and sustenance of a sense of obligation to abide by the law, and an acceptance of the legitimacy of the legal and the political systems. These are critical to the maintenance of a civil society because they mean that people will "self-regulate." In other words, they will follow the law even when they are unlikely to be caught and punished for breaking it. They do so because they feel obliged to do so and because it is the "right" thing to do. Ultimately, social order depends upon this kind of voluntary compliance with the law because law enforcement authorities cannot enforce all the laws against all the people all the time. Keeping everyone under constant surveillance is not only not feasible for many reasons, but attempting to do so would create an unacceptable police-state atmosphere.

Most people, most of the time, will obey the speed limits while driving and stop at stop signs, even when no police are visible. Indeed, most people, most of

4 Introduction

the time, will abide by other laws, even when they believe that their risk of being caught is extremely low. They do this because they realize doing so is in the best interests of the society at large, even when it may be detrimental to their own interests in particular instances, such as when they are running late for class or work. Please note that I am saying most people, most of the time—not all people, all the time!

The more recent studies of legal socialization mentioned above added the dimension of contact and interactions with authority figures (à la Tyler) to the original cognitive development premises of legal socialization. These studies showed that procedural justice is indeed a significant antecedent to legal socialization. They also demonstrated that when people feel they have been treated fairly in their dealings with legal authorities, they are more likely to comply with the law in the future. Fagan and Piquero added vicarious experiences into the interactions with the legal system equation as well. This means that perceptions, beliefs, and even behavior, are influenced not only by what one experiences for oneself, but also what one observes or otherwise learns about the treatment of others—vastly multiplying the universe of possible influences. These later studies have thus expanded the perspective of how legal socialization evolves.

Perceptions of authority as being legitimate lead to trust and obligation, whereas cynicism about legitimacy leads to an unwillingness to accept and regard rules and laws as binding. Such cynics feel alienated from the legal and political systems; they become what have been called "legal nihilists," about which I will have much more to say. The failure to accept laws and legal authorities also provides a rationale (a rationalization) for violating them, which can in turn lead to deviant behavior.

The more recent research has also expanded the scope of legal socialization to encompass a broader notion of socialization. This wider concept includes the development and internalization of a range of norms and values, including attitudes toward democracy, views about other social groups, and tolerance of diversity. These in turn influence active engagement in communities and involvement in the political process. All this is especially relevant to our look at what has been happening in Russia and its effects upon today's Russian youth.

The idea of a culture of lawfulness, a concept that springs from the work of Roy Godson (see, for example, Godson, 2000), leads us to think about a bridge between individual-level legal socialization (what an individual experiences, believes, feels, and acts upon in terms of their own law-abidingness) and the posture toward law and justice of the larger society. What constitutes a culture of lawfulness? In essence, it is one in which the population in general follow the law, feel they are part of the process and that they can use the law to improve their lives, and have a desire to access the justice system to address their grievances. This ambitious ideal has been described as follows:

> When the population starts to feel part of the process, they connect to their society, thus strengthening social cohesion and their investment in

promoting the rule of law, and they begin to trust in their government and the justice system, both of which are essential for planting the seeds of a culture of lawfulness and respect for the rule of law.

www.usip.org/publications/2009/11/guiding-principles-stabilization-and-reconstruction

Society is comprised of several elements that influence whether and to what degree it has a culture of lawfulness. These elements include what have been called the centers of moral authority, meaning largely the educational, religious, and governmental institutions. Also influential are the mass media, which consist of all the news and information sources that are available in multiple formats seemingly all the time. Then there is the popular culture, which makes up a large part of the content of the media sources—music, television shows, movies, and the increasingly prevalent social networking sites. Recent cellphone videos of police–citizen encounters in the U.S. are an example of how a medium with particular content can influence perceptions of law enforcement. It is via these various elements that the norms and values of society with respect to law and justice are both conveyed and maintained.

After the legal socialization studies in the U.S. and Russia described above, I subsequently had occasion to work with Godson and his colleagues on the development and delivery of a curriculum designed to teach culture of lawfulness (COL) principles. The initial subject students for this curriculum were middle-school adolescents on the one hand, and police academy trainees on the other. Following what is called a train-the-trainers model, we actually taught middle-school teachers and police academy instructors who, in turn, were to pass on this instruction to their respective charges. Over a period of years, members of the COL team taught at various locations in Mexico, in Bogota, Colombia, in Panama City, Panama, and in Beirut, Lebanon. We instructed teachers (usually those who handled civics instruction) in Mexico, Panama, and Lebanon, and police instructors in Mexico and Colombia. Why these countries? First, because they were interested and willing to commit time and resources to carrying out the project. And second, because law and justice and safety where seen to be seriously problematical in each of them.

Whether or not the project was successful depends largely upon what measuring rod is used. The curriculum was developed and continually fine-tuned as the project went along. Its delivery to the teachers and instructors was generally well-received and well-regarded. How well and with what effect the teaching in turn was delivered to the students and trainees is a greater unknown. And an even bigger black hole is what effect, if any, the project had upon the culture of lawfulness of the respective countries. It should be obvious that a school or academy curriculum is only one of a myriad of factors bearing on a culture of lawfulness.

To illustrate the challenge our efforts and others like them face, I recall the comments of a young adolescent boy during a focus group that we held at one of

6 Introduction

the sites in Mexico. The purpose of the focus group was to get feedback on the COL instruction the students had received. The boy said that he agreed wholeheartedly with the content. He agreed that a rule of law was critical for society; that all people should value and abide by the law; and, that their doing so would create a better and more just society for all. That said, this boy then went on to describe how this was impossible in his community and perhaps in Mexico in general. He attributed this to what he described as a culture of corruption in which people like him were themselves forced to be corrupt and to break the law in order to survive. He described several examples to quite convincingly illustrate the reasons for his pessimism.

Ironically, it was this same pessimistic notion of "connive to survive" that had been described to me years earlier as being a necessity for the average citizen living in the then-USSR. A Russian colleague had concluded that it was much easier for Americans to be moral and law-abiding because expectations would generally be met if one followed the rules and abided by the law. That was not the case, he said, in the Soviet Union, where rules and laws were routinely ignored, and instead goods and services got allocated based upon bribes, connections, insider knowledge, etc. The question now is whether any of this has changed, and if so, how? With all this as a kind of context and conceptual guide, let us turn to contemporary Russia and Russian youth.

Law and Legality in Post-Soviet Russia

One of my conclusions in *Russian Youth* was that as of the mid-1990s there was considerable ambiguity about the future status of Russia. Now, after 25 years of economic and political turmoil, that still remains largely the case. Many, many changes have taken place, but how these will ultimately turn out remains to be seen. What is clear is that any initial thoughts and hopes by many that with the collapse of Communist rule, Russia was going to quickly adopt democratic principles and become a thriving market economy, have proven to be both naïve and unrealistic. These hopes ignored the fact that Russia had no history of ever being a democracy, but rather had only experienced different forms of authoritarian rule, beginning with the tsars and then Lenin and Stalin, etc. It had also had nearly 75 years of a state-command economy. Thus, the kind of laissez-faire, free-for-all messiness that characterizes democracies and market economies was totally alien to the Russian experience and to the Russian mindset.

Before tackling the specific situation vis-à-vis the law, it is also helpful to see what happened to the Russian economy during this period, and how that had a big effect on people's lives and attitudes. Masha Lipman, in her *New Yorker* magazine article recounting the 25th anniversary of the August 1991 coup that was the beginning of the end for the Soviet Union, said this about the Russian economy:

The transition from the egregiously inefficient Soviet economy to a market economy gave an opening to those with entrepreneurial spirit, but the economic reforms of the early nineties also led to corruption, inequality, impoverishment, and a collapse of the Soviet life style, which may have been shabby but was at least stable and habitual. The Soviet middle-class—teachers and engineers—suddenly found its salaries eaten up by inflation, and had to look for other ways to make money.

Lipman, 2016

I personally observed these economic repercussions during several of my visits to Moscow in the mid-1990s. For example, I was struck by seeing elderly women standing in the entrances to the Moscow metro stations selling puppies or bottles of beer or personal items of jewelry, etc. Pensioners who had either lost their pensions or had them severely cut back had to try to survive however they could. It reminded one of the depression years in the U.S. Perhaps the most poignant example for me was a visit I paid to the flat of my colleague Alexander and his wife Valentina.

Alexander was a senior lawyer with the Institute of State and Law of the Soviet Academy of Sciences, and it was he who had facilitated my earlier research on Russian youth. Valentina had been the principal or director of a high school (a prestigious position) in Moscow, where I had delivered a commencement address some years earlier. In my subsequent visit with them I was shocked and saddened to see the low state to which they had fallen. Because of some sort of problem with the public utilities, their flat was both quite cold and quite dark. Valentina, who I learned had lost her job at the school, was huddled under some blankets in an attempt to stay warm, and seemed to me at least to be quite depressed. Alexander was attempting to stay upbeat, but had had to resort to any kind of law-related work he could dig up (and there was not much) to provide some minimal income. These were two well-educated professionals who had had relatively high status positions, but who had been left by the wayside in the new Russia. Unfortunately for them, they were not entrepreneurs; they were not able or perhaps not willing to resort to selling things as their means of survival.

The aforementioned Masha Lipman—as well as many others—labeled the 1990s in Russia "a nightmare of lawlessness and poverty." Alexander and Valentina did not resort to lawlessness because of their near-poverty status, but many others did.

One of the key factors with respect to law that was alien to the Russian experience is with respect to the fundamental legal principle known as the rule of law. As explained in introducing the foundations for the studies described in *Russian Youth*, rule of law is a Western legal concept referring to the idea that the law is pre-eminent. Under this principle, no person or institution is above the law, and thus the rule of law is a check against the abuse of power. Government officials are not immune from liability for their actions. This is obviously a

8 Introduction

critically important protection for individual citizens in their dealings with governmental authorities.

A contrasting notion to the rule of law is what has been referred to as rule *by* law. In this latter instance, the law is a mere tool of the government. Governmental authorities create and enforce laws as needed to protect their authority and to suppress the citizenry, who have no legal basis to challenge that authority. Whereas under the rule of law, the law is something the government serves, under a rule by law, the government uses law as the most convenient way to govern, and the law is ignored when it is inconvenient. I can illustrate this contrast and the challenges Russian progressive reformers faced in the 1990s with the following example.

I had the opportunity to visit Moscow during the latter period of U.S. President Bill Clinton's term. This was around the time of Clinton's impeachment hearings and the scandal involving White House intern Monica Lewinsky. If impeached and convicted, the president would be removed from office. Just a few years earlier, there had been in Moscow, in the Kremlin, a dispute between then Russian President Boris Yeltsin and the Russian Supreme Soviet or parliament. The contrast between the experiences of the United States and Russia in how these presidential-level crises played out and were resolved provides a telling distinction between a country that has historically been a democracy governed by a rule of law, and a country that had no history of either of those.

In the U.S., President Clinton was indeed impeached, but after a vigorous and full-throated adversarial process, he was not convicted at trial by the U.S. Senate—a trial presided over by the Chief Justice of the U.S. Supreme Court. The entire proceeding was carried out publicly and in accordance with the law and the U.S. Constitution, and when it was over all parties (albeit some begrudgingly) accepted the result, went on about their business, and President Clinton completed his term.

In contrast, in Moscow, following a series of confrontations, President Yeltsin unlawfully ordered the dissolution of the Supreme Soviet parliament, which in turn voted to remove him from office. Military troops were called out in support of the two opposing sides, with the Yeltsin-supporting military forces ultimately using tanks to actually shell the parliament building. There were a number of deaths. After finally coming out on top in this constitutional crisis, Yeltsin then scrapped the existing Russian constitution and banned his political opposition.

Such an outcome would have been unthinkable in the United States— President Clinton ordering the army to shell the Capitol Building! Scrapping the U.S. Constitution! Banning the Republican Party! Unimaginable! Yes, unimaginable in a country ruled by laws and not by men—a rule of law and not a rule by law.

The current state of law-related affairs in Russia continues to reflect its complicated legal history. Most observers conclude still that there is no rule of law in Russia, and indeed under the current president, Vladimir Putin, the notion of a "dictatorship of law" has been introduced (sounding very much like rule by law). President Putin's advocacy of a dictatorship of law came early in his presidency (www.brookings.edu/opinions/vladimir-putin-and-the-law). Exactly what he had in mind was unclear, and developments over his years in office have certainly not seemed to move in the direction of a rule of law. Instead, his initial idea seems to have been in reaction to the economic and political chaos of the Yeltsin years. Putin proposed, for example, that there could be opposition political parties, but that they should use democratic (meaning okayed by the state) means toward political change. There could also be legal dispute resolution, public organizations could sue governmental officials, and court proceedings would be publicized. The Russian state, he said, should act in a law-based manner; and that this adherence to the law was necessary to insure Russia's democratic development. A number of subsequent actions by Putin and his government over the intervening years have belied any notion that there would indeed be true democratic development. Instead, as many observers have noted, what has arisen, or actually just been continued, is rule by law. William Pomeranz of the Kennan Institute had this to say about Russia's post-Soviet legal reforms:

> As we reflect back on twenty years of Russian legal reform, it is possible to identify genuine accomplishments—achievements many observers would not have thought possible in just two decades. Most notably, Russia has made significant steps in the transition from socialist law to a more recognizable, continental-based civil law system, in the process opening new avenues of constitutional and commercial law. At the same time, the persistent abuse of criminal law, corruption, and the return of certain deep-rooted authoritarian tendencies continues to undermine—and even negate—any progress that has been made in establishing a law-based state. In many ways, the fundamental question that confronts Russia today after twenty years of independence is the same question that confronted the Soviet Union after 70 years (at the beginning of glasnost and perestroika) and Imperial Russia 50 years after the Judicial Reforms of 1864, namely is the Russian state subordinated to—or does it stand outside of—its own laws. Until Russia makes this essential choice, the rule of law will remain a perennial, and ultimately elusive, goal.
>
> *Pomeranz, 2012: 146–7*

Legal nihilism is the phrase often used to describe the post-Soviet contemporary state of legal affairs in Russia. This characterization has been put forward even at the highest levels of the Russian government. For example, when Dmitri Medvedev (a trained lawyer) was running for the Russian presidency in 2008, he described what he called the struggle for the rule of law in his homeland. Medvedev said Russia had a "culture of legal nihilism that in its cynicism has no equal anywhere on the European continent." Further, he said that if Russia were

10 Introduction

to become a truly civilized state, it first needed to become a lawful one (Horton, 2011). This Medvedev observation is especially interesting because he and Vladimir Putin have played a kind of musical chairs with the presidency and prime ministership of Russia for nearly 20 years now. First, Putin was president and Medvedev was prime minister, then they reversed roles for some years, and now Putin is back as president and Medvedev as prime minister. The point is that Medvedev has been in powerful positions to do something about the legal nihilism he decried, but so far not much has happened. His calls for overhauling legal education, and especially for the independence of judges and the media, are far from being achieved.

The independence of judges is related to the principle of the separation of powers in governing. Not being beholden to the executive or legislative branches, an independent judiciary can exercise objective and final judgment on the actions of the other two branches. An independent appellate or constitutional court at the highest level will have ultimate say over what is the law and how and to whom it is to be applied. Contrary to this idea, the Soviet Union had a long history of what was called "telephone law." In reaching a decision about the outcome of a criminal case, Soviet judges would be directed, either literally or figuratively via the telephone by Communist Party officials, what the decision was to be. That this practice has continued, albeit by other government officials since the Communist Party is no longer all-powerful, is alleged by a number of observers (e.g., Horton, 2011). Far from being independent, the courts continue to be considered "lapdogs" of the Kremlin—as some have called them. Consequently, any reliance on formal law or legal institutions in Russia is considered by many to be foolhardy and to be avoided; and the Russian government's commitment to the law is considered questionable at best.

As for the independence of the media—which, as I pointed out earlier, is one of the major factors influencing a culture of lawfulness—here again the contemporary Russian situation falls far short of achieving this ideal. Because the media are both politically and economically dependent upon the government and its associated businesses, journalists and artists and performers have to toe the line of political correctness if they want to continue to stay in business, to work, and to stay out of jail (see *Demokratizatsiya: The Journal of Post-Soviet Democratization*, No. 2/Spring 2014, special issue on the media). Russian television, which is considered to be the most influential form of media in the country, is regarded by many as being little more than a mouthpiece for the Kremlin. Similarly, one of the other centers of moral authority considered essential to a culture of lawfulness, the Russian Orthodox Church in this case, is likewise currently considered to be subservient to the state, and thus lacking in moral stature and prestige. This too is an echo of the earlier Soviet period, when that Church was allowed to continue to exist only as long as it did not challenge the Party or the State.

In sum, three factors critical to the rule of law and a culture of lawfulness are either weak or pretty much missing from the current Russian scene. It should be

Introduction **11**

no surprise then if the legal nihilism referred to by former President Medvedev is still very much present. When the state itself behaves in a lawless fashion, it sets a poor example for its citizens and provides an acceptable rationale for those citizens to themselves evade the law. Kathryn Hendley refers to "the pervasiveness of legal irregularities during the 1990s . . . [when the] law was often an afterthought in the process of privatizing state enterprises, which enriched a very small stratum of Russian society, leaving the vast majority of citizens deeply disillusioned" (Hendley, 2012: 156). Certainly, my earlier-mentioned colleagues Alexander and Valentina fell into that category.

So, what exactly is legal nihilism and what does it say about the contemporary attitudes and behavior of Russians? At its core, writes Hendley, legal nihilism is a lack of respect for the law; more than that it is condescension toward the law: "legal nihilists obey the law when convenient, and otherwise ignore it." Further, she says, "if a significant number of Russians are, in fact, readily prepared to disregard law, then progress towards a legal system that reflects the ideals of the 'rule of law' is going to be stymied" (Hendley, 2012: 150). This assessment clearly speaks to the issue of self-regulation and a sense of obligation to obey the law that I discussed earlier. But it will be a concern, as the quote above implies, only if legal nihilism is truly a major problem in Russia.

There have in fact been various efforts to look at the prevalence of a kind of disdain for the law and legal institutions in contemporary Russia. For example, the Levada Center in Moscow does periodic public opinion polling, and one of its topics has been the public's level of trust in various institutions, including the courts. Over a number of years during the post-Soviet period, less than 20 percent of those surveyed have said they had confidence in the courts. Even smaller percentages in other surveys believe the courts to be independent. Similarly, the Russian police have long been seen as being one of the most corrupt of Russian legal institutions, as well as being overly violent—and are thus generally held in low regard. These kinds of perceptions can provide a rationalization for citizens to themselves disrespect and disregard the law and law enforcement.

But Kathryn Hendley, who again is among those who have looked most closely and recently at the legal nihilism phenomenon in Russia, challenges some of the findings and the conclusions of those, such as Prime Minister Medvedev, who have criticized the Russian people for not respecting the law. Hendley used data collected in 2004 and 2006 to measure the incidence of legal nihilism in Russia and to find out who the legal nihilists are and what demographic factors characterize them. Her findings suggest a more complex and nuanced picture than is generally thought to be the case.

Piggy-backing on a larger study, Hendley asked approximately 10,000 respondents (fewer in 2004 and more in 2006) to agree or disagree on a five-point scale with the following statement: "If a person considers the law unjust, he has the right to 'go around it.'" Those who agreed with the statement were labeled as legal nihilists. Hendley's rationale was that if respondents believed in the moral

12 Introduction

sanctity of law, then they would be unlikely to agree that going around it would be legitimate. She argued:

> They would recognize that allowing people to pick and choose which laws they will obey could lead to societal chaos. On the other hand, those who lack fundamental respect for law would see no problem with substituting their own moral code for that of society. Such a view lies at the very heart of legal nihilism.
>
> *Hendley, 2012: 152*

Based upon this admittedly very limited query (using but a single question), Hendley found that in her total population, the largest proportion (around 34 percent) were "somewhat" law-abiding. On the other hand, about 25 percent were strongly or somewhat nihilistic. Whether one in four persons saying they would go around the law is a little or a lot is difficult to say because there are not comparable data from other countries. When Hendley broke the sample into generational cohorts, with those born after 1988 being the youngest, she found the proportion of nihilists among youth to be about the same as for the total sample (approximately 24 percent). Interestingly, and perhaps surprising to some, the least nihilistic and the most law-abiding cohort was made up of those Russians born before 1940, in other words, those who had lived more than 50 years in the USSR.

With reference to my earlier point about conniving to survive, Hendley found that those respondents who were prepared to go around the law were also more likely to believe the courts were less than honest and that one had to violate the law in order to live in contemporary Russia.

The effects on youth in particular of 25 years of legal developments (both positive and negative) has been described by, among others, Martha Olcott, who wrote that it was Russian youth who seemed to suffer disproportionately from the numerous social disorders in the USSR at the end of the 1990s; and Igor Ilyinsky, who described the moral decay in Russia during its first decade of independence resulting in a lack of direction among many young people—and leading to their poor understanding of freedom, lack of faith in politicians, and a sense of injustice (see Åslund and Olcott, 1999; Riordan et al., 1995).

The height of the tumult and disorder in Russia occurred during the first decade after 1991—the Yeltsin years—and since then, since Vladimir Putin assumed power, there has been much greater stability. As pointed out earlier, however, this stability has come at a price in individual rights and freedoms. Given Putin's very high favorability ratings, most of the Russian people—including the young—appear to be willing to pay this price, at least for now.

In 1996, another of my Russian colleagues, Alexander Yakovlev, published a book aptly named *Striving for Law in a Lawless Land*. This Alexander, who I knew as Sasha, was very much in the middle of the legal reform efforts of the early

Yeltsin years, and his book provides an insider's look at what was going on during that time. Writing with his usual eloquence, Sasha concluded his book with the following words:

> Russia, my country, is predominantly a northern one, with a severe climate. In winter the rivers are frozen, and solid ice covers them. But in the spring comes a day when the neighborhoods shudder with thunderous sounds. Then everyone understands that spring has come; the ice is broken. In spring the winds are moist and chilly. And so it is with us now. We Russians are experiencing a political spring after decades of totalitarian winter. The winds are chilly and make us shiver, but the ice is broken and the wind is the wind of freedom.
>
> *Yakovlev, 1996: 225*

Perhaps there has been some melting of ice and some warming of the wind, but the hoped-for spring thaw clearly still has a very long way to go!

1

LEGAL SOCIALIZATION IN DISPARATE LEGAL CONTEXTS

What are the links, if any, among knowledge of the law, attitudes toward law and its enforcement, legal reasoning, and deviant behavior? The essence of this work is to try to sort out and answer that complex question. The conceptual paradigm that incorporates each of the aforementioned elements is a form of social learning called legal socialization. Legal socialization is learning about rules and laws; it is developing attitudes concerning those rules and laws; and it is reasoning about why certain laws are necessary and legitimate regulators of behavior. Ultimately—and most importantly—legal socialization is concerned with complying (or not complying) with the rules and laws that define one's legal environment. Legal socialization research can help us to understand why certain persons obey the law and others do not, and why some people obey some laws and not others. Legal socialization recognizes that the law has an educative function, that it is important as a socializing institution.

The conditions for legal socialization are assumed to be embedded in the law-governed environment (Cohn and White, 1990: 22). Cohn and White argued that the theory of legal socialization "must incorporate the salient features of the legal environment" (Cohn and White, 1990: 189). These salient features include fair enforcement of rules, the legitimacy of rules, and the role of authority. It is in the process of legal socialization, a process that involves interaction with our legal environment, that we learn which attitudes and behaviors are encouraged and rewarded, which are merely tolerated, and which are sanctioned—and under what conditions and circumstances. This interaction and learning take place at both a formal and an informal level. Formal here refers to those norms and rules that are codified into law; informal refers to everything else. The formal rules—the laws—operate at the level of legal authority that is government. The most important informal rules, some of which may actually be in conflict with the formal ones, are those set and enforced by family and peers, and in school. We are all governed by numerous laws and rules, both formal and informal, that are generally part of the regulatory structure of every society.

For young children, legal environment or context consists mostly of rules and rule-enforcement by parents, grandparents, other adult family figures, siblings, teachers, and daycare workers. Older children and adolescents are exposed to a much broader legal environment. In addition to family and teachers, peers become very important, and there is often the first exposure to the formal legal system— usually the police—at this stage. The law thus comes into play. With this broader exposure—when combined with their increasing emotional maturity, political and social sophistication, and knowledge—teenagers begin to be concerned about such issues as personal identity, justice, fairness, individual rights, legality, the role of the individual in society, and so on. As adults, they continue to have these concerns. Legal socialization is continuous, proceeding with the increased knowledge and wisdom that comes from learning and experience. Beliefs about law and justice therefore evolve over a person's lifetime, influenced by changes over time, place, and experience (Tapp, 1987a).

Given its vitally important role, the choice of legal environments, of legal cultures and contexts, in which to seek answers to questions about legal socialization is a crucial one. With that in mind, if one were to think of macro-level examples of disparate legal and political systems, say just in the twentieth century, the Soviet Union undoubtedly would come to mind as an example of one of the most totalitarian, coercive, and repressive legal cultures of the past 75 years. Other examples could include totalitarian regimes in Germany, Italy, China, and Cambodia. But one significant difference between each of these and the Soviet regime is the longevity of the latter. Some four generations of Russians were born and raised as Soviet citizens.

The greatest repression in Soviet Russia occurred during the 30-year reign of Joseph Stalin as the leader of the USSR. The most egregious and perverted uses of Soviet law and the Soviet legal system ended with his death in 1953. The legacy of that period, however, remained for many years—and there are still residues to be found today in Russia.

Conversely, over this same period, the United States would probably be considered to be among the more liberal and the least authoritarian of legal environments. This distinction is important when one wishes to examine the effects of ideological content on legal reasoning, attitudes, and behavior. From the ideological perspective, the meaning of law

> reflects how dominant groups in a society view social and political life and how they define and apply the values of justice and fairness. Legal reasoning [thus is believed to be] a matter of the manipulation of legal symbols by those in power to legitimize their authority and the acquiescent employment of these symbols by members of the community.
>
> *Cohn and White, 1990: 188*

16 Legal Socialization

In addition to their formal legal differences, the U.S. and the USSR differed also in other respects that are germane to legal socialization. These disparities are found more at the informal or micro-level. Most important is the contrasting emphases upon individualism versus collectivism. Whereas Soviet society extolled the virtues of the group, the *"kollektiv,"* and community values—downplaying individual rights and interests—American society has always been blatantly individualistic. Some consider the "undervaluation of the individual" in Soviet society to be the greatest difference between the two (Gray, 1989: 9).

The communal nature of Russian society actually predates the Bolsheviks. The pertinence of the Russian idea of community to issues of ethics and morals is argued by Berdyaev (1992). He says that the ethical ideas of Russians are very different from Americans, for example: "Russia's moral values are defined by an attitude towards man, and not towards abstract principles of property or State, nor towards good in the abstract" (Berdyaev, 1992: 267). As a result, Russians are said to adopt a different attitude toward sin and crime, being more sympathetic to the sinner and the criminal. The collective was a prime agent for the political and moral socialization of Russian children throughout Russian history (Clawson, 1973). It received special emphasis in the USSR, however, under the teachings of Anton Makarenko, whose educational and childrearing theories were endorsed by Stalin (see Makarenko, 1967). Makarenko believed that the collective was the most important factor in Soviet childrearing. According to his teachings, the Soviet child had to come to depend on the collective for guidance and direction, must learn from it to exercise self-discipline, and must subordinate his interests to those of the collective (McClellan, 1987: 8).

The contrast between the individually oriented childrearing practices of the United States, where children are encouraged and rewarded for being different, for standing out and thinking for themselves, versus the group-oriented practices of the former Soviet Union where children are taught to subordinate their individual desires to those of the group, and where teamwork is emphasized, will enable us to test the differential effects on legal development. This cultural disparity is particularly pertinent because the theory of legal development is itself derived in part from moral development theory (e.g., Kohlberg), which in turn has been associated with (some would say accused of) extolling individual rights and autonomy over the submission to the values and behavioral norms of the community or of a cultural group (Cohn and White, 1990: 186).

Apropos this disparity, there is the intriguing hypothesis that rules (and laws), and their attendant enforcement apparatus, may have more legitimacy and moral validity in engendering acceptance and compliance, when collectivism is valued more highly than individualism. Members of communal societies are expected and pressured to subordinate their personal interests to those of the group. It is the group that promulgates and enforces the rules and laws. To achieve the desired acceptance into the group, one has to accept its moral authority and abide by its rules. Conformity is encouraged and rewarded; doing your own thing is discouraged. This is not to argue that this is exclusively present in the former USSR and absent in the U.S., but rather that the emphasis is different. Smith (1992a: 89) makes an argument along these lines about Soviet society: "among many Soviet citizens," he writes, "there is a greater tendency than in the West to consider the consequences of one's behavior for the society as a whole." We will examine this general issue in terms of the effects that the informal rule-governed environment have upon legal socialization.

The contrasts in legal cultures and legal attitudes between the United States and the former Soviet Union are further exemplified in the contrasting views of individual rights and the relationship between the state and the individual. Shelley (1993) points out that law was never considered to be fundamental in the former USSR. Individuals had little recourse against abuses of power by state authorities. "According to the ideology, law was always considered part of the superstructure. There were no inalienable rights [for the individual]" (Shelley, 1993: 129). Soviet law, unlike American law, did not operate on the premise that whatever was not expressly prohibited was permitted (see Nove, 1989: 173, 175). In Soviet legal thinking, the "rights" of Soviet citizens were expressly spelled out and granted by the state. If not recognized by the Soviet state, they did not exist. In contrast, in the U.S. Constitution rights are presumed to exist naturally. These can only be denied or curtailed in specific circumstances and under specific conditions, as consented to by the American people. Although both countries certainly had and—following the dissolution of the USSR—continue to have their share of corruption and lawless behavior, the Soviet Union especially was the land of the "necessary criminals," and the "survivors and connivers" (Rosner, 1986); of the notorious black market; and of a government dominated by the "Soviet mafia" (Vaksberg, 1991). The latter, as we will see, was a special, unique kind of organized crime operating at the highest levels of the Soviet government. Each of these infamous characteristics had at least the potential for undermining respect for the morality and legitimacy of the law and its enforcement in the former USSR.

Given these and other dissimilarities, it may be assumed that both the macro (formal) and micro (informal) contexts for legal socialization were very different in America and the Soviet Union. Because of these distinctions, the opportunity to examine the legal socialization of our respective youth sets up a most interesting and important cross-cultural comparison. Such a comparison was in fact carried out in 1987, and its results will be reported here. Now that Russia is in the process of shifting away from its old Soviet traditions to some new but as yet undefined legal and political form, adding a further contrast between Russian youth at two points in time, one before and one after the USSR's demise at the end of 1991, makes that comparison an even more meaningful examination of the effects of shifting legal contexts upon attitudes and behavior. The still evolving rule/law environment in Russia was very different in 1992 than it was in 1987. A corollary to our principal research question will thus be whether the post-Soviet Russian youth of 1992 perceive, believe, and behave differently with regard to law than

18 Legal Socialization

did their Soviet-Russian predecessors of five years earlier. And, how do they compare in these respects to American youth?

I am not, by the way, suggesting that 1987 is a "representative" baseline year for the "old" Russia. That year was chosen for study simply because that is when the opportunity presented itself. By 1987, which was the second year of Mikhail Gorbachev's leadership of the USSR, there were already evolutionary changes in societal norms taking place. Splits and differences between the official, formal norms and the unofficial, informal norms were becoming apparent. Socialization— in the home, in the school, and in the formal institutions charged with that responsibility—was already in a state of flux. The Soviet legal and political order, however, was still very much in place.

Legal Socialization at the Macro-Level

One thesis providing a conceptual framework for this work is the idea that voluntary compliance with the law issues in part from a legal order and justice system that is seen to be legitimate, and is believed to be deserving of respect and compliance (Friedrichs, 1986; Gibson, 1989, 1991; Tyler, 1990; Tyler and Rasinski, 1991; Pilon, 1992; but see Hyde, 1983). This legitimacy generally derives from the autonomous consent of those subject to the law, and from the perception that legal authorities and procedures are fair.

A second tenet of our underlying thesis is that compliance/non-compliance is also based upon one's own sense of personal morality (Tyler, 1990). Here the motivation is more complex. The person subject to the law essentially asks the question: how does the law, or a particular law, accord with what I believe to be right and wrong? How wrong do I believe an action to be? According to this notion, principled legal reasoners are motivated to resist unjust laws that violate their moral values. They make their own judgments about the wrongfulness of specific behaviors and respond accordingly. The result of higher-order legal reasoning may thus be unlawful behavior.

The third motive for obeying the law derives from the principle of simple self-interest (Hyde, 1983). People obey because they are afraid of being caught and punished (deterrence). Self-interest also includes other reasoning about what actions may be in one's best interests in a particular instance—gaining the approval or avoiding the disapproval of one's peers for example—but deterrence is the major element. A concern for and a responsiveness to the influence of peers would be an example of the effects of the informal legal context on attitudes and behavior.

If legitimacy and moral congruity (between personal beliefs and the laws of the country) are absent, or only minimally present, then it would follow that coercion, even extending to the use of mass terror and a police state, would have to be society's recourse to engender lawful behavior. That compliance would, however, be mostly of the self-interest and perhaps involuntary kind. Although rebellion, civil disobedience, and crime may be the usual negative responses to authority in the face of coercion (Cohn and White, 1990: 2), what if the coercive force is so great as to be overwhelming? And what if the population is so apathetic, cowed, cynical, and lacking in traditions of dissent and disobedience that it stoically accepts whatever it gets? Under such circumstances, brute force may be able to effectively deter and repress unlawful behavior. The former Soviet Union provides a good case example for considering these possibilities.

In his writing about the relationship between morality and law, the dissident Soviet psychiatrist Semyon Gluzman suggested that this relationship is determined by the nature of the state. "Morality and law overlap in varying degrees according to the type of state," Gluzman argued. "[I]n totalitarian societies [e.g., the USSR] the overlap is minimal, in an open, powersharing society [e.g., the U.S.] it is at its greatest" (Gluzman, 1989: 11). This suggestion offers a good argument for doing a comparative study of the effects of the two political systems.

All governments in practice (including the governments of the U.S., the former USSR, and now Russia) have some combination of elements operating at the macro-level from each of the three foregoing bases for compliance. They all depend upon the perceived legitimacy of their laws and law enforcement, upon a degree of congruence between law and the personal morality of their citizens, and upon control and deterrence, in order to bring about lawful behavior. Rigby addressed this issue with reference to the USSR, limiting his comments to legitimacy and self-interest:

> [I]n most systems the compliance of the population with the demands of their rulers depends not only on the threat or actuality of coercion, but also on a measure, at least, of belief in the 'legitimacy' of such demands, and . . . the Soviet Union is no exception to this.
>
> *Rigby, 1983: 9*

We will assume that Soviet and post-Soviet Russia and the United States have a mix of all three of these elements, but also that the mix is sufficiently different that the contrasts in legal cultures provide a valid basis for a comparative examination of the effects of disparate legal contexts on legal socialization.

In sum then, the theoretical premise here is that people (in this case youth) can be expected to behave in accordance with the law because (1) they believe in its moral validity, that is because they believe the law serves some essential social purpose with which they agree (moral values/obligation); (2) because they believe that laws should be obeyed simply because the law is the law (legitimacy); and/or (3) because they fear sanctions (deterrence), or are acting out of some other motive of self-interest. These motives correspond roughly with the post-conventional (law-creating), the conventional (law-maintaining), and the pre-conventional (law-obeying) levels of legal reasoning that are the developmental stages of legal socialization (Tapp, 1987a, 1987b). This research will thus test the

20 Legal Socialization

various propositions derived from or related to legal socialization theory in legal contexts that are very different across place and across time.

The two phases of the research that is described in the chapters that follow took place during enormous changes in Russia. These changes occurred in every sphere of Russian life—economic, political, social, and legal. Perestroika (restructuring) and glasnost (openness) became household words to both Russians and Americans during the last half of the 1980s. The Communist Party, which had been the dominant force in the USSR for seven decades, first lost its primacy and then was outlawed. Ethnic and national unrest began undermining the unity and sovereignty of the old Soviet empire, and then broke into open warfare. There was the failed coup attempt against Soviet President Mikhail Gorbachev in August 1991; an event that is seen as the last gasp of the old guard hardline Communists. This was followed finally by the breakup and disappearance of the Soviet Union itself in December, 1991. Each of the 15 constituent republics of the old USSR, including Russia, became independent states. Russia, the largest and most dominant of these new states, and Boris Yeltsin, its first democratically elected president, became the heirs apparent of the legal and political reforms initiated by Gorbachev and the Soviet Congress of People's Deputies in the late 1980s. The new era began amid grave concern in Russia about maintaining law and order, and combatting corruption and crime, while at the same time continuing economic, political, and legal reforms, which it was hoped would continue to advance the principles of the rule of law and the creation of a rule-of-law state (*pravovoe gosudarstvo*) (Thorson, 1992).

Because the sweep of the various developments of this period furnished the backdrop for the studies—and most particularly for their implications—we will begin by briefly tracing those issues that are most relevant to concerns about sociolegal context at the macro-level. These have to do with law and legal reform, with crime and delinquency, and with corruption, the black market, and the shadow economy. Each issue will then be discussed more fully in subsequent chapters. The emphasis will be on Soviet and post-Soviet Russia, with only some contrasts drawn for illustrative purposes with the United States. We begin with a little history in order to try to get some sense of the possible bases for the attitudes, opinions, and perceptions of Russian youth.

Soviet Law and Order

The Soviet Union, from its beginnings, was not a state based upon the rule of law, or what was called *Rechsstaat* in its mid-nineteenth-century German interpretation (Markovits, 1989; Butler, 1990, 1991; Brown, 1992; Thorson, 1992)—that is, a state in which the power of government is limited and subject to the law. Under the *Rechsstaat*, rule-of-law ideal, there is an independent judiciary, the government is bound by general rules, and individuals have both entitlements and obligations conferred upon them (Unger, 1976: 186). As will be seen, in the USSR in contrast to this ideal, there was no independent judiciary, and limitations on the power of the state as well as entitlements for Soviet citizens existed more on paper than in reality. As a consequence, the Soviet state and Soviet law did not have those legal foundations in justice, fairness, and due process that would be expected to give them legitimacy and moral validity in the eyes of the Soviet people. It was the monopoly domination by the Communist Party that was the major—although by no means only—impediment to the existence of a truly law-based Soviet society. Other obstacles became more apparent only after the Party lost its authority. Hazard, for example, referring to other impediments to reform, said there were "deep-seated cultural restraints on change," including legal change, which went well beyond the control by the Communist Party (Hazard, 1990: 526). A strong attachment to authority and order are among these other restraints.

Partly through repression, partly through secrecy and underreporting, and partly by redefining crimes as administrative offenses, the Soviet Union was fairly successful in keeping a lid on crime for most of its history. This is a history, however, that reflects a considerable reliance upon the use of terror and coercion to force compliance with the law. Beginning in 1917, the principal Soviet tools to enforce law and order were deterrence and the fear of harsh punishment. The indiscriminate use of punishment, particularly during the Stalin years in what is known as the Great Terror, is said to have "corrupted the Soviet people's sense of justice and spawned cynicism. People feared unjust laws, but did not respect them" (Yakovlev, 1990: 130).

The Effects of Glasnost

Beginning in the mid-1980s, the residual effects of the Great Terror began to change substantially. When he came on the scene in 1985, first as leader of the Communist Party, and then as president of the USSR, Mikhail Gorbachev (the first leader of the Soviet Union to be trained as a lawyer since Lenin) began to institute a series of fundamental reforms in the Soviet Union. One of the more important of these was the policy known as glasnost, or openness. Glasnost was intended to open Soviet history and current affairs to public scrutiny, and to help move toward democratizing the USSR. The publication of previously banned literary works was allowed; a multitude of investigative news media sprang into being; open discussions of history, politics, economics, and so on were encouraged; and limited forms of democratic elections were held. Glasnost dramatically removed the cloak of secrecy from the hypocrisy, corruption, and amorality of the Communist Party's totalitarian domination of Soviet society, and exposed its corrosive effects upon the Soviet people. What had been widely believed about the Party's lawlessness for 70 years—but had largely been spoken about only behind closed doors—was rather suddenly exposed and became openly discussed. One unexpected and unintended result was that "the Myth, was now transformed into the Lie" (Z, 1990: 315). According to the then anonymous author "Z," the moment of truth about the illegitimacy of the Soviet state had arrived, and constituted one of the great unresolved contradictions of perestroika. "Z" has subsequently surfaced as historian Martin Malia. "The collapse of the Lie [originally Solzhenitsyn's term for the fraud of Soviet socialism] under glasnost is destroying acceptance of the system itself, especially among the young, just as Gorbachev is trying to save it by restructuring" (Z, 1990: 315).

By opening the floodgates of self-criticism, glasnost simultaneously erased the old ability of the police state to coerce compliance with the law, and undermined any vestiges of legitimacy and moral validity which that state might have possessed to encourage voluntary compliance. The old order broke down, but there was little to replace it. Public confidence fell, and fears of crime, of civil disorder and disruption, and of moral decay rose. Moscow joined such cities as Amsterdam and New York in its openly available pornography. Currency speculation, long subject to severe enforcement and punishment, became rampant. As in some American cities, people began to feel that they had to be armed to go out on the streets at night. Such things had been practically unknown in the Soviet Union just a few years before. There was much less fear of punishment, but there was also little respect for the legitimacy of the law. In this sense, the worst of both possible worlds seemed to have been achieved.

Glasnost and perestroika liberated the Soviet people to think for themselves, but much of what they had to think about they did not like. Expectations were raised, but remained unfulfilled. Problems were explicated, but without solutions. Although many did not like where they seemed to be going, there appeared to be no possibility of a retreat from perestroika—simply because there was no retreat (see, for example, Nove, 1989; Smith, 1990; Miller et al., 1990–91, for discussion of the disillusionment in the waning days of the USSR).

A study of Soviet public opinion, reported in 1990, found high levels of dissatisfaction, especially among young people, in all the geographical areas surveyed (Rukavishnikov, 1990). The survey found that black marketeers, the "dealers and representatives of the shadow economy," were ranked as being the most powerful force in the Central Asian city of Tashkent; and, were considered second only to the Communist Party in their power in Moscow and in the western Ukrainian city of L'vov. A belief that criminal and quasi-criminal elements had practically taken control would certainly seem to have undermined beliefs in the efficacy of law enforcement and the legal authorities. It is not the intent here to imply that this circumstance was or is unique to Russian cities. One could hear somewhat similar beliefs by questioning residents in, for instance, Washington, D.C., Miami, or Los Angeles. There is certainly a qualitative difference, however. Americans in Miami and elsewhere, although certainly concerned about the ability of the police to control crime, are unlikely to agree that criminals are *the* dominant force in their cities. They would not agree that criminals have totally taken over the government and the economy. What is of particular interest here is that this openly expressed type of public dissatisfaction was new and different for the Soviet Union.

Whither the Russians?

In the latter years of the 1980s, many Soviet citizens, but especially the Russians who comprised just over 50 percent of the Soviet population, criticized the chaos of Western-style democracy, and what they called the ugly face of freedom and permissiveness. These they saw as the bitter fruits of glasnost (see, for example, Keller, 1990). For instance, during a visit to Moscow in September, 1990, I was walking near the Kremlin with a young Russian university student named Sergei who was working with me as an interpreter. We passed by the tent city that had been set up there by a collection of dissident and disaffected persons who were apparently living there and sporting signs airing their grievances against the Soviet state. Sergei was extremely disturbed by this display. He felt it was an embarrassment, and said that the protestors really had no legitimate grounds for their protests. When I asked him what he would do about them, he answered that he would send in the police or the military to clear them out. This kind of freedom and democracy made him very uncomfortable, and he believed that the forces of law and order should be used to get rid of such unnecessary demonstrations (and at the end of December 1990, this is exactly what happened as the protestors were removed and the tent city razed).

Sergei's own disaffection for the Soviet state was, however, reflected in his pessimism about getting a job as a translator/interpreter in Moscow. Without such a job, he would be forced to leave Moscow and return home where there was no chance of his finding suitable employment utilizing his education and training. The disillusioning effects of unemployment and underemployment are also certainly not unique to the Soviet Union, although being forced by law to leave one's chosen city is atypical. What is important is that the specter of something that had been practically unheard of—and in fact was contradictory to the cradle-to-grave social security blanket guarantees of Soviet socialism—namely widespread unemployment, was just beginning in 1990. Unemployment undermines confidence in and respect for the system. It is feared as one of the major risks of Russia's fitful moves toward a market economy.

One of the negative sides of glasnost was the emergence of extremist nationalistic groups like the Russian Pamyat (Memory) society. This is a violent, anti-Semitic group reminiscent of Hitlerite organizations in Nazi Germany. Pamyat is the extreme fringe of a powerful, chauvinistic Russian nationalism. It has not yet become a political force, but it has been attractive to disaffected Russian youth.

It was Russian youth, according to Olcott (1990), who seemed to suffer disproportionately from the numerous social disorders in the USSR at the end of the decade. This is pertinent to our discussion here, because it is Russian youth who are the subjects in the legal socialization research that will be reported. From her examination of youth and nationality in the Soviet Union, Olcott concluded that "the political culture of Russian youth appears to be the most fragmented" (Olcott, 1990: 136). "Russian youths," she said, "seem most attracted to extreme

24 Legal Socialization

political ideologies, such as fascism," as espoused by Pamyat. She also concluded that the political re-education of Russian youth was going to be the most difficult, because unlike non-Russians, they did not have a non-Soviet past that could be reclaimed and reinterpreted, and that could thus form the base for a new political identity. One may disagree with Olcott's conclusion that the Russians do not have a non-Soviet past. But whether that past—in which Russians were united by their culture, their church, and fealty to the tsar—can be the foundation for a new state remains to be seen. After all, Russians have never known a nation-state in the West European sense.

It is ironic that the special relationship and intertwining of Russians and the Soviet state may make it more difficult for Russians to build a legitimate, rule-of-law entity separate from the former Soviet Union, because it is the separate entities and identities—Armenians, Lithuanians, Tatars, Uzbeks—that may offer the best base for building a law-based state or states having legitimacy and moral validity. Mickiewicz (1990) indicated that the most powerful shaper of values in the Soviet Union was membership in a particular ethnic or national group. So putting aside the special case of the Russians, it is at the old republic level (or perhaps at the level of other configurations of national identities) where the best hope for laws and legal systems seen to be deserving of respect and compliance perhaps exists. The Russians, meanwhile, were left "feeling robbed of a sense of place, of purpose and of identity" (*The New York Times*, June 14, 1992).

The Rule of Law

It is perhaps appropriate at this point to define what is meant by "rule of law"— that critical Western legal concept that was absent in Soviet criminal justice processes, and that became a goal of Soviet legal reforms. It is a concept intricately tied up with public perceptions of legitimacy, with acceptance of the necessity of law, and with compliance. Rule of law implies principally the absence of arbitrary power and the limitation of discretionary authority. The values underlying the rule of law include fairness, impartiality, independence, equality, openness, rationality, certainty, and universality (Marshall, 1977). Impartiality and independence require that the processes of justice be divorced from undue political influence and control. Fairness, equality, and rationality require that like cases be treated alike, and that there are sound reasons for all decisions and actions, including any departures from equal treatment. Openness prohibits or restricts the use of confidential or secret materials in criminal cases. It also means that procedures should be open to public scrutiny. Certainty is the opposite of capriciousness; it means that people can plan, predict, and control their lives and behavior so that they are subject to criminal punishment only where they have had fair capacity and opportunity to avoid such punishment. Certainty means that sanctions should "be applied only to persons who have broken a reasonably specific law, who had the full capacity and opportunity to obey the law, and who could reasonably have been expected to know that such a law existed" (Richards, 1981: 274). Finally, universality means that no person is above the law.

In his analysis of the rule of law, the legal philosopher John Rawls (1971) delineated a set of precepts that are useful in the consideration of Soviet law and the subsequent law reforms in the USSR and Russia. Rawls argued that, "other things being equal, one legal order is more justly administered than another if it more perfectly fulfills the precepts of the rule of law" (Rawls, 1971: 236). And, it follows that a more just legal order is (and is believed to be) more deserving of and entitled to compliance. The causal chain thus begins with the rule of law → that leads to more just legal processes → that create a legal environment characterized by fair enforcement of laws and rules, legitimacy of laws, and a carefully delimited role for authority → that, in turn, shapes and determines the three factors comprising legal socialization: legal reasoning, attitudes toward the law, and law-abiding behavior.

Rawls' precepts of the rule of law are:

1. The actions which the rules of law require or forbid should reasonably be actions which people would be expected to do or avoid anyway;
2. Consistent with the role of legitimacy in effecting compliant behavior, "not only must the authorities act in good faith, but their good faith must be recognized by those subject to their enactments. Laws and commands are accepted as laws and commands only if it is generally believed that they can be obeyed and executed."
3. Similar cases should be treated similarly. This precept limits discretion and forces the justification of distinctions made between persons "by reference to the relevant legal rules and principles."
4. There is no offense without a law. "This precept demands that laws be known and expressly promulgated, that their meaning be clearly defined, that statutes be general both in statement and intent and not be used as a way of harming particular individuals."
5. "[T]he rule of law requires some form of due process: that is, a process reasonably designed to ascertain the truth, in ways consistent with the other ends of the legal system, as to whether a violation has taken place and under what circumstances ... judges must be independent and impartial ... [t]rials must be fair and open."

Rawls, 1971: 235–43

Examples from Soviet legal history and practice that will be discussed in Chapter 3 will illustrate the point that the administration of criminal justice in the USSR was not governed by the principles outlined above—thus it lacked legitimacy and moral validity. For more than seven decades, laws were framed, interpreted, and implemented in the service of Communist ideology (Brown, 1992: 1). We will also look

26 Legal Socialization

at some legal reforms that were intended to remedy these problems—to restore justice and, in the words of a Russian colleague, to instill "moral values in the law" (Yakovlev, 1990: 130).

Crime Defines Legal Context

In August 1989, the USSR Supreme Soviet passed a resolution calling for a stepping up of the fight against crime. The resolution said: "Crime in the country, including organized crime, has increased sharply. This is causing justified alarm among the population and is complicating the course of restructuring" (*The Current Digest of the Soviet Press*, 1989). It is necessary to examine just what the crime situation in the Soviet Union was. How much crime was there? What kinds? Most importantly, what were the public concerns regarding crime? And what were the effects of these concerns?

Several threads here are tied to our overall theme: (1) the policy of glasnost included releasing crime data to the public, and also resulted in massive news media coverage of crime stories; (2) democratization and the shrinking of the police state created new criminal opportunities, as well as lessening the deterrence that sprung from fear of that police state; (3) criminal behavior was justified or rationalized by some violators on the basis of their belief that Soviet laws and the Soviet legal system were illegitimate; and (4) as reflected in the above resolution, the fear of crime, along with perceptions of permissiveness on the part of the authorities, led to demands to "get tough" that, in turn, complicated the reform process and undermined what were seen to be overly liberal legal reforms. Shelley (1991), for one, believed that the glasnost revelations "clearly undermined citizen confidence in their safety and the integrity of the system and its officials." She posed the question of whether Gorbachev's policy of glasnost about crime and corruption undermined the very confidence in the system that was needed for its reform. The final answer to that question, as far as Russia is concerned, is still not apparent.

Exposing the Reality of Crime

Soviet crime data were not published after 1928. That is until February 1989, when national crime data were released to the public through the news media. These data indicated that there had been 1.8 million recorded crimes in the USSR in 1987. This represented a rate of 558 crimes reported for every 100,000 people. This figure is extremely low when compared to the 13.6 million reported crimes in the United States in that same year. The comparable U.S. rate per 100,000 in 1987 was 5,550 reported crimes. In other words, the United States had ten times as much reported crime as the Soviet Union. For purposes of this discussion, the reliability and validity of the Soviet figures are not at issue here. The 1987 number increased by 3.8 percent to nearly 1.9 million crimes in 1988; the reported crime rate increased to 657 per 100,000 people. Within this relatively small overall increase, however, there were some ominously large increases: murders and attempted murders went up 14 percent, assault and batteries up 32 percent, violent robberies up 43 percent, and break-ins and holdups up 44 percent. In other words, the crimes that people fear most—the violent crimes against persons—were all up rather dramatically. This trend continued in 1989, when there were 2,461,692 total crimes recorded (an increase of 32 percent over the previous year). Murders, which numbered 14,651 in 1987 and 16,702 in 1988, grew to 21,467 in 1989 (*The Literary Gazette International*, 1990). The rise of crime continued in 1990 when a total of 2,786,606 crimes were reported, an increase of 13.2 percent over 1989.

The fact that these figures reflected a relatively smaller reported crime problem than in the United States is of little or no consequence in terms of its impact upon the perceptions of the average Russian citizen. In the first six months of 1992, following the breakup of the USSR, there were 1.3 million crimes reported in Russia alone, a one-third increase over the 1 million reported in the first six months of 1991. The biggest increases in Russian crime were in burglaries and property thefts. A Russian Interior Ministry official was reported saying of these increases: "People do not believe they will be punished any more for committing crimes . . . They know the system has broken down, and they are less afraid of this system then they used to be" (*The New York Times*, August 2, 1992: 10). This kind of social breakdown presents a situation in which rules/laws cannot be "legitimate" when they are being visibly and massively violated by a large proportion of the people. Russia may have gone from one kind of illegitimacy to another; the earlier dominant role of deterrence seemed clearly to have been lost; and moral validity remained a question mark.

One of the clear byproducts of the earlier glasnost about crime was that the Soviet public became very fearful; and, as was the case in the United States beginning in the late 1960s, Soviet citizens consequently toughened their attitudes about crime and criminals. For example, a 1989 poll by the *Moscow News* newspaper reported that 33 percent of Moscow residents (as compared with 38 percent of New Yorkers) were afraid of going out alone at night (*The New York Times*, September 17, 1989). This same *Times* article reported frustration among Soviet citizens at "the sociological subtleties that underpin proposals for reforming criminal law now being considered in the Supreme Soviet, proposals such as eliminating the death penalty for economic crimes." That article noted an essay in the then-Communist Party newspaper *Pravda* that equated humanizing justice with protecting lawbreakers' rights. This raised the thorny issue that, as is the situation in the U.S. and other democracies, the chief direct beneficiaries of expanded rights and due process are offenders. Non-offenders for the most part do not need to avail themselves of the right to remain silent, of the right to be presumed innocent, and of the right to have an attorney.

The average law-abiding citizen, whether Russian or American, questions the need for and the value of expanding due process rights for criminals, particularly

28 Legal Socialization

during a time of rising crime, violence, and victimization of innocents. In the U.S., this problem has usually been resolved, at least for most American citizens, by the recognition that their constitutional rights ultimately protect all of them, and that these frustrating contradictions are one of the prices that have to be paid for living in a democracy. The key difference between the American and Russian situations is, of course, that Russia has no history of democracy and no history of limitations on arbitrary applications of governmental power—limitations that would give its laws legitimacy, and help to encourage acceptance and support.

Solomon (1992c) argues that the 1989 crime scare—the social panic—was, to a degree, manufactured by conservative officials and compliant journalists. Conservative law enforcement officials, according to Solomon, used the crime figures to attack "the new protections of the rights of defendants; the 'humanization' of the criminal law . . . and even democratization in general" (Solomon, 1992c: 247). He agrees that public calls for law and order create an unfavorable climate for liberal criminal law reform.

In addition to the difficulties and complications already described, there is also a "self-justifying ideology" that has long infected the Russian population. This infection is said to have been the basis for some of the criminal and delinquent behavior in the Soviet Union in a manner not unlike the techniques of neutralization that Sykes and Matza (1957) claimed characterize American juvenile delinquency. The Center for Humanization of the [Soviet] Penal System offered an illustration of this idea. They indicated that this self-justifying ideology rested upon the belief that everyone in the Soviet Union stole. There was a belief

> that the distribution of goods in our society depends not on how well you work or serve, but on how well you can steal and establish relationships with "the right people." The press today serves to strengthen this ideology as it reveals corruption throughout all aspects of society.
>
> *Chesnokova et al., 1990: 20*

The result was what appears to be a sort of perverse combination of "the ends justify the means" rationalization, with an excess of newly developing illegitimate opportunities amid limited legitimate opportunities, combined with a belief that "everyone is doing it." Thus, young people in particular were believed to justify their deviancy because of the corruption and perceived illegitimacy of the Soviet system.

The Center for the Study of Public Opinion conducted a survey of more than 3,000 people from throughout the country just before the August 1991 coup. It asked whether it was possible to live in the Soviet Union without violating the law. Just over half the respondents (51 percent) answered no. Among young people under 24, 66 percent said no (*Nezavisimaya Gazeta*, November 1991). Have such beliefs changed since the demise of the USSR? No! On the contrary, matters have only gotten worse.

The Soviet Mafia

The New York Times reported in 1989 that:

> Western-style cooperative enterprises [in the Soviet Union] . . . are being harassed by protection racketeers and organized criminals looking for ways to launder their money . . . Police officials . . . are dramatically announcing that, unless drastic changes can be financed, they will lose the struggle against organized crime that is being highlighted in press reports on tsar-like "godfathers."
>
> *September 17, 1989: E2*

The very idea that there was such a thing as organized crime in the USSR was perhaps amazing and incredulous to many outsiders. After all, American images of organized crime, linked as they usually are with the Italian or Sicilian Mafia and Cosa Nostra, and with *The Godfather*, seemed antithetical to at least the stereotypical view of Soviet society and of the Soviet political and legal systems. Soviet society was seemingly not plagued by drugs, gambling, prostitution, loansharking, and so on—the staples of Western organized crime. It is true that organized crime in the Soviet Union was not like organized crime in the United States. But, it was organized crime nonetheless.

The chief difference between the two was that, whereas in the U.S. organized crime is principally engaged in the provision of illegal goods and services, in the USSR the most elite form of organized crime was that involving the illegal provision of what were otherwise legal goods and services but that were subject to chronic shortages. The top echelon of Soviet organized crime was occupied by Communist Party chiefs and top-level government bureaucrats. This *apparat* abused and exploited their positions and power in a kind of white-collar crime that was the main Soviet version of organized crime. It was the glasnost exposure of this abuse of power in particular, of the rampant corruption that accompanied it, and of the hypocrisy of it all, that contributed a great deal to the disillusionment of the Soviet people (Miller et al., 1990–91). Beliefs in the moral validity of the law and in the legitimacy of the system were badly battered by these revelations—revelations that fueled the self-justifications and rationalizations mentioned earlier.

We will examine this strange animal—the Soviet mafia—in some detail in Chapter 5. We will also look there, in depth, at organized crime in Russia today, and at our next topic as well.

Corruption and the Shadow Economy

Corruption in the United States involves principally the extortion and/or acceptance of bribes by politicians and public officials, including law enforcement officials. In return for payoffs and favors, officials grant public contracts, circumvent the law, overlook violations, suppress prosecutions, and so on. American organized

30 Legal Socialization

crime, for example, employs corruption to immunize itself from arrest and prosecution. Because the regulated market economy of the U.S. assumes a basically free, competitive process to produce the best economic outcomes, any introduction of corruption distorts that process and thus changes the nature of the outcomes. Rigged bidding on public contracts tends to result in a product of lower quality, but at higher cost. The ultimate losers are the American public consumers.

Much of the organized crime and no small amount of the corruption in the USSR similarly arose out of the peculiarities of the Soviet economic system. Because of the massive shortages and dislocations produced by the Soviet economy, there was always a thriving black market there. It should be noted that one of the principal aims of the Gorbachev and now Yeltsin reforms has been to revitalize the economy by changing it from a command, centrally planned form to a mixed public-private market form that encourages private enterprises, such as cooperatives. There has been considerable controversy over just how this should be done, and over what it will ultimately look like. Historically, scarce goods and services that were unavailable through normal channels could usually be gotten through "*blat*" or connections, or "*na levo*," literally on the left. A second so-called shadow economy and a black market evolved to operate in tandem with the official, state-run economy.

Because goods are priced much higher on the black market, there is incentive to siphon off goods from the official market for sale on the black market. During the Soviet era, government bureaucrats and party apparatchiks were best positioned to do this siphoning, and were also in the best position to obtain and market goods not available at all from Soviet production. The latter included such things as fine wines, liquors, designer clothing, automobiles, electronics, and so on. It was in these ways that corruption crept in. It also came in the more traditional forms of arranging (for a fee or possibly some other quid pro quo) for housing, jobs, university placements, and medical care. So, the political system did the positioning, and the economic system allowed and even encouraged and rewarded the exploitation. Unfortunately, these same apparatchiks, reborn as democrats and/ or nationalists, are still best positioned to exploit the Russian economy.

Shlapentokh described the black market:

> Corruption is generally based on the exploitation of a position in an organization or the consumers of its services . . . The black market is a direct outgrowth of the process of privatization inside the state because the better part of the goods circulated on the market are offered by those who in one way or another may have exploited their official position.
>
> *Shlapentokh, 1989: 208, 211*

Just as in the United States, and despite official protestations to the contrary, the Soviet political and socioeconomic system always bred illegal dealings.

These illegal dealings, which in many instances as just indicated, involved organized crime, were simultaneously the result and the cause of the shortages. The existence of the shadow economy brought about theft, bribe-taking, and abuse of official positions because of the great potential for personal profit. Breakdowns in the central planning process resulted in official abuses because managers of state enterprises were forced to resort to illegal means in order to fulfill state-mandated production plans. These illegal means included theft, bribery, and fraud. Theft, bribery, deception, and cheating, along with shortages and poor-quality goods, were all inherent elements of the Soviet economy.

The insidious effects of more than 70 years under this model result in the conclusion that those who believed that everyone in the Soviet Union stole—whether they used this belief as a justification for their own unlawful behavior or not—were not too far wrong! After studying the Soviet black market, two Soviet scholars, Belikova and Shokin, concluded: "The most negative practical result of trafficking [on the black market] may be [a] shift of moral accent, [a] blurring of the borderline between 'bad' and 'good,' respectable' and 'unworthy'" (Belikova and Shokin, 1989: 32). This kind of moral ambiguity goes to the heart of the point about legitimacy and perceptions of legitimacy being one of the cornerstones of legal socialization. Lest one be too quick to assume, however, that moral and legal hypocrisy were/are unique to Russia, we are reminded that "[t]he . . . tendency to wink at successful evasions of the moral code—the psychopathy of everyday life—is [also] as American as apple pie" (Rieber and Green, 1990: 85).

These bitter fruits of Soviet legal history, notwithstanding that they are not peculiar to Russia, are among the products of a unique system in which the law was subordinated to the desires of a monolithic Communist Party and its self-appointed state officials. This system glorified and attempted to furnish ideological legitimacy for itself, while denying the existence of serious social and economic problems. Dobson (1991: 232) described one further effect of this political schizophrenia: "The pervasive mendacity about Soviet history and society led many young people to develop a 'dual morality' (one for public display, another for their private lives)." It could be argued that what was actually being produced was a kind of amorality. In any event, whether it is amorality or dual morality, we will examine it and its effects.

Russia struggles to survive and to make economic and political progress while experiencing what has been described as a disintegrating collective consciousness. It is within this framework of history and current events that the study of legal socialization was undertaken.

2

FOUNDATIONS FOR THE STUDY OF LEGAL SOCIALIZATION

Having framed the structure of the Soviet legal context, we will now turn to the other half of the picture that I am trying to paint here. This is the half that deals with legal socialization. We will examine legal socialization from a number of different angles, and I will press my case that this special form of socialization does not occur in a vacuum. Instead, it is very much influenced by the sociolegal environment in which it takes place. To complete the picture, this chapter reviews and summarizes four main bodies of literature: (1) legal socialization theory; (2) legal socialization and delinquency research; (3) cross-cultural and comparative studies; and (4) legal socialization in the former Soviet Union. This literature both provided the conceptual foundation and influenced the design of the present research.

Theoretical Perspectives

Legal socialization has been defined as "the development of values, attitudes, and behaviors toward law." Legal socialization "focuses on the individual's standards for making sociolegal judgments and for resolving conflicts, pressing claims, and settling disputes" (Tapp and Levine, 1974: 4). The theory of legal development is derived primarily from cognitive developmental theory.

Four strategies for socialization into a legal system can be identified: (1) the legal knowledge strategy giving substantive information about the law and the legal network through some form of legal education; (2) a mismatch and conflict strategy providing challenging experiences in the form of legal or ethical dilemmas that force the questioning of one's existing reasoning and problem-solving; (3) participation that stimulates legal development through role-taking, communication, reciprocity, and so on, in a form of participatory democracy; and (4) a legal

The Study of Legal Socialization **33**

continuity strategy that allows for seeing the relationship among various rule systems and having the individual actively engaged in the development of a network of rule/law systems (Tapp and Levine, 1977: 174–6). One example of this latter kind of continuity would be that between the formal law system and the informal rule system(s) that were described in the first chapter.

Legal socialization builds particularly upon the work of Piaget (1932) and most especially that of Kohlberg (1958, 1963, 1964, 1968a, 1968b, 1969). Consistent with Kohlberg's moral development theory, legal socialization is said to progress across three levels: pre-conventional law-obeying, conventional law-maintaining, and post-conventional lawmaking (Tapp and Kohlberg, 1971; Tapp and Levine, 1974; Levine and Tapp, 1977).

Individuals operating at the first (Level I) of the three stages of legal reasoning are said to be guided in their reasoning by a focus on external consequences and authority. Afraid of punishment and physical harm, they are particularly deferential toward power. Such persons are deterred from criminal or delinquent behavior by their fear of punishment. Laws and rules do not have any particular inherent goodness or value; they are to be obeyed (unless that can be avoided) simply because of the negative consequences one could suffer through disobedience. This pre-conventional law-deferring stance has been shown empirically to be especially characteristic of younger children (Hess and Tapp, 1969; Minturn and Tapp, 1970; Tapp, 1987a,1987b).

Level II is a law and order, conformity posture. Persons operating or reasoning at this level are concerned with role expectations and their fulfillment. Most youth, by preadolescence, reason from this conventional, system maintenance perspective. In fact, it is the predominant level of legal reasoning through adolescence and into adulthood for most adult groups (Tapp, 1987b). At this level, people are influenced by both the informal (micro-level) and formal (macro-level) social control coming from rules and laws. These rules and laws define what behavior is acceptable and permissible and what is not. You follow a rule because you want to be accepted as a member of a particular group, or you follow a law because you want to be an accepted member of the society. It is what you are supposed to do. Rules/laws and their enforcement are perceived to be legitimate.

Post-conventional (Level III) reasoning is engaged in by "[p]rincipled, thinking individuals [who] . . . see the need for social systems and yet can differentiate between the values of a given social order and universal ethics" (Tapp and Levine, 1974: 22). The rare individuals at this level of legal reasoning see that all laws are not the same. They discriminate among laws and evaluate them in terms of universal principles of justice and fairness—of moral validity. This level captures the notion of the principled obligation to violate unjust laws, America's "Jim Crow" laws for example, in order to contest their unjustness. In the Soviet Union, dissident Andrei Sakharov's human rights activities and exercise of free speech that landed him in exile might also be considered an example of Level III functioning.

34 The Study of Legal Socialization

Previous research shows relatively few persons, even among adult samples, reasoning at this third level. The results of research on legal socialization generally parallel those produced by moral development research in this regard—as well as in other respects (Rest, 1979). In both instances, most persons are found to reason at the middle, conventional level.

Just as there are age-related changes in conceptions of morality, there are age-related changes in conceptions of legality. It appears that the meaning of law loses its absolutism between childhood and adolescence, and that children become more flexible as their legal reasoning shifts from the concrete to the abstract (Radosevich and Krohn, 1981).

Cross-cultural research by Tapp and others over two decades supports the existence of a progressive legal reasoning construct in the growth of ideas on justice and law. This research shows the following: (1) the same levels of development have occurred in all the cultures studied; (2) the pattern of legal reasoning progresses from a pre-conventional law-deferring to a conventional law-maintaining, and in rare cases, toward a post-conventional law-making level; (3) the progression is marked by some variation showing the effects of socializing and educational experiences; and (4) these experiences can take such forms as participation in legal conflict resolution and law-related education (Tapp, 1987b: 4–5). A more recent study by Cohn and White (1986) found legal developmental level to be a predictor of the normative and enforcement statuses of certain destructive, disorderly, and social disturbance behaviors. Such behaviors (in the abstract) were found to be more accepted at lower levels of legal reasoning, and less accepted at higher levels.

The work of both cognitive developmental psychologists and other social scientists interested in political socialization supports the notion of age- and knowledge-related trends toward more democratic attitudes and more complex reasoning. Age and knowledge are positively correlated, and both are associated with higher levels of reasoning. The age- and knowledge-related trends show shifts in attitudes toward wrongdoing, punishment, and the law that are progressively more liberal and humanitarian and less authoritarian (Adelson, 1971; Gallatin and Adelson, 1977; Brown, 1974; Kohlberg and Elfenbein, 1975; Mussen et al., 1977; Wilson, 1981; Nelsen et al., 1982).

Legal Knowledge

As indicated earlier, one of the ways in which a person becomes socialized—that is, develops a sense of ethical/moral legality—is through gaining legal knowledge. The role of legal knowledge (and legal education) is particularly interesting here, because law-related education is a popular pedagogical technique for attempting to enhance ethical legal socialization. This was especially true in the Soviet Union. The position of the principal legal socialization theorists on legal knowledge was stated as follows:

The Study of Legal Socialization **35**

We do not contend that knowledge about law determines either attitudes or behaviors. In fact, research suggests that factors such as peer influence are more important than legal knowledge . . . In general, it is not knowledge per se but one's mode of reasoning with available information that determines the making and acting upon specific legal decisions. In our view, [however] acquiring knowledge about law (whether one endorses the law or not) is essential because information about rights, rules, expectations, and so forth expands the ability to understand problems, relate to events, and structure choices.

Tapp and Levine, 1974: 32

Tapp and Levine argued that knowledge is a necessary, but not by itself a sufficient element in promoting progressively more sophisticated levels of legal reasoning. It is necessary because it provides the basis for understanding the need for the rules and principles embodied in the justice system. Numerous law-related education efforts, undertaken in the U.S. and elsewhere, have not, however, always been mindful of its limitations. One theoretical rationale for assuming a relationship among knowledge of the law, positive (law-conscious or law-abiding) attitudes, and law-abiding behavior follows:

A common argument is that increased knowledge of the law will produce greater conformity to the law. At least three mechanisms for this effect can be suggested. One is simple reduction of error; those who know the law are less likely to break it by mistake . . . A second argument is that greater knowledge of the law produces greater cognitive and moral support for law; a person's behavior comes to be characterized by his intellectual convictions about the law. Both studies of moral development (e.g., Kohlberg) and social control theories of delinquency (in their inclusion of "belief in the moral validity of the law") work this vein. Finally, it may be proposed that greater knowledge of the law will produce a greater fear of the consequences of breaking it—the perceived certainty, quickness, or severity of punishment will rise with gains in knowledge, thus reducing the probability of law violation.

Law-Related Education Evaluation Project, 1983: 171

The research evidence testing the links among knowledge, attitudes, and law-abidingness is very mixed. While studies of legal knowledge and attitudes have revealed that children's knowledge of the law increases with age (Bargman, 1974; Klar, 1974; Markwood, 1975), attitudes toward the law seemed to become increasingly negative from childhood to preadolescence and adolescence (Portune, 1965; Klar, 1974; Markwood, 1975). This has been the case especially for blacks, males, those from lower socioeconomic backgrounds, and for urban youth (Bouma, 1969; Park, 1970; Torney, 1977; Liebshultz and Niemi, 1974; Fox,

36 The Study of Legal Socialization

1974). Jacobson and Palonsky (1981) found that greater legal knowledge did not lead to more positive attitudes toward the law. Rafky and Sealey (1975) found that legal knowledge was unrelated to either respect for the law or to disruptive behavior. Markowitz (1986), likewise, reported that there was no relationship between increased knowledge of the law and either improved attitudes or behavior.

A three-year national study carried out by the Law-Related Education Evaluation Project demonstrated that law-related course content alone did not improve students' attitudes, build "good citizenship," or reduce delinquency. It provided, however, what was called a "convenient and effective hook" upon which to hang some features that could achieve these objectives. These features included using outside resource persons and good illustrative case materials, and promoting student interaction around controversial issues (Law-Related Education Evaluation Project, 1983). The latter are examples of the legal socialization strategies of mismatch and conflict, and of participation, referred to earlier.

Some promising results come from other studies as well. Brown (1974) found that positive orientations toward the law, police, and the courts were negatively related to certain self-reported delinquency measures. Huba and Bentler (1983) reported that low "law abidance" (law abidance was defined as a generalized tendency to respect the rules of law-setting institutions in society) causally pre-ceded drug use and other deviant behaviors. Other research from the Law-Related Education Evaluation Project (1983) indicated that measures of belief (e.g., favorable attitudes toward the police, unfavorable attitudes toward deviance, rationalizations for deviance, etc.) were strongly correlated in the expected direc-tions with self-reported delinquency. These findings suggest that if young people believe in the law and the justice system, and in its equity and fairness, they may be less likely to engage in delinquency. The research does not, however, provide much support for the idea that simply by means of some formal instruction in the law (i.e., using only the legal knowledge socialization strategy), one can significantly influence the law-abiding behavior of children and youth.

In their study of law-related attitudes, Palonsky and Jacobson (1982) included in their sample a group of juvenile offenders confined in a state training school. They found that these offenders were more negative toward the law than the comparative group of elementary and junior high school students. Chapman (1955–56), Portune (1965), Fox (1974), and Bowlus et al. (1974) reported similar findings. In the Palonsky and Jacobson study, the junior high student/juvenile offender comparisons did not produce differences that were statistically significant. Both groups, however, were more negative than the younger elementary school students. This finding confirmed the importance of age as a predictor of negative attitudes toward the law. Knowledge was positively, albeit modestly, correlated with attitudes. The researchers concluded that "The students who know the most about the law are not necessarily those with the most favorable attitudes toward the law" (Palonsky and Jacobson, 1982: 27). But they also concluded that the

The Study of Legal Socialization **37**

condition of delinquency was a "moderate" predictor of negative attitudes toward the law.

What influences what among knowledge of the law, attitudes toward the law, and delinquency results in a kind of chicken and egg argument. For example, youth who become involved in juvenile delinquency may, as a result, gain more knowledge about the workings of the juvenile justice system and juvenile law. They may also, again as a result, develop more negative attitudes. This complex issue of the relationships of legal knowledge, attitudes, and behavior leads us to our next area of discussion.

Legal Socialization and Juvenile Delinquency

The Tapp (and Kohlberg and Levine) model of legal socialization has been criticized for a lack of evidence supporting the behavioral consequences of legal judgments; and, for making the assumption that judgments are the cause of actions (Hogan and Mills, 1976). Kohlberg and his colleagues, who have been similarly criticized about the lack of fit between moral judgments and moral behavior (Blasi, 1980), have argued that the relationship between moral reasoning and moral behavior is complex, but that there is a significant, although not direct relationship between them (Jennings et al., 1983). The legal reasoning-legal behavior connection, on the other hand, has received much less attention and empirical investigation. Whatever the merits of these discussions, Levine (1979) concurred that the research had produced mixed results in finding relationships between moral and legal reasoning processes and behavior. All this is good cause to investigate the issues further—particularly with respect to the relations among knowledge of the law, belief in the moral validity, justice, and fairness of the law, other aspects of legal socialization, and juvenile delinquency.

One interesting difference between the limited legal socialization research results, and those from moral development research, is that the one legal socialization study that included "law deviants" as subjects, in this case prison inmates, reported no differences in their reasoning and the reasoning of college youth, teachers, or lawyers (Tapp and Levine, 1974: 30; Levine and Tapp, 1977). Unfortunately, given our particular interest in youth, in addition to being one of the only findings on law deviants, the study involved adult criminals as opposed to juveniles.

Turning of necessity to the moral development literature, as the closest kin to legal socialization, we find that some research on the moral development of juvenile delinquents indicates they do reason at a lower moral level than do non-delinquents (Fodor, 1972, 1973; Jurkovic and Prentice, 1977; Jurkovic, 1980; Sagi and Eisikovits, 1981; Jennings et al., 1983; Hains, 1984). This has not, however, been a uniform finding. For example, Emler, Heather, and Winton (1978) found that the degree and seriousness of involvement in delinquency was unrelated to immaturity of moral reasoning.

38   The Study of Legal Socialization

Blasi's comprehensive and critical review of this literature reached three conclusions: (1) there is support for the hypothesis that delinquents use lower modes of moral reasoning than do matched non-delinquents; (2) it is clear that a range of moral reasoning stages can be present among delinquents; and (3) moral reasoning is an important aspect of delinquency, but does not by itself explain delinquent behavior (Blasi, 1980: 12).

Some Kohlbergians argue that lower moral reasoning is a necessary, but not sufficient cause of delinquency in that "higher reasoning makes one a more reliable moral agent and thus better able to withstand some incentives to illegal conduct" (Jennings et al., 1983: 311). Further, they say pre-conventional thinkers may feel less obligated to conform to any conventions—either of the larger society (in the form of society's laws) or of a subcultural group (in the form of informal rules). Damon (1988) also agreed that there are no simple answers to the question of whether higher moral reasoning leads to moral behavior, but concluded that moral judgment does make a difference. "But it does not operate in a vacuum. It shares its influence with many social-contextual factors that also play some role . . . in determining a person's behavior" (Damon, 1988: 46).

Although Tapp (1970) had earlier indicated that, as with moral development theory, failure to develop beyond pre-conventional legal reasoning between the ages of 10 and 14 may lead to delinquency, to date there has been no empirical evidence to support this belief. To the contrary, Morash (1981, 1982) found that legal reasoning was not significantly associated with seriousness of delinquency. She concluded that there was no support for "the proposition that delinquency results from failure to develop beyond a preconventional reasoning level" (Morash, 1981: 367). Morash admitted, however, that her studies had a number of limitations that called for further research.

Notwithstanding the many similarities between moral development/ socialization and legal development/socialization, Levine (and Tapp and others) claim that "legal reasoning and moral judgment are not identical constructs but depict distinct, albeit related, valuation processes" (Levine, 1979: 182). All this seems to provide good and sufficient scientific and social reasons to investigate the relationship of "the distinct process" of legal socialization to juvenile delinquency (Yakovlev, 1988). Does legal reasoning have any relation to delinquency? Is this relationship similar to that of moral reasoning? If not, how and why is it different? And are there differences in the relationship as between different legal contexts?

A related theoretical construct that also supports the argument for further research comes from the work of Travis Hirschi (1969). It is this construct that might help explain the earlier-mentioned findings associating belief in the law's justice and fairness with law-abiding behavior. Hirschi's social control theory comports with moral development and legal socialization theories. Kohlberg and his colleagues concur that "[t]he portion of delinquent behavior that is explained by immature moral reasoning is most theoretically and empirically compatible with social-control theory" (Jennings et al., 1983: 347). One key component of social control theory is the principle of "belief in the moral validity of social rules." This principle proposes that there is variation in the extent to which people—including children and young people—believe they should obey the rules of society, and that the less a person believes he should obey the rules, the more likely he is to violate them (Hirschi, 1969: 26).

In testing his thesis, Hirschi learned there was variation in the extent to which the boys in his study believed they should obey the law. The less they believed they should obey it, the less likely they were to do so. Respect for the law was strongly related to the commission of delinquent acts, so that where estimation of the moral validity of the law was less, there was greater likelihood of law violations (Hirschi, 1969: 204–5).

Here we will attempt to build on these foundations. Legal socialization involves young people internalizing the normative rules, social conventions, and moral codes of their society—at least partially through a combination of the four socializing strategies described earlier. The completeness and effectiveness of this socialization in engendering higher estimates of the moral validity of law may be measured by their rule-breaking and law-breaking behavior. Thus, it can be hypothesized that those operating at Legal Level III (if there are any) may be less likely to engage in delinquent acts than those operating at Legal Levels I or II; and those at Level II may be less delinquent than those at Level I.

The work of Cohn and White (1990), referred to earlier, suggests, however, that such hypotheses are very tenuous and simplistic. They found no relationship between legal reasoning level and whether their research subjects (university students) were rule followers or violators. It was not the case, they concluded, that people at lower levels of legal reasoning are more inclined to violate rules than are people at higher levels of reasoning. Does that mean that legal reasoning is therefore irrelevant to legal behavior? No!

"[L]egal reasoning," according to Cohn and White, "is related to rule-governed behaviors through attitudinal mediators" (Cohn and White, 1990: 130). Legal context, the way rules and laws are made and enforced, shapes attitudes toward those laws and their enforcement. These attitudes, in turn, enter into the reasoning process. For example, experiencing authoritarian rule or law enforcement can create negative attitudes and undermine the connections between legal reasoning and rule- or law-governed behavior. In doing legal socialization research, then, one must pay close attention to the variations (along a spectrum of authoritarian to non-authoritarian) in legal environments, for example, the U.S. and the USSR. The moral authority of the law enforcer, say Cohn and White, comes from the willingness of the subject to accept the legitimacy of enforcement. "[Enforcement] without legitimacy decreases the moral content of the situation," and a person under those conditions with a capacity for Level III reasoning may actually be reduced to Level I reasoning (Cohn and White, 1990: 177).

So, legal context is variable, and at least one of its forms of variability is its degree of authoritarianism. Legal context also operates at two levels: a formal,

40 The Study of Legal Socialization

law–governed level, and an informal, rule–governed level. Likewise, legitimacy is variable, and does not, according to Cohn and White, translate into a generalized or fixed concept of obligation to obey the law. "We conclude that the distinction between conventional and postconventional legal reasoning, while it may hold in terms of reasoning in the abstract, does not make sense in the social context in which the interaction between reasoning and the environment takes place" (Cohn and White, 1990: 179). What is needed according to these authors, is research that focuses on the ideological forces that shape the content of legal reasoning; which focuses on social structure and the role of political domination in the legal environment. The research reported here will do that.

The hypotheses mentioned earlier are further complicated by the differences between belief (as defined and operationalized by Hirschi, for example) and reasoning (as operationally defined by the moral development/legal socialization theorists, e.g., Tapp). Reasoning is very much dependent upon intellectual capacity, upon intelligence and education; whereas belief is not. Reasoning is a rational–empirical process. The greater a person's cognitive skills, the better able they are to judge their own and others' behavior and the reasons for that behavior.

Belief, on the other hand, is often blind; we can and do, for example, believe in myths. And beliefs in myths (the "gnarled thickets of dubious ideas that do not readily yield to contrary evidence") govern behavior, perhaps just as effectively, if not even more effectively, than the cognitive processes of moral or legal reasoning. Religious beliefs, for example, have been a great constraint on human behavior down through the ages.

Yakovlev (1988) and others (Cohn and White, 1992) have also pointed out that legal reasoning may actually involve the rationalization of deviant behavior, the neutralization of rules and laws, and after-the-fact justification for behavior. Thus, law–abiding behavior need not follow from more sophisticated legal reasoning. Even the smartest lawyers can and do become criminals. It may also be that as Cohn and White suggest, some behavior must occur first in order to be the catalyst for the cognitive processes involved in legal reasoning. A young person thinks about why he or she should obey the law only after having broken the law, and been caught and punished. If the conclusion is to avoid further punishment (special deterrence), the youth is a pre-conventional reasoner. If the conclusion is because the law has moral validity, and is morally congruent with the youth's own sense of right and wrong, then he or she is a conventional or even a post-conventional reasoner.

It is obviously necessary that the differences among and between knowledge, belief, and reasoning be sorted out, and that the relationships among attitudes, reasoning, and behavior likewise be examined. It is further obvious that this should be done while taking account of the legal environments in which socialization occurs.

Cross-Cultural and Comparative Studies

The major cross-cultural and comparative study of legal socialization was commenced in 1965 (Hess and Tapp, 1969; Minturn and Tapp, 1970). In that study, almost 5,000 youngsters were subjected to both attitudinal and surrogate behavioral measures to determine their socialization into compliance. To understand further the reasons for their initial answers, 406 preadolescent (ages 10 to 14) children from six countries were interviewed and scored for legal levels (Tapp, 1970; Tapp and Kohlberg, 1971). In addition to the United States, the countries represented by the sample included Denmark, Greece, India, Italy, and Japan. That research collected information on children's perceptions of and attitudes toward authority, rules, and aggression in various compliance systems such as the home, school, government, and community. This research demonstrated a "universality" in modes of legal reasoning, that there were clear cross-cultural commonalities among the preadolescents in the six countries and seven cultures investigated—both black and white samples were employed in the United States (Tapp and Kohlberg, 1971; Tapp and Levine, 1974).

There are a number of characteristics and factors concerning this original research that make new cross-cultural studies imperative. First is the concern that these results are dated, and that the conclusions therefore may no longer be valid. Have there been relevant historical or contextual effects over the past 25 years that would influence or change these findings for contemporary samples?

Second, the countries from which the samples were drawn included only a limited number of Western-style democracies, albeit with different cultural and religious traditions. Would children and youth from other countries with very different cultural, economic, political, and legal traditions—and thus legal environments—respond differently? In particular, do Russian youth experience their legal worlds and construct their maps of legality differently than do young people in the West?

The original rule-law interview used by Tapp and her colleagues in the 1960s is now available in a shorter, ten-item, closed-ended format. Although that form has produced reliable and valid results in the U.S. with adults, it has not been utilized with youngsters nor in cross-cultural research.

The data collected in the earlier cross-cultural studies did not include information on knowledge of the law of the respective countries, on attitudes toward the law and the justice system, on beliefs in the justice and fairness of the legal system, nor on behavior (except in the most abstract way). In considering this research, Cohn and White (1990: 184) agreed that those who criticized it as "narrow, tepid, and irrelevant to the learning process are correct."

Finally, and most particularly, the prior research dealt with young people who were all ostensibly non-delinquents, and thus did not encompass delinquency as a variable nor delinquents as a sample—although it superficially probed law-breaking through surrogate variables. The relationship between legal socialization and juvenile delinquency has not been examined.

42 The Study of Legal Socialization

Legal Socialization in Russia

Although there have been no specific studies of the Tapp et al. theory of legal socialization in the former Soviet Union, there have been a number of genre-related studies of law or legal consciousness (see, e.g., Chyapas, Dolgova, Groshev, Guskov, Igoshev, Noskova, Pavilonin, Ratinov, Efremova, Yermakov, and Yutskova—all cited by Ivanov, 1988; the originals are unfortunately unavailable in English).

Among the results compiled by Ivanov from the Soviet studies he cited are the following:

1. Ratinov found that basic differences between law-abiding individuals and offenders were not based upon their knowledge of the law, but rather on their attitude toward the law and its practical implementation.
2. Dolgova found that youthful offenders rated law rather low as a social value, and that offenders lacked clear understanding of the social meaning of legal rules and were not "sufficiently" aware of the unfavorable consequences of violating the criminal law.
3. Convicted offenders have been shown in some cases to have a greater knowledge of criminal laws and legal institutions and norms than more minor offenders or non-offenders.
4. Contrary to the above result, Guskov discovered that youthful recidivists knew less about the criminal law than did first-time offenders and non-offenders.
5. Offenders have been found to have a more guarded and distrustful attitude toward judicial authorities, and to believe that punishment is too severe; but to also perceive a lesser risk in committing crimes than do non-offenders.
6. Young offenders were seen to have a low view, a sort of rationalized view of crimes and criminal behavior. Theft and misappropriation of socialist property, for example, were not seen to be particularly wrong—nor was the use of alcohol or participating in a fight. Offenders also had a hostile attitude toward the police, and paid more attention to the unwritten laws of their peer group.
7. On the issue of belief, Ratinov and Efremova found that only one-third of convicted offenders felt that people follow the law because they believe in it, whereas among law-abiding youth the figure was 70 percent. The former, more so than the latter, believe it is people's fear of punishment that motivates them to obey the law.

Ivanov concluded that from this series of studies by Soviet criminologists in the 1970s and 1980s, young offenders were shown to differ from non-offenders on the nature and scope of their legal knowledge, their degree of commitment to the law, the depth and stability of their unlawful orientations, and the degree of their social and legal activity. "Results of the study have confirmed the general hypothesis that legal consciousness, as one of the sources of social activity, is a factor which directs [the] lawful and unlawful behavior of people" (Ivanov, 1988: 12–13).

The Study of Legal Socialization **43**

There were also cross-cultural studies of general socialization in the Soviet Union (e.g., Bronfenbrenner, 1970; Whyte, 1977); of political socialization (e.g., Hahn, 1969; Clawson, 1973; Cary, 1974; Berman, 1977); of moral judgment (e.g., Ziv et al., 1975); and of legal education (e.g., Ioffe, 1978; Gerbich, 1978; Sukharev, 1978; Fomin, 1978). Cary, Clawson, Hahn, and Whyte all spoke to the particular importance of primary groups—the collectives—in the socialization of Soviet children. The informal groups of parents, peers, and teachers, were generally considered to be more influential than the formal groups, such as, for example, the Komsomol or Young Communist League.

In a study that has been criticized by some because they believed he was taken in by Soviet authorities,[1] Urie Bronfenbrenner compared sixth-graders in selected Soviet and American schools, and concluded that the strong emphasis on collective upbringing and collective discipline in the Soviet schools produced more conformity to adult standards. This was in contrast to the American children, who were more autonomous and individualistic, and who were more subject to deviant peer group norms. The collective, according to Bronfenbrenner, is an effective device for enforcing group norms on individuals. And the result is relatively obedient, disciplined young people willing to conform to the demands of their society. This conclusion is relevant to the contrast between group-oriented versus individually oriented societies pointed out earlier. Bronfenbrenner's study demonstrates how the authority (both coercive and moral) and the legitimacy of informal social control networks may counteract or overcome the kind of disrespect and lack of acceptance that might be expected to follow from living in a "lawless" and "immoral" formal legal environment.

Is there reason to doubt that Bronfenbrenner's somewhat rosy picture of upbringing in the USSR, if it ever existed, existed at the time of our research? Perhaps. In a 1987 piece that he entitled "Russia's Restless Youth," *New York Times* correspondent William Keller cited evidence of the beginnings of alienation, disillusionment, and rebellion among Soviet youth, including a growing drug problem. Describing what he called the "malaise" of these young people, Keller said: "Soviet analysts have discovered a general failure of the institutions designed to mold Russian children into bright-eyed young Socialists. Komsomol [the Communist party's youth organization] doesn't work, school doesn't work, the army doesn't work, even work doesn't work" (Keller, 1987: 27). As a kind of counterpoint to Bronfenbrenner's approving appraisal of Soviet schools, Keller indicated that Soviet schools had come under assault from academic reformers "who argue[d] that teaching is regimented and stifling, and does not encourage the creative thinking necessary if the Soviet Union is to catch up with the age of high technology" (Keller, 1987: 27).

Soviet-born psychiatrist Boris Segal said flatly that Bronfenbrenner's assumptions about collective upbringing producing good behavior and conformity in Soviet youths were wrong (Segal, 1990).

It is fear of punishment [pre-conventional reasoning and self-interest] and not collective upbringing [conventional reasoning and legitimacy] that

44 The Study of Legal Socialization

makes Soviet children behave more or less well in the controlled environment of the classroom. Once Soviet children and teenagers expect no immediate punishment, they will cheat, steal, or do damage to "socialist property" to an extent which exceeds Western patterns of antisocial behavior.

Segal, 1990: 249

Segal believed that in spite of the differences in American and Soviet educational practices, "both systems produce teenagers who regard old taboos over-lightly" (Segal, 1990: 249–50). Current developments in Russia can be interpreted as lending support to Segal's views. This we shall attempt to either confirm or refute.

Some Russian scholars have considered the issues of the public consciousness of youth as it relates to crime and punishment. One such legal scholar is Yakovlev. In one paper, prepared for a U.S./USSR conference on legal knowledge and values clarification, Yakovlev (1988) indicated that there are three sources of or influences on legal consciousness/knowledge: the law itself, the mass media, and the attitudes, beliefs, and opinions of individuals. Each of these influences, he said, constitutes an appropriate topic for study. Why should one study this area at all? Because it is critically important to establish what correlation there is, if any, between the law and the behavior of individuals and groups in society.

From the perspective of the individual, according to Yakovlev, there are three dimensions of legal consciousness: first is knowledge of the law—what he calls the rational or conscious element in legal consciousness; next is the emotional element—the evaluative component encompassing attitudes toward laws and rules; and third is the behavior (both legal and illegal). Although knowledge ("informedness") with respect to law is the basis of rational perception and rational behavior, "[i]t is obvious," Yakovlev believed, "that a mere knowledge of the rule of law by no means guarantees that it is observed" (Yakovlev, 1988: 6). This can be due to the effect of an emotional, attitudinal element. Adolescents, in particular, may develop negative attitudes toward the rule of law because they are influenced by the youth subculture—a system of particular social values, tastes, and preferences. But to complicate matters further, even if one has knowledge *and* a positive attitude toward a particular rule or law, that does not guarantee that they will abide by that rule or law.

The complex interactions among the three dimensions are portrayed by Yakovlev in a schema that has six different ways or patterns in which legal or illegal behavior can come about. This schema, as adapted, is shown below:

The first three patterns in this schema seem straightforward and unsurprising. The fourth pattern may be explained by the subject's fear of punishment—a Legal Level I Type. It is the last two patterns that, according to Yakovlev, are "more characteristic for the majority of cases . . . both for lawful as well as unlawful behavior" (Yakovlev, 1988: 10). The individual who abides by the dictates of a rule without knowing that there is such a formal rule, may do so because the rule is consistent with other behavioral norms and mores that are part of the individual's

The Study of Legal Socialization **45**

TABLE 2.1 Dimensions of Legal Consciousness

Rational Dimension	Emotional Dimension	Behavior Dimension
Knows content of rule/law	Approves/has positive attitude	Follows rule/law
Knows content	Disapproves/has negative attitude	Violates rule/law
Does not know content		Violates rule/law
Knows content	Disapproves	Follows rule/law
Does not know content		Follows rule/law
Knows content	Approves	Violates rule/law

culture—and as such are acceptable guides to behavior. This is a form of moral congruity. The last pattern, in which a person has a positive attitude toward the law but nevertheless engages in illegal behavior, may reflect the influences of neutralization (nullifying the law in a particular instance or as far as "I" am concerned) and rationalization (justifying or excusing illegal behavior). These latter two patterns, according to Yakovlev, "bring us much closer to the essence of the problem of a practical functioning of legal consciousness . . . [o]nly there . . . is where the scientific approach to [the] study [of] problems of legal consciousness commences" (Yakovlev, 1988: 15). Yakovlev's paper touches on a number of issues and questions that will be addressed by the research reported later on. These include the influence of knowledge of the law in effecting legal reasoning, attitudes, and behavior; the distinct roles played by both the informal and the formal legal environments in shaping this reasoning, and these attitudes and behavior; and the various causal orderings that can exist among knowledge, reasoning, attitudes, and behavior.

Concluding Comments

We have obviously covered a lot of territory here. There is much to be investigated and studied, and the research described herein will really only make a beginning. The principal implications of all this literature (only a few of which such implications have been incorporated in the immediate research), which lay the foundations for far-reaching new research initiatives, are as follows:

- The Soviet collective-centered system of childrearing, with its emphasis upon character education, should theoretically (or at least if Bronfenbrenner was right) have produced children who were more compliant, and less anti-adult, rebellious, aggressive, and delinquent than U.S. children. But, first with perestroika and glasnost, the loss of faith in the ability of the Soviet government and of the Communist Party to bring the good life, and then with the collapse of the USSR and all the turmoil that has followed that collapse, there may be

46 The Study of Legal Socialization

less belief in the legitimacy of the legal system and less legal compliance than before. With this, one might expect increasing juvenile delinquency, hooliganism, and other kinds of antisocial behavior. There is, as already indicated, some evidence that this indeed is what has happened. We will find out just how American, Soviet, and post-Soviet Russian youth of the late 1980s and early 1990s compare on these dimensions.

Both Russian and outside observers have noted a growing alienation among Russian youth, and a possibly consequential rise in juvenile crime, drug use, and other deviant behavior (e.g., Keller, 1987; Finckenauer, 1988). Is this the case? How does the situation compare with that in the United States? Just what are the effects in this regard of Russia's moves to become a more open, and an economically, politically, and socially restructured society?

- Cultural socialization processes in Soviet Russia (as elsewhere) will have had a strong influence on moral judgment. One of the results of these processes in particular is that although the Piaget/Kohlberg developmental sequences may have appeared in Soviet society, the progression to higher levels may have been slower. That is, Russian youth might have taken longer to reach higher levels of reasoning than Western youth. This expectation arises in part from the lesser emphasis in the USSR on individualism and independent thinking, and the greater emphasis on respect for and conformity to group norms and rules. If there has been a slower progression in legal development, we should expect to find a stronger correlation between age and legal development in the former USSR than in the U.S.

  A kind of retardation in legal development might also be the expected result of the disenchantment and the moral malaise that characterized Soviet society and continues today. Will the absence of the rule of law, and the reliance upon police state tactics at the societal level, result in a concentration of children and youth whose legal reasoning and development is fixed at the pre-conventional, fear of sanctions stage?

- Formal legal instruction of students is intended to shape the civic views of young people, and to develop in them a sense of personal responsibility, convince them of the inevitability of punishment for crime, and to prevent legal infractions. Such instruction was deemed especially necessary in Soviet schools when surveys indicated that students were almost completely ignorant of the law. Some Soviet officials and educators believed that "[k]nowledge and understanding of the law strongly influence young people's behavior" (Ioffe, 1978); and that organized legal education would reduce criminality and other antisocial behavior among young people. How do American, Soviet, and post-Soviet young people compare in their legal knowledge? Are the relations among knowledge, attitudes, and behavior different in Russia than in the old Soviet Union, and in the United States?

- Variation in belief in the moral validity of society's rules and laws is believed to be related to the propensity to obey or violate those rules and laws.

The Study of Legal Socialization **47**

One of the sources of such variation may be the degree of participation, or perceived degree of participation, in the rule- and law-making process. The so-called participation hypothesis is that the more the members of a group perceive themselves as participating in decision-making and other group processes, the more supportive they will be of the group (Hahn, 1969). The more benefits they receive from a system, the more supportive they will be of that system. It will be recalled that participation is one of the legal socialization strategies. Following this idea, there are several developments in Russia that might be expected to influence beliefs and behaviors. There should (or at least could) be a greater sense of participation at the macro-level now, given the moves toward democratization. Political trust and belief in political efficacy, as engendered by political socialization, and by having a vested interest and consequent commitment, may increase legal compliance. On the other hand, most people in Russia now are receiving fewer benefits from the system than they did before. We will be looking at beliefs and attitudes both before and after these developments began.

The possibilities of making cross-cultural comparisons on measurable characteristics, such as those outlined above, are, I believe, empirical and methodological issues of social science, and not moral or ideological issues. This is not to deny that any discussion of the history of legal development and legal practices in the former Soviet Union has perforce a moral and ideological perspective. I do not believe it could be otherwise. On the other hand, the empirical data address empirical questions. These data will either support or refute whatever theoretical premises underlie the questions. And that is as it should be. Given the chance to compare Russian and American youth at one point in time; and then to add Russian youth at a second point makes it most opportune to go forward with important, groundbreaking research in all these areas. That is what we will be about.

Note

1   This criticism included the complaint that Bronfenbrenner allowed Soviet authorities to read his manuscript, and subsequently deleted material that they found offensive.

3
LAW AND LAW REFORM

In this chapter we will further develop the idea that legal socialization is shaped and determined by the legal culture in which that socialization occurs. One major element of that culture is the formalized rules—the laws—by which a society defines what is and is not acceptable behavior. Laws are the codification of norms and values, and as such they have symbolic as well as utilitarian purposes. They establish standards of conduct. Laws tell us a great deal about what a society considers important—about what its priorities and goals are.

The law and the criminal justice system were used in the USSR not only to prosecute and punish ordinary crimes, but also as tools to promote Party and State control in politics and the economy. The legal apparatus was also used to suppress dissidents' movements and to prevent democratic developments. Soviet law had the peculiar characteristic of being subordinate to politics, which were determined strictly by the Communist Party. The Communist Party of the Soviet Union (CPSU) was not a political party in the normal sense of that term. It did not compete for power with other political parties. Such other parties were outlawed. Instead, it had a monopoly on power—ratified in the Soviet constitution. Thus, the law was not paramount—the Party was. Soviet citizens were expected to obey the law because it was "just," and laws were supposedly universally applicable to all (except, of course, to Party members). In the case of criminal charges against the latter, the cases were screened (by the Party), and Party membership was taken away before the charges could proceed. Party officials and the so-called nomenklatura (party functionaries) had special privileges and immunities that enabled them to evade the law.

In all societies, law has a guiding, educational role, as well as a punitive one. But the Soviet legal system in particular emphasized this educational role (Berman, 1963). Berman pointed out that in the Soviet view, the educational function of the law was central to the concept of justice itself. According to this view, Soviet citizens had to be protected against the consequences of their own ignorance, and had to be guided, trained, and disciplined. The Soviet legal system, said Berman, was parental. Smith reiterates this point: "Soviet law, apart from governing the interactions of citizens and the relation of their rights and duties, is concerned with the development of citizens' moral well-being and their law-consciousness" (Smith, 1992a: 224). Let us review some case examples and issues from Soviet legal history and practice to get a sense of the messages communicated, and the legal (and moral) lessons seemingly taught by Soviet law.

Soviet Justice in Russia

Crime by Analogy

We begin with a legal principle mentioned earlier, that there is no offense without a law—"*nullum crimen sine lege*." In violation of this principle, the 1922 Criminal Code of the Russian Soviet Federative Socialist Republic (RSFSR) incorporated an expedient way of covering unanticipated crimes called *crime-by-analogy*. This meant:

> If this or that socially dangerous act is not explicitly provided for by this Code, then the basis and limits of responsibility for it are determined by the application of those articles of the Code which define crimes generally most similar.
>
> *Patterson and Doak, 1980: 33*

In other words, any act construed as being "socially dangerous," whether or not the act was proscribed by law, could be prosecuted and punished. If the particular act was not against the law, the courts were to find the act most analogous to it in the criminal code, and use that proscription as the basis for prosecution. This was said to be necessary at the time because it was impossible to construct a code that anticipated all dangerous acts.

The analogy notion was finally abolished from the Soviet criminal code in 1958, but its effects and its legacy are present even today. When legal offenses are defined in part by presidential decrees, as is currently the case in Russia; and when there are whole areas and behaviors not covered by any law, as is also currently the case, there is danger of resort to a form of analogy. Thus, the formal elimination of crimes by analogy in 1958 Soviet law, and from the criminal code of the Russian Federation in 1960, did not, and has not, totally removed the danger of arbitrary or bureaucratically inspired extensions of criminal sanctions.

During the nearly four decades of its formal use, analogy is criticized for undermining legality, depriving the laws of stability, and weakening the culture of the administration of justice (Kogan, 1989). In addition to convicting persons

50 Law and Law Reform

of acts that were not against the law, it was often used to convict offenders of more serious crimes than the ones they had actually committed. Crime-by-analogy clearly violated the rule-of-law precepts of certainty and rationality. That these contradictions were not unknown at the time is illustrated in Solomon's description of the 1930s legal debate about the retention or abolition of analogy as a principle of Soviet criminal law:

> The theoretical discussion revolved upon the interpretation of the phrase "stability of law." [Professor A. A.] Gertsenzon claimed that by allowing judges to legislate in individual cases, the principle of analogy placed judges above the law and thus undermined the law's stability. One of analogy's proponents, V.M. Chikhvadze, answered that analogy was inconsistent not with the "stability of law" but only with the slogan of the classical school, the "bourgeois" principle nullem crimen sine lege, which, Chikhvadze claimed, had no place in Soviet law. In other words, Chikhvadze believed that, to achieve "stability of law," it was unnecessary to accept the "rule of law." But P.S. Romashkin challenged Chikhvadze's assumption and made explicit what Gertsenzon had only implied—that stability of law did require the adoption of "rule of law." In insisting that the "rule of law" had a place in socialist legality, Romashkin was quietly supporting a change in the relationship of the Soviet legal system to the political order. For a legal system characterized by "rule of law" would have to be relatively autonomous from politics, so that politics [only] determined the rules of its operation, through legislation, but not the details of that operation through intervention in individual cases.
>
> *Solomon, 1978: 156*

The analogy principle allowed the Soviet state to proceed in a much more unbridled fashion against its citizens. The state's arbitrary discretion was less limited. And as would be the case in any similar situation, the people were left unsure about what was and was not against the law, and thus could not govern their behavior accordingly. That crime-by-analogy, despite its being so antithetical to the principles of the rule of law, died hard in the former Soviet Union, is reflected in Kogan's observation that as late as 1987, some 30 years after its repeal, more than 40 percent of Soviet judges surveyed were in favor of restoring it (Kogan, 1989).

Telephone Law

As previously indicated, impartiality and independence, and the universal application of the law, are core values of the rule of law. The independence of Soviet judges and people's assessors (laypersons elected to sit with judges to hear criminal cases) was guaranteed under the Soviet constitution and Soviet law.

Not only were judges and people's assessors to be independent, but they were to be subordinate only to the law.

> The judges and people's assessors are independent and this means that they are not subordinate to anybody, except to the law in adjudication of cases cognisable by them. The formula that the judges and people's assessors are subject only to the law means that in the hearing of cases they are guaranteed full independence from any interference.
>
> *Law: Studies by Soviet Scholars, 1984: 159*

Soviet legal scholars vigorously rejected Western criticisms that interference by the Communist Party in the processing of criminal cases undermined the notion of judicial independence and the principle that judges should be guided only by the law (Bassiouni and Savitski, 1979: 15). The work of such Western students of Soviet law as Fletcher and Solomon, however, indicated that this criticism indeed had validity.

From the Soviet Interview Project, where he interviewed former judges and court or other justice officials, Solomon concluded:

> party bosses . . . expected that investigators and judges would co-operate with their occasional requests with regard to particular criminal cases—to drop charges or pursue a case with vigor; to punish harshly or leniently. While the requests sometimes involved *justifiable* goals like protecting managers whose peccadilloes served the fulfillment of the economic plan, as often the interventions served selfish motives such as protecting friends or punishing enemies. In acceding to the call of the party secretary, judges made "telephone law" real and dangerous.
>
> *Solomon, 1988–89: 84, emphasis added*

Solomon's use of the term *justifiable* here refers to interventions as seen from the perspective of high Communist Party officials. They were certainly not justifiable from the broader perspective of such rule-of-law principles as impartiality, independence, and universality.

Despite the legal reforms of the Gorbachev era beginning in 1986, legality and the rule of law remained very tenuous. Solomon observed that:

> As of 1990 legal values still did not have a strong hold over the Soviet public . . . many citizens appreciated how the law could protect personal rights and stand in the way of injustices perpetrated by public officials. But few Soviets were willing to place abstract principles of legality ahead of satisfaction of their own views of what was morally correct. For most Soviet citizens the law remained an instrument, if not for their masters, then one that could serve their own views of morality and justice. This popular

52 Law and Law Reform

> conception . . . remained as the legacy of a decades-long expedient approach to law on the part of state officials, what . . .[some] observers described as "legal nihilism."
>
> *Solomon, 1992b: 281.*

Following his observations of Soviet criminal courts, and his interviews with Soviet court officials and criminal justice experts, Fletcher concluded that "[w]hether the judge will defer to anyone, particularly to the local Party officials, [became] a central question of criminal justice under Gorbachev." Fletcher reported that "Party officials intervened in about 12 percent of the criminal cases by telephoning advice that the judges were expected to take" (Fletcher, 1989: 12). Savitski was one of the Soviet legal reformers who challenged the attempt to portray telephone law as a myth.

> Do not think that the judge is ordered to sentence the defendant for so many years or, alternatively, to acquit. Influence is now exerted more subtly by requests to "sort out the case carefully," "not to hurry with conclusions," and so on.
>
> *Savitski, 1990: 102*

Judges and other officials who were subordinate to the Communist Party and dependent upon the Party for their positions could not, of course, be independent and impartial. And if Party members were above the law, the justice system could not be fair and equitable. It was exactly those circumstances that characterized Soviet legal history. They were part of the legal environment in which the Soviet people were socialized.

Social Dangerousness

The element of social danger was important in defining what was a crime in the Soviet Union. The label *socially dangerous*, is, however, a kind of umbrella or catch-all that can encompass a variety of acts—in this case acts that "infringe[d] the Soviet social or state system, the socialist economic system, socialist property . . . or any other socially dangerous act provided for by the criminal law, which infringe[d] the socialist legal order" (Criminal Law Fundamentals of the USSR and the Union Republics). The socially dangerous included at various times drunkards, hooligans (itself a catch-all category of deviants), and counter-revolutionaries. The latter was made up of class enemies (the bourgeoisie), malingerers, parasites, saboteurs (e.g., people who refused to work on religious holidays), intellectuals, speculators (people who resold merchandise for profit), and kulaks (private farmers).

The 1922 Code of the RSFSR adopted the principle that the defense of the state required not only combating crime, but also combating socially dangerous elements. The Code thus gave the courts the right to punish those "who are dangerous because of their links with the criminal environment or because of their past activity" (Kogan, 1989: 8–9). The court, according to Kogan, was empowered to banish persons who were acknowledged as being socially dangerous irrespective of whether they had committed a crime, and even persons who may have been acquitted of a crime. Under Stalin, special boards of the Ministry of Internal Affairs could imprison or exile for up to five years anyone considered to be socially dangerous. "It is much easier," as Kogan quotes one of the proponents of this social defense idea arguing at the time, "to judge the social dangerousness of a person by his mentality, by his petty but characteristic deeds, and by his way of life, habits, and social position, then by his individual actions that may be proscribed by the criminal law" (Kogan, 1989: 9). This is because under such an approach, one is not constrained by such legal niceties and necessities as due process, the rules of evidence, presumption of innocence, and so on. The well-known Soviet dissident and human rights advocate Andrei Sakharov exemplified persons who, by law, were sent into "administrative exile" without the benefit of due process of law.

As Kogan concluded, justice thus was replaced by expediency. Crime and criminal behavior became socially dangerous acts and social dangerousness. Punishment became social defense. Adopting this stance put the Soviet legal system at odds with the rule of law. Under that system, individuals were denied a fair opportunity to make their own decisions and to order their own lives. Liberty was governed less by individuals' voluntary acts, and more by the state's assessment of individuals' propensities for some forms of future conduct. This violated principles of fairness, certainty, and rationality.

Kogan suggested that this victory of expediency over justice at least partly explained the subsequent state-administered terror begun under Stalin. In that vein, Solzhenitsyn described how the article of the criminal code pertaining to socially dangerous elements was used in 1946–47 against Soviet girls who went out with foreigners; and also against Spanish persons who had come to the USSR as children after the Spanish Civil War, but who were later deemed as fitting poorly into Soviet life, and as longing to go home (Solzhenitsyn, 1973: 86). Both categories of persons became targets for social defense measures. Such measures, and the construed legal bases for them, violated the notion that "no act that is not, on examination, morally wrong is properly the subject of serious criminal penalties"; and that "to the extent the criminal law does criminalize such acts, it is justly the subject of moral criticism" (Richards, 1981: 279).

One type of socially dangerous behavior was defined by the crime of parasitism. Ostensibly intended to punish persons who refused to work and to contribute to the building of Soviet society, it was also used as a legal weapon against dissidents. Jews, for example, who were denied other employment opportunities, were charged with parasitism for teaching and writing Hebrew. Under Khrushchev there were created informal tribunals called "antiparasite courts," which were

54 Law and Law Reform

to deal with social parasites such as prostitutes, beggars, vagrants, and speculators. Of the antiparasite laws, Smith writes:

> The case of the antiparasite legislation illustrates several aspects of the Soviet legal system. The antiparasite laws were originally initiated to punish antisocial behavior and to socialize Soviet citizens by enlisting their assistance in combating parasitism and hooliganism . . . The case of the antiparasite laws also illustrates the use of law in the USSR as a means of social engineering—that is, as a means of ordering human relations to further the values of Soviet society.
>
> *Smith, 1992a: 225*

The definition of crime as socially dangerous action was retained in the 1991 Fundamental Principles of Criminal Legislation. This was done over the objections of some legislators who argued, as I have here, that the concept is inconsistent with the idea of a law-based state. These critics, according to Quigley,

> were evidently concerned that if crime definitions are construed in light of how the activity in question affects socialism, courts may define an act as criminal even if it does not meet the elements of the offense, so long as the act is a threat to socialism.
>
> *Quigley, 1992: 285*

Presumption of Innocence/Right to Counsel

Whether the principle of presumption of innocence was ever a maxim of Soviet criminal law, and if so in what sense and form, has been a subject of considerable controversy to legal scholars (see, for example, Fletcher, 1968; Berman, 1980). The constitution of the USSR and the Fundamentals of Criminal Procedure seemed to clearly adopt and endorse this principle. All courts were said to be required to

> strictly observe the constitutional principle according to which the accused is deemed to be innocent until his guilt is proven in the [court] order provided for by the law . . . The law places the burden of proof on the accuser. So it is impossible to place the burden of proof on the accused. A conviction cannot be based on assumptions. All doubts that cannot be resolved should be interpreted in favor of the accused.
>
> *Bassiouni and Savitski, 1979: 49–50*

Presumption of innocence entails the fundamental ideas that the accused has no obligation to prove his innocence, but rather that the state is obliged to prove guilt according to a stipulated standard of proof; that all evidence of innocence must be considered; that the court itself must not endorse any indications of guilt prior to rendering its official judgment; and that any doubts must be resolved in favor of the accused. A major impediment to the application of this principle in the USSR had to do with certain characteristics of Soviet criminal procedure—mainly the role of the Procuracy. The Procuracy is an administrative agency that oversees all questions of legality (previously in Soviet courts and the Soviet bureaucracy, and currently in Russia as well). In addition to its general supervision of legality in a kind of ombudsman function, the Procuracy was in charge of the preliminary investigation of crimes, leading to indictment; and it prosecuted criminal cases. According to Fletcher,

> These procedural factors bestow[ed] an unusual trial posture on the court prosecutor: he [was] at once an advocate seeking to demonstrate the guilt of the accused and a representative of a state agency that had impartially [already] found the accused to be guilty.
>
> *Fletcher, 1968: 1215*

Accepting a presumption of innocence at trial thus conflicted with the finding of guilt in the preliminary investigation, as well as interfering with the prosecution.

American prosecutors also carry out preliminary investigations and prosecute cases, and they also presumably generally believe in the guilt of persons brought to indictment and trial, but an important distinction is that they do not have the omnipotent role that their counterparts had in the Soviet system. Current political and legal changes seem to have had little effect on the Procuracy, but we will come back to a discussion of its current status in Russia.

The biggest problem with Soviet criminal procedure, in the view of Berman, Solomon, and others, was that the hidden preliminary investigation—which lacked a fully adversarial character—resulted in abuses of pretrial detention and in the indictment of innocent persons. Right to counsel attached usually only at the end of the preliminary investigation, which could proceed for as long as nine months (or longer with extensions) with the accused held essentially incommunicado. In fact, persons under investigation were not only denied counsel, but were generally also not permitted to see relatives and friends (Berman, 1980).

> For the Soviet Union, the scope of the presumption of innocence at the pre-trial stage is perhaps the most acute aspect . . . It bears on the severe limitations placed by Soviet law on the right to counsel during the preliminary investigation or police inquiry. It bears on the justification for detention of persons during preliminary investigation or police inquiry, on the length of the detention, and the right to be released after indictment

56 Law and Law Reform

and before trial. It bears on the conditions of such detention. It bears on such demeaning practices as the shaving of the prisoner's head and the posting of armed guards on both sides of him during trial.

Berman, 1980: 623.

In a similar vein, Solomon concluded that the presumption of innocence did not penetrate into Soviet legal culture.

According to recent surveys most advocates [Soviet lawyers] saw little sign of the operation of presumption of innocence in Soviet courtrooms . . . Only half the judges surveyed agreed with the proposal of admitting defence counsel at the beginning of the preliminary investigation.

Solomon, 1988–89: 89–90

Reforms in the Soviet criminal procedures that were adopted by the Supreme Soviet in 1990 put a number of limits on the use of detention during the preliminary investigation and also provided for the accused to be represented by counsel not later than 24 hours after their arrest. If there is full implementation of these reforms in Russia, that will give much greater credence to the meaning of presumption of innocence.

Historically, the accusatorial crime control Soviet model, which had its roots in nineteenth-century France and Germany, stood in contrast to the adversarial, due process model found in other countries with Anglo-Saxon legal traditions. Under the accusatorial system, for example, the range of evidence that can be introduced into a criminal proceeding is much broader than under the adversary system. Further, the proceedings can extend beyond the accusation, and the findings are also not limited to the pleadings. These and other characteristics serve to grant much more power to the state and to provide fewer protections for the accused individual. Smith points out that Russian law belongs to the family of civil legal systems which generally grant greater authority to state officials than do common law systems (Smith, 1992a: 203). The emphasis in Soviet criminal procedure was on efficient and effective control. The definition of crimes to be controlled could be arbitrary and capricious. The state—the procurator—in addition to commanding the lion's share of the resources, played the investigation and prosecution game according to rules he himself made up *and* enforced. The due process model (the one most consistent with the rule of law), in contrast, attempts to equalize the resources available to the prosecution and the defense, to put the burden of proof on the prosecutor, and to in effect create a minefield of obstacles to the conviction of the accused. The contrasting goals might be best summed up as ensuring the conviction and punishment of the "guilty" on the one hand, versus ensuring that no innocent person is convicted and punished on the other.

The Political Abuse of Psychiatry

The systematic abuse of psychiatry for political purposes began shortly after the Russian Revolution of 1917 (Podrabinek, 1980). We will examine this abuse by addressing questions of how and why psychiatry was abused, why the psychiatric profession went wrong, and what the effects are of the political abuse of psychiatry.

Like all other Soviet institutions, psychiatry was completely subordinate to the state. Beyond that, and unlike the situation in other countries, Soviet psychiatric hospitals were not under the jurisdiction of mental health authorities, but rather under the Ministry of Internal Affairs—the agency that housed the law enforcement apparatus. In addition, therefore, to psychiatry not being autonomous in the field of mental health, it was placed into an institutional structure that facilitated and then mandated collaboration with law enforcement authorities—especially the KGB, who were the political police.

Soviet criminal law and procedure also contributed and led to abuse. Under Soviet law, people could be arrested for political crimes such as "anti-Soviet agitation" or "spreading deliberate fabrications discrediting the Soviet political and social system." If such "dissidents" had "questionable mental stability," they could then be referred by the criminal investigator for examination by a forensic psychiatric commission (Faraone, 1982: 1105). There is a certain inherent—albeit perverted—logic to the belief that anyone who persists in political dissent under the repressive and punitive circumstances that characterized the Soviet Union must be mentally unstable. Different types of dissident behavior often came to be officially labeled "sluggish schizophrenia." This convenient and useful equating of nonconformity and mental illness was the brainchild of Andrei V. Snezhnevsky, the then-head of the Serbsky Institute of Psychiatry. It was the Serbsky Institute that carried out the forensic examinations.

The results of the psychiatric examination of the accused were reviewed by a court and, if the court accepted the commission's judgment, the accused person could be sentenced to an indefinite period of detention for further psychiatric examination in a psychiatric hospital. The accused was neither informed of the commission's findings, nor permitted to participate in the court hearing. There was also a civil procedure for involuntary psychiatric confinement that was used to incarcerate dissidents in psychiatric hospitals.

Why was psychiatry used as a way to get dissidents? Oleszczuk (1988: 78) says that the authorities decided that psychiatry could be used to punish dissidents with internment for their activities, at the broad discretion of the coercive apparatus, while at the same time being unencumbered by legal safeguards or due process. Adler and Gluzman offer a specific rationale for the practice:

> The misuse of psychiatric hospitals, techniques and medications with the aim of repressing political dissidents was widely practiced in the former USSR. By claiming to "treat" political adversaries in either "Special" or

"Ordinary" psychiatric institutions, the failures of the political system were relocated from the institutions of State to the psyche of the individual so that the Soviet system could deny its own structural failings.

Adler and Gluzman, 1992: 1

The above two authors—one of whom (Semyon Gluzman), a psychiatrist, was himself incarcerated in a Soviet labor camp—also point out that it was administratively easier to put dissenters in mental hospitals than in prisons. Hospitalization essentially deprived dissidents of the opportunity for legal recourse. Psychiatrists went along with, and in some cases enthusiastically supported this political abuse of their profession because they believed "that the Party and its interests were paramount, and that career advancement was dependent on Party loyalty" (Adler and Gluzman, 1992: 15). The powerful role of the Communist Party and the gross departures from the principles of rule of law are both in evidence here.

Adler and Gluzman reached a chilling conclusion to their discussion of what they call "psychonoxious psychiatry":

One of the most flagrant violators of commonly accepted medical and legal standards was the Soviet Special Psychiatric Hospital system, which was at worst criminal, and at best, had lost contact with scientific reality. Its dissident inmates were neither criminal nor insane but were treated as if they were both. Many mentally healthy individuals entered Special Psychiatric Hospitals only to be eventually released from them as patients—with nightmares, symptoms of depression and difficulty in communicating. They are living proof of how the Soviet system had triumphed in the transmogrification of the science of psychiatry.

Adler and Gluzman, 1992: 19

Each of these issues and examples are major parts of the legal environment, of the context, which shaped and molded legal values and perceptions of moral validity and legitimacy during the 75 years of the Soviet regime. Before turning to the changes that have taken place in recent years, we need to look at the agency that has been the centerpiece of both the Soviet and now the Russian justice systems. I single out the Procuracy for special attention because it is quite without counterpart in the United States.

The Procuracy

The Procuracy was the most powerful institution—the linchpin—in the Soviet criminal justice system. It so far continues to be so in the Russian system of administering justice as well. Its formal responsibilities include: general responsibility for the legality of actions of all institutions; supervision of the judicial

Law and Law Reform **59**

process; and prosecution of offenders. To give a sense of the enormous influence of this office, it has the power to do the following:

- demand any document from any government institution;
- stay the execution of any criminal penalty;
- direct investigative agencies, including removing investigators/agencies from an investigation;
- end a criminal case before trial and during supplementary investigation;
- advise the courts on the legality of the courts' actions, as well as the actions of others;
- suspend court decisions considered illegal or inappropriate;
- inspect jails, labor camps, and other correctional facilities, and suspend illegal actions in these facilities;
- free anyone illegally detained.

There is nothing comparable to this institution with these powers in the American criminal justice system. The Procuracy's oversight of the courts means that they cannot and do not operate as an independent branch of government, autonomous from the executive branch. The courts thus do not have equal standing with the executive and legislative branches, and cannot overrule their actions. In its combined roles as sort of inspector-general, ombudsman, and prosecutor, the *prokuror* is supposed to protect the procedural rights of individuals. How well did it perform this task?

> although the procurator bears the most responsibility for the defense of legal norms and the protection of the rights of individuals, his position as representative of the state prevailed. In many cases . . . legal safeguards were disregarded. Blatantly arbitrary interpretations of laws and personal behavior went unchallenged by the procurator, who was recruited and supervised by the party organization. This ignoring of rules and logic is the germ of the charges of arbitrariness leveled against Soviet law.
>
> *Oleszczuk, 1988: 180*

Again, the overpowering role of the Communist Party in governing the administration of justice is evident. Among his rule-of-law proposals made in 1988, Gorbachev considered transferring all remaining criminal investigations from the Procuracy to the Ministry of Internal Affairs (which was already handling the bulk of investigations). This proposal did not go anywhere. It in fact, fell short of what most reformers wanted anyway, which was to have criminal investigations removed from both the Procuracy and the MVD, and instead made the responsibility of the Ministry of Justice or of another separate agency.

Glasnost also revealed at that time that the public did not trust the Procuracy, but regarded it as a principal organ of state coercion (Smith, 1992b: 3). Despite

60 Law and Law Reform

this, and despite the attempts of the most liberal legal reformers, the law on the Russian Federation Prosecutor's Office, passed on January 17, 1992, basically confirmed the existing powers of the Procuracy, with few if any restrictions. "Most significant, the prosecutor's oversight [nadzor] powers over the courts remain in force" (Thorson, 1992: 45). This means that the prosecutor will continue to dominate judicial proceedings.

Let us conclude this discussion of the laws and the legal issues and history that helped shape the environment for legal socialization by getting up-to-date on the reform efforts in general. Some of these have fared much better than the attempts to scale back the powers of the Procuracy.

Law Reform in Russia

Beginning in 1989, and extending through the waning days of the Soviet Union, law reform was a very active pursuit. Among the revisions and proposed revisions in the various Soviet legal codes were a number pertaining to the criminal law in particular. These reforms were intended to correct the kinds of abuses described earlier, and to begin the construction of a new legal culture. This still-evolving legal culture is to embody rule-of-law principles. At the nineteenth Conference of the CPSU in June, 1988, Gorbachev and other leaders of the party had pledged their commitment to creating a state governed by the rule of law (*pravovoe gosudarstvo*), in which "not one governmental agency, official . . . party or public organization, not one person would be freed from responsibility to obey the law." President Boris Yeltsin of Russia then continued this commitment. Ironically, it was just over three years after that 1988 Party Congress that the Communist Party itself was outlawed by Yeltsin for its failures to obey the law in the failed coup attempt against Gorbachev.

With the end of the Soviet Union, the Soviet legal system also died. But Russian law, in the interim, has struggled to fill in the resulting legal gaps because it does not yet cover all the areas that Soviet law once did. Nor has law reform in Russia been able to keep up with the rapidly changing conditions and new realities. For example, despite the official moves to create a market economy and to encourage private enterprise, old laws against speculation and the possession of hard (foreign) currency remain on the books. Lawyers and judges are thus left to choose from a confusing maze of old Soviet laws, Soviet-era laws that have been explicitly carried over, new Russian laws, presidential decrees, or some combination of these, as the bases for their legal decisions. There were numerous drafts of a new Russian constitution that began to be discussed as early as January 1992. But it was not until two years later (in December 1993)—after Yeltsin had dissolved the Russian Parliament and then used the army to put it out of business; and after the parliamentary elections and the concurrent referendum on the constitution—that a new Russian constitution was finally ratified.

Law and Law Reform **61**

What is clear is that toward the end of creating a fairer and more just system of law enforcement and administration of justice, a number of proposals for reform were adopted in the USSR between 1989 and 1991. These remain in place for the most part. Legal reform plans of the new Russian government have been even bolder; but so far there has been little concrete action (Thorson, 1992: 41). The implementation of new laws and new policies is never simple, even under the best of circumstances; and the turmoil in Russia has presented far from the best of circumstances.

Judicial Independence

The system of appointing judges was changed by the Supreme Soviet so as to protect judges from political pressure; that is, "telephone law." Instead of judges being nominated by local Party officials, to whom they then became beholden, they were to be selected by authorities at higher levels. Unfortunately, and as evidence of the difficulty in accomplishing judicial reform, these higher authorities (legislative deputies) who voted on nominations of judges, would themselves summon nominees, question their handling of particular cases, and even order directed verdicts. Thus, *telefonnoe pravo* was replaced by *deputatskoe pravo* (Solomon, personal communication, 1993).

The terms of office for judges were extended to ten years—and there was and still is some consideration to giving them life tenure as in the higher courts in the United States. They have been given contempt powers and, to further immunize them from political influence, they were given higher salaries and some special guarantees of housing (of which there tends to be a chronic shortage). However, in the wake of the collapse of the USSR, and the harsh economic reform measures imposed by President Yeltsin, judges and the courts are said to be suffering (Thorson, 1992). When Yeltsin signed a decree on emergency measures to improve Russian courts on September 3, 1991 (which decree was not acted upon until February 1992), "an estimated 4,000 judges were unable to survive at all on their state salaries and another 7,000 judges had a very low standard of living" (Thorson, 1992: 45).

There is considerable criticism in Russia that there has been no effort to remove judges who were appointed under the old regime. There is concern that these old judges are not reformable. The question of reforming legal education has also not been tackled. Thus, the judiciary is still dominated by old appointees of the Communist Party—appointees who were trained through such institutions as the Ministry of Internal Affairs correspondence school, which, according to Thorson, "does little to establish their credibility in the eyes of the public" (Thorson, 1992: 46). The latter point is, of course, pertinent to the issue of legitimacy.

Russia established a new 13-member Russian Constitutional Court in 1991, as a separate and presumably independent branch of government. Thorson called

62 Law and Law Reform

this "the most promising indication of the new leadership's commitment to an independent judiciary and a law-based state." Ironically, one of the first cases before that Court was one to decide the legality of the CPSU, and of President Yeltsin's banning of it. The importance of the outcome of this case for the future of a democratic Russia was stressed by a Russian colleague: "If [that outcome] is based on ruling passions," he said, "it will have very little value for the future. If it is grounded in law, regardless of result, it will be valuable, showing we are building a rule-of-law state" (Yakovlev, 1992a). In what was referred to as a "Solomonic" judgment, the Court in the end walked a fine political line—upholding the president's ban of the Party's organizational structures, but not of the territorial primary Party cells. The court did not rule on the constitutionality of the CPSU, declaring that since it had ceased to exist with the collapse of the USSR, this was a moot question. This and other court actions led one observer to conclude that the Russian Constitutional Court had not yet become a "bastion of legality." "It will probably be a matter of generations before any court in Russia develops the habit of putting the constitution and laws of the country above political considerations" (Wishnevsky, 1993: 8). The prescience of this judgment is evidenced by Yeltsin's dissolving of the court—allegedly for playing politics—in October 1993.

Counsel for the Defense

Never in Russian history did accused persons have the right to be represented by legal counsel from the very beginning of their preliminary investigation. As indicated earlier, the right to counsel has been expanded, and a defense attorney can now begin to represent his client 24 hours after the beginning of the preliminary investigation. The 24-hour stipulation represented a compromise between liberal reformers who wanted immediate representation, and law enforcement authorities who wanted to delay attorney involvement for as long as possible. Under the old Soviet legal procedure, defense attorneys did not become involved in criminal cases until after the preliminary investigation, the gathering of evidence, and the questioning of witnesses was complete. Nor could attorneys provide advice to the accused during this period. Russian defense attorneys now have immediate access to materials gathered by the procurator both during the preliminary investigation and after the case has already been prepared for prosecution.

It is still the case—unlike in the U.S. with its Miranda warnings—that neither the police nor the prosecutor have any obligation to inform a suspect of a right to counsel. Obviously, the rights of an accused become real and meaningful only when there is someone (a competent someone) charged with the responsibility of overseeing and protecting these rights. This is the proper role of the legal counsel for the defense.

Reformers hope that these changes will be retained, and that they will help move the legal procedure a considerable distance along the road toward becoming a more adversarial rather than an accusatorial process. Unfortunately, there is now a tremendous shortage of defense lawyers in Russia, as there is elsewhere in the former Soviet Union. This is especially true outside of the major cities. Further, among the existing legal force are a number of lawyers who are at best ill-trained—having, for example, gotten their degrees through correspondence courses. David Lempert (1992) indicated that there are only about 16,000 defense attorneys in Russia, and that market reform for the legal system has so far meant only that "access to justice is sold to the highest bidders," and thus the "same elites are favored in the legal system as before." The defense lawyers (*advokats*) are also not immune from the corruption that permeates Russian justice. One current practice involves the police detaining an accused person while "encouraging" that person (or the person's family) to retain a particular *advokat*. If the accused succumbs, the police and the *advokat* then split the legal fees. All such practices do not bode well for dramatic improvement in the administration of Russian justice any time soon.

Pretrial Detention

There was general agreement among critics of the Soviet legal system that custodial detention during the preliminary investigation had been greatly overused and much abused. Hazard called this practice "the primary peril point of Soviet criminal procedure," particularly because it was "bereft of counsel for the suspect" (1990: 524). The importance of establishing guarantees against capricious arrest and unlawful detention was connected with a history of practice in which law enforcement agencies had exercised uncontrolled power to arrest any suspect; these suspects had no appeal of their arrest; and they were often kept in pretrial confinement for long periods of time. Nicholas Lampert was one who criticized the practice:

> [A]bout one-third of the people who come into the hands of the law enforcement agencies are detained for a considerable period before being charged . . . the periods of custody have tended to be long and the [statutory] limit of nine months . . . regularly extended . . . [and] conditions in remand prisons are typically awful . . . All this is a major source of concern, not just because of the human degradation to which it leads, but also because it provides favorable conditions for the extraction of confessions.
>
> *Lampert, 1988: 11–12*

A Russian colleague said that the previously unrestricted power to detain had resulted in a tendency to orient criminal investigations not toward a search for objective evidence, but on an intensive interrogation of the suspect. Pretrial detention was used as a tool for extracting an admission of guilt. This procedure deprived the suspect of any guarantee against self-incrimination. It also resulted

64 Law and Law Reform

in a situation where to be arrested nearly automatically meant to be convicted (Yakovlev, personal communication, 1991).

Proposals for changing pretrial detention practices, which were adopted in 1990, included giving the accused the right to appeal his arrest to a court, and putting limits on the detention period. Despite these changes, however, the procurator still has considerable power to use and to extend pretrial detention.

Trial by Jury

One of the important ways in which legal socialization comes about is through citizen participation in the legal system and process. One form of such participation for those citizens living in countries that use jury trials is through jury duty. Jury trials had been used in Russia before the Bolshevik Revolution in 1917, but were later eliminated. In fact, this was just one of several features of the legal reforms put forth by Tsar Alexander II in the 1860s. These latter reforms ironically incorporated such principles as equality before the law, due process, and judicial independence.

Participation by ordinary citizens in criminal trials during the Soviet period came in two forms: comrades' courts and peoples' courts. The former, *tovarishcheskii sud*, were described this way:

> The comrades' court is a Soviet phenomenon, a popularly staffed judicial institution that gives citizens a role in solving local disputes. Discipline on the job, drunkenness, petty theft, and slander are among the issues under the court's jurisdiction. Available sanctions include public reprimand, censure, and the imposition of small monetary fines. These courts are found at most Soviet economic enterprises, collective farms, social organizations, educational institutions, and housing complexes. Court members—the judges—are elected by the community. They consider cases in open hearings at the place of work, study, or residence of [the] accused offender.
>
> *Rand, 1991: 21*

Peoples' courts—the basic criminal courts of first jurisdiction—are staffed by one professional judge and two lay assessors. In theory, the assessors are to have equal decision-making authority with the judge, and to help ensure a form of "popular justice." The practice, however, has been somewhat different.

> While bench decisions are made on the basis of majority vote, the assessors, who are not trained in the law, almost always follow the professional judge's lead . . . they rubber-stamp judicial pronouncements, depriving defense counsel and defendant of two impartial and objective voices.
>
> *Rand, 1991: 42*

Despite this shortcoming, it was argued by defenders of Soviet justice that the lay assessors, as citizen representatives, were acting in lieu of a jury of peers and represented legal democratization.

In the 1990 reforms adopted by the Supreme Soviet of the USSR, the various republics were empowered to institute jury trials in cases where the law provided for capital punishment or deprivation of liberty for more than ten years. The republics were given the option of providing jury trials in other criminal cases as well. Jury trials remain to be implemented, however. A combination of ignorance, resistance, and a shortage of funds seems be responsible for this failure thus far. Some thought was given to simply expanding the number of lay assessors as a way of approximating a jury, but this did not get very far either. A justice of the former Supreme Court of the Soviet Union described to me, in late 1991, the great difficulties already being experienced in finding a sufficient number of people's assessors to staff all the people's courts. Attempting to create and draw upon a pool of potential jurors seemed to him to be an impossible bureaucratic nightmare that would be doomed to failure.

The idea of jury trials is, however, still alive, despite the obstacles that had to be overcome. Legislation has now been passed to permit the accused the option of a trial by jury. Unlike the case with the American jury system, conviction will be by majority vote—seven jurors out of twelve.

Criminal Punishment

Alternatives to incarceration and new forms of isolation in lieu of banishment and exile have been adopted or proposed. Capital punishment, a popular and widely used form of punishment throughout Soviet history, has been severely limited. During the heyday of the Stalin years, it has been estimated that upwards of 700,000 executions were being carried out each year. Later, Van den Berg (1985) reports that capital punishment was used in about 2,000 cases annually between 1960 and 1966. Even this exceeded by more than tenfold its greatest use in any one year in the United States. By the last decade, however, the number of death sentences and executions had declined sharply. For example, the number of capital offenders sentenced to death in the USSR declined from 770 in 1985 to 445 in 1990. In Russia, convictions for capital crimes rose from 2,814 in 1989 to 4,977 in 1991, but actual executions for this period fell from 93 to 59 (Motivans and Teague, 1992: 69). The death penalty in Russia is now limited to five offenses under criminal code revisions adopted in July 1991: high treason, premeditated murder in aggravating circumstances, rape of a minor in aggravating circumstances, violent kidnapping of a child, and "crimes against peace and the security of humanity." It is not clear exactly what the latter crimes are. In addition, two categories of offenders are exempt from the death penalty—juveniles under the age of 18 when their crimes were committed, and women.

66 Law and Law Reform

The motives for the various legal reforms provide a perspective on how the legal culture and context is changing—or not changing. Fletcher (1989) cited the argument of one reformer to the effect that "justice" will not do as a justification for, or end of, the criminal justice process. It was said to be too abstract and too far removed from real human interests. Instead, it is humanism, a compassionate concern for people's needs, which should be the principal goal of legal reform. So far, however, neither justice nor humanism appear to have been achieved in Russia.

Although democratic reformers have advocated a law-based state in the abstract, thus far the government has been rather halting and inconsistent in its response to demands for substantial legal reform. Some significant measures have been passed, but many legal changes seem to have been made on the basis of political expediency rather than as a matter of principle. In order to establish a law-based state, the Russian leadership must conquer the longstanding propensity to use the law as a tool for personal and political gain and the tradition of sacrificing the rights of the individual for the so-called good of the state (Thorson, 1992: 49).

The rule of law in Russia is, as of yet, an illusory goal.

4

CRIME, DELINQUENCY, AND YOUTH PROBLEMS

In this chapter I want to further develop the argument that crime, criminal behavior, juvenile delinquency, and other forms of youth deviance—and especially the reactions to them—shape the process and products of legal socialization. Criminal and other forms of deviant behavior help both to define and reflect the legal environment. Children learn of this behavior; they observe it. They hear, see, and read the justifications and rationalizations for it. They also find out how (and even if) enforcement authorities respond. Vicarious learning experiences of this kind are shared by all of us, and they are one of the premises underlying general deterrence.

Young people also learn legality directly through their own personal experiences of breaking rules and laws. They may feel guilty because their behavior violates their personal moral code. They may, however, experience feelings of excitement, adventure, and risk-taking. They receive approval or disapproval from peers and from adults. They may or may not get caught and punished. If caught up in the legal system, they experience firsthand the justice and fairness of that system. From these experiences they judge whether the costs and benefits are worth the risks. It is clear that both the vicarious and the actual learning experiences are important to the legal socialization process.

To get another sense of the legal context in Soviet and post-Soviet Russia, it is instructive to look at the overall crime picture, particularly the picture that began to emerge at the end of the last decade. It is especially important to examine the problems of juvenile crime and delinquency, because these are direct indicators of youthful legal compliance. We will look first at juvenile misbehavior during the bulk of the Soviet period. Then we consider especially the Gorbachev—glasnost and perestroika—era. Finally, and most important, is what is happening now in Russia. Recent increases, really dramatic upward trends in juvenile

68 Crime, Delinquency, and Youth Problems

delinquency, suggest that whatever combination of moral validity and congruity, legitimacy, and deterrence that worked to help keep juvenile deviance relatively low in earlier periods of Soviet history seemingly began to break down in the late 1980s. We must be cautious in adopting the latter conclusion too readily, however, because of the gaps and changes in defining and recording the data required to measure and test any assumptions about trends in youthful misbehavior.

It is also important, if one wants to get a comprehensive sense of law and deviance, to consider youth behavior problems broadly—to include such things as alcohol, drugs, prostitution, gang and youth subculture involvement, and school maladjustment. The latter go beyond just the narrowly defined criminal behavior for which juveniles are registered, that is have criminal cases initiated against them. Antisocial, but not necessarily criminal behaviors also mirror young people's reactions to the legal context in which they are growing up.

With respect to the official Soviet response to crimes and other social problems, including those involving youth, there were roughly four strategies that were employed. Especially during the first days of Soviet socialism, there was the ideological belief that the country would grow out of the problems inherited from the tsars. These problems included crime and lawlessness. Building socialism and the "new Soviet man" was the basic ingredient for an effective Soviet crime policy. Somewhat later, while there were still some "true believers" who continued to hold to the notion that achieving socialism was all that was necessary to eliminate crime in the planned Soviet utopia, others adopted the offshoot rationalization that the criminality that persisted was a remnant of the "bourgeois capitalism" that remained to be rooted out of the people's psyches. One element of this rooting out was the use of the law-related education approach discussed earlier. Next, but actually contemporaneous with both the former approaches, there developed the ironfisted repressive strategy for dealing with many social problems (including crime), that I have already described. This approach was focused on formal social control and deterrence. Lastly, when all else failed, there was unabashed resort to denial and cover-up. Information about crime and other social failings was simply suppressed or distorted.

Given this, it would not be surprising then to find that a kind of giant sham that incorporates rationalization, denial, cover-up, and suppression might spawn cynicism, especially among more idealistic youth. And further, that it might undermine both the morality and the legitimacy of the Soviet system in their eyes.

Crime in the Former Soviet Union

As I indicated in Chapter 1, there were dramatic increases in crime in the USSR toward the end of the 1980s. Registered crimes went from 1,867,223 in 1988 (an increase of 3.8 percent over 1987) to 2,786,606 in 1990 to 3,102,748 in 1991. "Registered" crimes are those in which criminal cases are initiated. "Reported"

Crime, Delinquency, and Youth Problems **69**

crimes, on the other hand, are apparently all those that are reported or known to the police.

Although the per capita Soviet figures were well below those for the West, the rate of growth was considered to be alarming (Dashkov, 1992). Most alarming were the increases in violent crimes such as homicides, assaults, rapes, robberies, and that quintessential Soviet crime of malicious and especially malicious hooliganism. Use of firearms and brutality appeared more and more often. More premeditated and sophisticated forms of organized crime also became more prevalent. Theft of state property increased 40 percent in 1991, and theft of personal property increased more than 20 percent. Some economic crimes—for example, speculation—on the other hand, declined. This latter development seems to be related to the transition to a market economy. Reselling goods and services for profit had been prohibited under the socialist command economy, whereas it has become a more expected feature of the new free market economy.

Interesting from the legal socialization perspective are some fairly typical observations about these developments:

> Soviet scholars and journalists are more and more open about the deeper political roots of the current crime wave—seventy years of totalitarianism. In a society, they say, where for over seventy years the state systematically eliminated all private mechanisms of moral uprightness—religion, charity, attachment to land and property—relying instead on fear and fear alone as a means of social control, even a slight diminution of fear led to a crime wave that is rolling over Soviet cities. As a Soviet criminal psychology specialist . . . puts it: "We are reaping the consequences of the totalitarian system." . . . the greatest obstacle in the "war on crime" [is] a broad and deeply engraved belief, upon which . . . "a whole generation of young people has grown up," the belief that "you cannot survive by honest labor."
> *World Affairs, 1989: 109*

> In addition to the growth in the number of crimes against the person connected with apparently motiveless cruelty and malevolence, there appears to be a general growth in disrespect for the law.
> *Dashkov, 1992: 161*

The crime wave has continued in the new post-Soviet Russia. In the first three months of 1992 in Russia alone, there were 18.6 percent more murders and attempted murders; there were 10.6 percent more crimes involving grave bodily injury; 38.8 percent more crimes with firearms; and 20 percent more street crimes than during the first quarter of 1991. Property crimes showed even greater increases: property thefts up 60 percent; burglaries up 70 percent; auto thefts up 60 percent; and, counterfeiting up 120.7 percent (Tapp and Kohlberg, 1992: 8). Toward the end of 1992, concern was being expressed over a 30 percent increase

70 Crime, Delinquency, and Youth Problems

in crime in Russia over 1991. In 1992, the first full year of its independence from the former Soviet Union, Russia experienced nearly 600,000 more crimes than it had in 1991. (This following a 24 percent increase in 1991 over 1990.) Of special concern were car theft and trafficking in stolen cars, trafficking in drugs and stolen firearms, muggings, and robberies; and generally the crimes of loosely organized criminal networks or groupings based on nationality or regions in central Russia. Both law-abidingness and social control appeared to be continuing their breakdown.

Juvenile Crime and Delinquency

Today, the effects on juvenile delinquency—and on other problems of Russian youth—of the enormous changes in the former USSR obviously cannot be fully discerned. It can be anticipated, however, that several of these changes are unlikely to have any effect, some changes may eventually alleviate causes of these problems; but still others may actually exacerbate the situation, at least in the short run.

What is clear is that these problems are not new in Russia; nor are they unique. Recent history shows that Russian scholars, journalists, politicians, and the general public first began to openly express concern about the rising tide of delinquency and deviance among young people in the late 1980s. Numerous newspaper articles recited tales of juvenile lawbreaking, and of youthful drug addiction and involvement in the black market.

Although the extensive media attention devoted to youth crime and delinquency in the past five years conveyed the impression that these problems were novel in Soviet Russia, the reality is that this is not a new phenomenon. Well before the Bolshevik revolution, Russian scholars were concerned with the youth problems, including delinquency, that accompanied the industrial revolution and the massive urbanization that had begun in Russia in the late 1800s (Juviler and Forschner, 1978). Major Russian cities experienced an influx of homeless youth and a consequent rise in delinquency. A second wave of youth migration to the cities occurred following the Bolshevik revolution, the ensuing civil war, and the famines of the 1920s (Juviler and Forschner, 1978; Zeldes, 1980, 1981). During the early 1920s, there was again a sharp increase in the number of juveniles convicted of crimes. Juvenile crime continued to rise through the mid-1930s, despite a number of prevention measures (including law-related education) that were adopted. According to Zeldes (although statistical data on these early periods are very limited), it appears that another juvenile crime wave occurred following the outbreak of World War II—an outbreak that lasted through the late 1940s. As with the period following World War I and the revolution, there again were large numbers of homeless children (*bezprizornost*) in Russia after World War II. This temporarily contributed to the juvenile crime rate. Then, similar to the American experience, the postwar baby boom in the Soviet Union

Crime, Delinquency, and Youth Problems **71**

resulted in yet another major increase in juvenile crime during the 1960s (Juviler and Forschner, 1978; Zeldes, 1980, 1981; Van den Berg, 1985).

That juvenile crime had always existed in the Soviet Union, and that it became an even more pervasive problem in the 1980s, was, however, only to be openly admitted under the policy of glasnost. As more attention came to be focused on the situation, it also became clear that the problems experienced by Russian youth were in many ways similar to those of their counterparts in the West. Juvenile delinquency, despite what might be its different origins, was once again demonstrated through this example to be a cross-cultural, universal phenomenon. It exists in socialist as well as capitalist societies.

The Scope of Delinquency

The actual extent of delinquency in Soviet Russia is difficult to assess because of the fact that statistics on crime and delinquency were tightly controlled by the authorities. Until 1989, the information on crime and delinquency that was made available to the public was limited to sketchy figures released through the state-controlled press. Specific statistical information detailing the actual amounts of crime was released only to party officials, and was considered to be a state secret. This was all part of the policy of denial and suppression. Academics, researchers, and scholars also had only very limited access to crime information (Zaslayskaia, 1987). Soviet officials were reluctant to discuss the true picture of crime because of the obvious contradictions such discussion would pose for one of the basic tenets of Communism, that is, that capitalism is criminogenic and that crime in a socialist state declines and eventually disappears. When this failed to occur in the USSR, government officials were "unable to reconcile ideology with the actual situation," and thus, "they refrained from discussing crime" (Shelley, 1991: 252). But they did more than simply refrain; they also put out false and misleading information. Butler reported that

> the public was for some three decades given only ritualistic incantations that crime rates were dropping, occasional press reports of particularly pernicious crimes (and executions), and a criminological literature that dealt in abstract weeded percentages rather than hard empirical data on the incidence of crime.
>
> *Butler, 1992: 144*

This was a part of the "Big Lie" referred to in the first chapter.

Beginning in 1985, glasnost permitted more open discussion of crime and social problems by Soviet officials. The Soviet Ministry of Internal Affairs even started providing weekly press reports to both foreign and state press regarding crime in Moscow. Government officials, scholars, and journalists, all began acknowledging the increasing crime rate among both adults and juveniles, as well as the growing problems of drug abuse and alcoholism. Despite such information

72 Crime, Delinquency, and Youth Problems

advances, obtaining accurate crime statistics remained and still remains a problem. One of the major contributing (operational) factors to the inaccuracy of Russian crime data is the failure by the militia to record all the crimes known to them. This problem arose originally because of the considerable pressure placed on the militia to solve 95 percent of all reported crimes. In order to maintain such an unrealistically high clearance rate, crimes that were unlikely to be solved were simply not recorded by the police (Van den Berg, 1985; Shelley, 1991). Another form of denial and cover-up.

But even under an honest reporting system, estimates of the level of delinquency are complicated by the fact that, as in the United States, not all crimes are detected by the police. It is unclear at present to just what extent Russia now maintains a standardized system of recording crimes. To date, little is known about how these data are collected and what methods are used to ensure their accuracy. According to Zeldes (1981), in the former USSR, there were several different systems of recording information on crimes and criminals at various stages of the criminal justice process. Each system was said to have had varying degrees of accuracy.

A number of Soviet researchers writing in earlier periods relied on court statistics for their estimates of delinquency; but this information is also seriously underestimated because not all juvenile cases are processed through the criminal courts. It is estimated that approximately a third to a half of all cases involving Soviet youth were dropped or handled informally by the various commissions on juvenile affairs (CJAs) (McClellan, 1987). Cases that were handled administratively or processed through the CJAs were not included in the court statistics.

Even in countries where there is a standardized crime reporting system, such as in the United States with its Uniform Crime Reports, it is still difficult to get a handle on the true amount of crime. It must be kept in mind that official statistics are at best a function of decisions by citizens and police to report crimes. Discretion is especially evident when it comes to minor offenses and to juvenile offenders. With respect to juveniles, the police frequently leave matters up to the parents or other adult authorities to handle. There is no reason to believe that Russian police are any different in this regard than police elsewhere. Thus, Soviet and Russian crime and arrest data must be viewed in this light.

With these caveats in mind, some assessment of the amount of juvenile crime can nevertheless be made. It is estimated that Soviet youth were responsible for roughly 10 percent of the total number of registered crimes in the mid-1980s; although again it is likely that the true amount of youth crime was actually higher (Shelley, 1991). A report from the Soviet Ministry of Internal Affairs in 1989 showed that juveniles aged between 14 and 17 accounted for 11.1 percent of the registered crimes in 1980. This proportion had dropped to 9.5 percent in 1982, but rose to 14.4 percent in 1988 (*Statestecheske Dane a Prestupnoste v Strane*, 1989); and to 16.3 percent in 1989–90 (Serio, 1992a). By way of comparison, during the 1980s, juveniles in the United States accounted for approximately 15–20 percent of the yearly total of arrests (Uniform Crime Reports, 1981–90).

Crime, Delinquency, and Youth Problems **73**

The Soviet Union experienced a general increase in the level of registered juvenile crime over the past three decades. In 1965, 14–17-year-olds committed 80,650 registered crimes. By 1985 (the beginning of the Gorbachev period), this number had increased 107.8 percent to 167,630. In 1989, it was 223,940—an increase of 177.7 percent over 1965 and 21.2 percent just over 1988; and in 1990, there were 232,701 registered crimes by juveniles (Serio, 1992a). Juvenile crime in the United States also increased through the 1970s (peaking in 1981), but then declined somewhat in the early 1980s, and leveled off. During the latter half of the decade, however, juvenile arrests for violent crimes in the U.S. increased significantly.

In the former Soviet Union, as in the United States, most juvenile offenses are property offenses. Russian juveniles likewise tend to commit their crimes in groups (Juviler and Forschner, 1978; Ovchinskii, 1989). Evidence suggests that the rate of involvement in violent crimes by juveniles in the USSR began increasing at the end of the decade. It was estimated that juveniles then accounted for 21 percent of all violent offenses (Shelley, 1991). In comparison, in 1990 in the United States, juveniles accounted for approximately 16 percent of all arrests for violent crimes.

Soviet females earlier accounted for only a small proportion of overall crime and delinquency. But their proportion of criminal behavior also increased dramatically (to more than 20 percent) by the end of the 1980s (Shelley, 1991). The latter figure is similar to the situation in the United States, where females accounted for 23 percent of all juvenile arrests in 1990 (UCR, 1990).

According to Arshayskii and Vilks (1990), the juvenile crime rate in the USSR rose from 4.2 per 10,000 population to 7.6 per 10,000 population between 1981 and 1987. During this time, the number of juveniles between the ages of 14 and 17 in the general population was actually declining. The absolute number of juveniles charged with crimes thus increased by one and a half times. In addition, the number of youth committing crimes who were below the age of accountability, that is age 14, also increased during this period. Arshayskii and Vilks projected that between 1989 and 1995, the juvenile crime rate in the USSR would increase an average of 3 percent per year. That this estimate is going to fall badly short is evidenced by the 21.2 percent increase recorded just in 1989 over 1988.

The 10 percent of crime attributed to juveniles in 1980 had grown to over 16 percent by 1990. According to current reports, this increase is continuing, and juvenile crime in Russia is becoming an ever more serious problem. The Russian newspaper *Izvestia* reported in April 1992 that juveniles accounted for 17 percent of all crimes committed in Russia in the first three months of 1992. Twenty percent of juvenile crimes were of a serious nature. On July 29, 1992, *Izvestia* had this to say about the crime picture in Russia:

> the criminal milieu is beginning to grow younger at a rapid rate. The number of teenagers arrested at crime scenes has topped 91,000, which is

74 Crime, Delinquency, and Youth Problems

23 percent higher than last year's [1991] figure. Grave crimes are increasing with shocking steadiness—premeditated murders, along with holdups and muggings involving the use of firearms, increase by almost 33 percent every six months.

Tapp and Kohlberg, 1992

During a 1992 visit to the Russian Ministry of Internal Affairs, I was given data on juvenile crime in Russia for the first six months of 1992. These data document the increasing problem. They showed 125,093 crimes involving juveniles, a 19.3 percent increase over the comparable period in 1991. The proportion of all reported crimes accounted for by juveniles was 16.7 percent. Crimes for which juveniles were registered amounted to 120,372, a 19.7 percent increase; and they accounted for 21.8 percent of all registered crimes. This suggests that juvenile involvement in crime had roughly doubled in the last ten years.

In 1992, juveniles were registered for 21,622 serious crimes—18.3 percent of the total in Russia. These included 351 intentional homicides, 802 cases involving intentional grave bodily injury, and 1,201 rapes. Juveniles were also charged with 11,768 robberies, and assaults with intent to rob, involving personal property; with 7,236 cases of hooliganism; with 23,428 cases of theft of state property; and with 58,451 cases of theft of personal property. Surprisingly, there were only 14 cases in which juveniles were registered for narcotics offenses. The latter is far lower than in the United States. It has been suggested, however, that there is reason to believe that the drug statistics drastically understate the true magnitude of that problem.

Causes of Delinquency

Sociological and criminological theory and research in Russia is still very much in its infancy. This is a legacy of the general suppression of the social sciences. As indicated earlier, glasnost eased restrictions on the media, thereby beginning more open discussions of crime and social problems among youth. In addition, glasnost also began to provide scholars with more freedom to explore the real causes of delinquency. Research workers were no longer bound to party rhetoric as they had been in the past. No longer were they compelled to portray Soviet society in a positive light. The research and writing on crime and delinquency that was done by criminologists, sociologists, psychologists, and others was framed and constrained by ideology well into the 1980s (Juviler and Forschner, 1978; Zeldes, 1981; McClellan, 1987). According to this ideology, because crime was disappearing, or certainly would disappear, there was little need to continue to examine its causes. Delinquency specifically, when and where it was acknowledged to exist, was attributed to parents passing on the old capitalist ideas to their children.

One problem that emerged out of the stifling of criminological research is that there are no real scientific studies looking into the nature and causes of delinquency.

Crime, Delinquency, and Youth Problems **75**

As a result, most of the existing literature from the Soviet period is, unfortunately, only descriptive and/or fraught with methodological problems. Zaslayskaia, in a critique of the state of Soviet social sciences in general, stated that "for a long time the social sciences, far from being the vanguard, brought up the rear of society. They have lagged behind practice, restricting themselves largely to repetition, explanation, and approval of already adopted party decisions" (1987: 8).

Arshayskii and Vilks also highlighted the absence of solid research into the causes of crime and delinquency:

> In studies of the illegal behavior of minors and young people, it is very rare to find a deep analysis of the current state or a determination of trends in the development of a social phenomena and factors associated with criminality: drug addiction, addiction to toxic agents, prostitution, and other social anomalies.
>
> *Arshayskii and Vilks, 1990: 89*

Soviet criminologists focused heavily on the contribution of micro-level social institutions (such as families, schools, workplace, etc.) to delinquency. Consequently, factors commonly cited as being correlated with delinquency included alcoholism in the home, domestic disputes and abuse, the lack of education of parents, parental criminal records, and the failure of schools (Juviler and Forschner, 1978; Zeldes, 1981). Without denying that these are truly factors contributing to delinquency, just as they are in other societies, the focus on them kept the focus away from the macro-level—from Soviet society at large.

Juviler and Forschner (1978), in their review of juvenile delinquency in the Soviet Union, found that Soviet scholars divided the causes of delinquency into long-term causes on the one hand, and short-term contributing conditions on the other. The long-term causes of delinquency included such factors as negative family influences, delinquent peer groups, and bourgeois propaganda. The short-term conditions were considered to be more immediately amenable to amelioration. They included the failure of the schools to deal with problem students, lack of parental supervision, too much unoccupied leisure time because of a lack of recreational facilities for youth, and lax enforcement of alcohol laws that restricted the sale of alcohol to minors. Juviler and Forschner concluded that, as of that time, that is, the mid-1970s, "the dynamics of Soviet delinquency underneath a different veneer, are not unlike [the dynamics in] Western countries" (1978: 21).

Walter Connor, in his groundbreaking 1972 book entitled *Deviance in Soviet Society*, characterized Soviet thought on the causes of delinquency as falling into two related perspectives: institutional malfunctioning and personality characteristics. The notion of institutional malfunctioning, which is a micro-level perspective and similar to Juviler and Forschner's short-term conditions, allowed Soviet officials to deny the possibility that factors inherent in their society were contributing

76 Crime, Delinquency, and Youth Problems

to delinquency. Instead, the Soviets argued that institutions responsible for the socialization of youth, such as the family, the schools, and the workplace, were malfunctioning. By improving the operation and efficiency of these institutions, it was said, delinquency could be prevented. Alexander Yakovlev, a noted Russian criminologist, was one of those who, while offering these arguments, also began early on to subtly move the focus to the broader stage. For example, he highlighted the importance of the role of social institutions in maintaining conformity and, although he did not call it that, seemingly advancing legal socialization:

> The most significant social institution is the system of upbringing, education, and training of the new generation . . . Social institutions ensure the possibility for the members of society or appropriate social groups to accomplish their goals. They regulate behavior, stabilize social relations, secure coordination and integrity in the actions of society members, and strive to attain higher levels of social conformity.
>
> *Yakovlev, 1979: 110*

Yakovlev argued that in times of rapid social change, social institutions may not keep pace with the changes occurring in the structure and needs of society. As a result, he said, social institutions may not be able to carry out their functions and societal members may seek alternative activities to satisfy their needs "at the expense of existing norms and rules, including legal norms" (Yakovlev, 1979: 111). Although he had no detailed data and empirical studies to support his arguments, or at least could not present any, Yakovlev suggested a criticism of the macro-level Soviet system by saying that sociological research showed that:

> an inadequate, inflexible general system of basic education, professional training, or university education leads to such social expenses as school dropouts, disadvantages in unemployment, and psychological difficulties. The totality of such factors may have a negative effect on the level of youth offenses.
>
> *Yakovlev, 1979: 113*

Returning to Connor (1972), the second trend in Soviet explanations of delinquency, he said, centered on the development of the adolescent personality. This approach was essentially a social-psychological explanation of delinquency that took into account the personality of the youth, as well as the context of the environment in which the adolescent found himself. The normal adolescent desires for self-assertion, excitement, adventure, and independence from parents could lead to delinquency. Once again, however, we see that the system is OK; it was the individual youth in this case who was not OK!

Years later, in 1988, I. M. Il'inskii, the then-director of the research center of the then-Komsomol High School of the Central Committee of the Komsomol (the official Communist Party youth organization), pointed to the declining moral

Crime, Delinquency, and Youth Problems **77**

responsibility among Soviet youth and the growing trend of consumerism, which he argued had resulted in "a decline in active, creative, and social involvement of individuals, a loss of intellectual values, an increase in selfishness, envy, lying, lack of principle, and finally criminality, including bribe-taking and thievery" (Il'inskii, 1988: 22). These trends, he said,

> are in many respects the consequence not only of certain costs of our developing society, the social conditions of life, the effect of bourgeois ideology and propaganda, but also of omissions and flaws in the functioning of the system of communist upbringing of youth—in particular, the educational activity of the Komsomol.
>
> *Il'inskii, 1988: 26*

According to Zeldes, "[i]n the opinion of Soviet criminologists, juvenile delinquency in the USSR [was] largely the result of both emotional and intellectual immaturity, poor upbringing, and socio-environmental factors and circumstances" (1980: 18). Zeldes emphasized that Soviet officials did not acknowledge the possibility that crime in the USSR was in fact rooted in the very essence of Soviet society, in the contradictions between the theory and practice of socialism.

A number of theories of delinquency that have been developed in the United States seem fitting to explain juvenile lawbreaking in the former Soviet Union. For example, in an earlier work I reviewed criminological explanations of Soviet delinquency in accordance with the precepts of two of these theories (Finckenauer, 1988). That review determined that there were striking similarities between the causes of delinquency that had been identified by Soviet criminologists and the so-called cultural deviance (i.e., social disorganization) and strain theories popular in the United States. Antonian, a Soviet criminologist writing in 1976, pointed to the weakening or breakdown of social institutions and their subsequent inability to exert control over youth behavior (which he attributed to urbanization and migration) as contributing to juvenile crime. This attribution of delinquency to social disorganization was very much reminiscent of the work of American sociologists Shaw and McKay on delinquency in urban areas. The latter work showed that urbanization, rapid industrialization, and immigration contributed to a breakdown of community-based organizations and to their loss of effectiveness in employing informal social controls.

Similarly, Babaev and Shliapochnikov, in 1979, discussed the differences between groups, particularly those living in urban areas, in their material well-being and living conditions, as being major factors contributing to Soviet crime. The essence of their argument was that those who had fewer possibilities (opportunities) available to meet their needs experienced a sense of deprivation and thwarted aspirations, which in turn could lead them to criminal behavior. This argument is similar to the differential opportunity theory of delinquency developed by Richard Cloward and Lloyd Ohlin (1960). The latter proposes that crime and

78 Crime, Delinquency, and Youth Problems

delinquency arise out of the shortfall between aspirations and achievements, from frustration of needs, and from relative deprivation. These conditions, in turn, are derived from the socioeconomic shortcomings and failures of the society to deliver on its promises.

Despite the few examples of more adventurous and risky thinking, in general the extant explanations of delinquent behavior steered away from even implicit criticism of Soviet society and Soviet law. The same was true of other problems involving youth.

Growing Up in the USSR

All societies in all countries present their children with a more or less hypocritical picture and a kind of mixed message during their growing-up years. The picture is hypocritical to the extent that there are gaps between the ideal and the real; that there are contradictions between what children are taught and what they observe. Children everywhere are in fact often directly cautioned by adults to "don't do as I do; do as I say!" They are also led to have expectations that are not—and sometimes cannot—be fulfilled. These contradictions and the gaps between aspirations and achievements may vary from place to place, from people to people, and from time to time, but they are seemingly ubiquitous. One result is that there is a disillusionment, mostly among adolescents, that comes from unmet promises and unfulfilled expectations.

The former Soviet Union was not alone in posing these contradictions to its youth. But the nature and the magnitude of hypocrisy in the USSR was unusual in the extent to which it was institutionalized. The contrast between the elders preaching ideals to the young, while surviving under the mendacious role models of the Soviet regime, was a stark one. A number of observers of the youth scene in Soviet and post-Soviet Russia have commented on this point (see, for example, Americans Dobson, 1991; Hollander, 1991; and Riordan, 1989; and Russians Kutsev, 1992; and Shubkin, 1992).

Riordan noted that it was the "unrelenting moralising, the hypocrisy, the double standards, the rigid monopoly of the mass media that . . . not only produced apathy among many young people . . . [but] pushed some to extremes" (Riordan, 1989: 135). Alluding to a loss of legitimacy, Dobson similarly described how Soviet commentators of the late 1980s began to openly admit that "falsehood, hypocrisy, and efforts to conceal problems [had] eroded the authority of the political leaders and of parents and teachers as well" (Dobson, 1991: 231).

Examples of such open Soviet admissions of these kinds of problems occurred at a meeting of the Central Committee of the CPSU in mid-1991. Professor G. F. Kutsev of the USSR State Committee of Public Education offered this lament:

> With full justification we can call young people the bewildered generation; young people are disillusioned with the ideals of socialism . . . The people's

moral level is going down . . . Crime is increasing, even among juveniles. These are all phenomena that elicit a disrespectful attitude to society and the law in young people—phenomena that can be considered as indicators of the level of moral upbringing.

Kutsev, 1992: 7–8

Professor V. N. Shubkin, at this same meeting, was even more directly critical:

In the course of seventy years, devastating blows have been inflicted on the spiritual and moral sphere. What we are left with are fragments of morality, a few individual centers of morality, while on the whole we have a rather demoralized society. It would be surprising if our young people were fine and not lost.

Shubkin, 1992: 14

Delinquency was just one of many problems associated with youth that began receiving wide public attention in the waning days of the Soviet Union. There was considerable concern over the proliferation of informal youth associations (said to be part of the youth subculture); over drug and alcohol abuse; over consumerism or the preoccupation with attaining material goods; and, most interesting for our purposes, over shifting political values and attitudes—some of which openly challenged official norms and institutions (Dobson, 1991; Frisby, 1989).

Richard Dobson and others suggested that in some respects Soviet youth experienced problems similar to those of youth in the West. Dobson identified three characteristics of Soviet society, however, which made their particular youth problems distinct. First, political controls had been much stronger, and deviations from official standards were considered to be a form of political opposition. Second, the economy's failure to meet consumer needs led to the creation and reliance on the illegal black market. Third, the economy's inability to provide youth with interesting, challenging, and satisfying jobs led to a great deal of job dissatisfaction and a high rate of job turnover among youth (Dobson, 1991: 229).

It was in this context that the new youth subculture emerged. Throughout the 1980s there was a proliferation of informal youth groups throughout the Soviet Union. Reasons given by youth for joining these groups were akin to the reasons offered by American juveniles for joining youth gangs. They included finding a sense of community with their peers outside the official institutions, and finding a place where they could express their individuality (Dobson, 1991). Included among the Soviet groups were rock music fans, hippies, religious groups, cults, *fanaty* (soccer fans), *afghansty* (veterans of the war in Afghanistan), *fashisty* (neo-Nazi youth group), youth gangs, vigilante groups, and others. Not all of these youth groups engaged in criminal activity, but many apparently did (Dobson,

80 Crime, Delinquency, and Youth Problems

1991). For example, the Liubery—a contemporary vigilante-type group that emphasizes physical strength—opposes all Western culture and influence. Their self-appointed mission is to rid the country of rock fans and groupies, of hippies, and of punks. They frequently travel to different Russian cities and physically confront such persons.

The Soviet Union was unique in its attempt to control and shape the development of its youth into "proper Communist citizens." The Komsomol, which was the official youth organization, had as its purpose "to organise and train young people in a communist manner, to build a communist society and to defend the Soviet Republic" (Riordan, 1989: 19). In theory, participation in the Komsomol was voluntary. In practice, however, the Party indirectly made participation compulsory by requiring character references from Komsomol for entrance into institutions of higher education or for job promotions.

In the late 1980s, the Komsomol (as with the Communist Party itself) became increasingly bureaucratic and its leaders were criticized as being

> careerists, corrupt officials, political "radishes" (red on the outside, white on the inside) who paid lip service to communism and young people while enjoying their fraise de representation: trips abroad, chauffeur-driven limousines, special (closed to the public) shops . . . and the rest.
>
> *Riordan, 1989: 38*

Such abuses of power and privileges further contributed to the alienation of youth from socialist ideology (Riordan, 1989; Dobson, 1991). The Komsomol became more and more out of touch with the needs and concerns of Soviet youth and lost what little remained of its credibility. After some futile and halfhearted attempts to reform the organization, in September 1991 the Komsomol held its last congress and then later disbanded (Lebedev, 1991).

Toward the end of the decade of the 1980s, Soviet officials were expressing a considerable degree of concern over the declining commitment of youth to socialist principles. Their ideals and beliefs were said to be changing. They had lost interest in public affairs; there was a decline in the moral incentives to work; and, an increasing number of youth had adopted as their main goal in life the attainment of material wealth. It was widely believed that it was the corruption and failure of various social institutions, such as the Komsomol, that undermined the ideological commitment of Russian youth (Il'Inskii, 1988). This corruption destroyed any remaining vestiges of legitimacy of these institutions and sapped any moral authority that they may have still retained.

Educational Problems of Youth

As the economy crumbles in Russia, the educational system is increasingly pressed for resources. Old thinking, old methods, and old curricula are out; but exactly

Crime, Delinquency, and Youth Problems **81**

what is going to replace them is not yet clear. Teachers now rely a great deal upon current events and the media for classroom materials, while history and other textbooks are being written and rewritten.

Soviet youth, regardless of social class, generally had similar aspirations in terms of going on to higher education. But despite official claims of equality of educational opportunity, there were always great disparities throughout Soviet history across classes in those who entered university. In the early 1960s, university students were predominantly from the higher classes or the professional working class (non-manual labor). As the number of children completing secondary education rose during this period, the number of students going on to higher education likewise increased; but the university system did not expand to keep pace with the increased demand. Connor (1991) noted, in yet another example of the contradictions between ideology and experience, that it was the urban, well-educated families with commensurate occupational status who were better able to ensure their child's place in higher education. Not only were such children more likely to get into an institution of higher learning, but they also were more likely to get into the best and most prestigious universities. One might observe that this practice is not totally dissimilar to that in the United States.

Emphasis in Soviet Russia was on academic education, especially in science and technology. This emphasis encouraged an increasing number of students to go on to higher education in hopes of securing a professional job. Unfortunately for these youth, the country had a large need for an industrial labor pool, and thus youth often found that these were the only jobs available to them when they entered the workforce. Just as they do elsewhere, Russian youth had a negative perception of these jobs. Now professional jobs in teaching, science, medicine, and so on, have lost status and prestige because of their relatively low current salaries. For example, a senior teacher and former secondary school director told me in October 1992 that her monthly salary (then 2,500 rubles) was sufficient to buy only the equivalent of two and a half boxes of candy. All this led to widespread job dissatisfaction and frustration that is evidenced in the rate at which young people switch jobs.

Now that the massive, inefficient, and unproductive state-supported industries are being cut back and closed down, the specter of wide-scale unemployment has also arisen. Just as in other societies, this new unemployment will hit the youth hardest—especially those youth who are without experience, education, and skills. This is expected to create even more dissatisfaction and frustration, and inevitably lead to more deviance.

In 1992, I had the opportunity to visit a Moscow school and talk with teachers and students. I also visited Moscow State University and spoke with professors and students of the law faculty there. With regard to the question of law-related education in the secondary schools, I was advised that there is no longer any mandatory law curriculum focusing on "fundamental principles of Soviet law." Instead there is a requirement that 20 hours of such subject matter be presented

82 Crime, Delinquency, and Youth Problems

a year. The content within these 20 hours is optional, to be decided at the discretion of individual schools.

Echoing concerns expressed earlier, the school director of the particular school I visited indicated that her students have now become very materialistic. She said that they were mostly interested in seeking any and all ways to make money quickly. Others plan marriage immediately after finishing school. The latter youth intend to seek jobs, homes, and families, rather than going on for higher education.

Corruption apparently also plays its role in education, just as it does in other spheres of Russian life. A student at a technical institute (comparable to a college with a vocational orientation) described to me the widespread practice of professors soliciting and accepting bribes for passing students on their examinations. He said that 3,000 or 4,000 rubles was the going price in October 1992 for a four or five (the highest grade) on an examination. He also said that it was possible for him to not go to his institute for an entire semester, but by paying a deacon (dean) he could receive passing grades for courses that he had not taken. Needless to say, such practices (which actually began to be acknowledged during the Brezhnev era of the mid-1960s through the beginning of the 1980s) would undermine respect for the legitimacy and integrity of the educational institution.

Urbanization and the Changing Nature of the Family

Rapid urbanization and migration has resulted in a breakdown of the extended family support network in the traditional Russian family. It is estimated that nearly 70 percent of the population of the former USSR now resides in urban areas (Juviler, 1991), and that two-thirds of all youth between the ages of 14 and 29 are city dwellers (Dobson, 1991). Again as in other countries, there are fewer informal social controls in urban settings. Both parents are likely to be working, and the community controls that were present in the small villages of Russia do not exist in the larger cities (Antonian, 1976; Dobson, 1991).

One in three marriages ends in divorce (Juviler, 1991) and the divorce rate in cities is even higher—one in two marriages (Frisby, 1989). Housing shortages exacerbate the problem by forcing many separated and divorced couples to continue to reside together (Juviler, 1991). An average of 950,000 divorces annually leaves 700,000 children in single-parent families. Most urban Russian children are an only child, and their single parent is their mother. The result? Large numbers of children, living in drab and crowded urban apartments with their mothers who are forced to work long hours to make a living, are left unsupervised and exposed to the numerous temptations and deviance that saturate big cities. Just as in urban America, this contributes to juvenile delinquency and other problems.

Crime, Delinquency, and Youth Problems **83**

Alcohol and Drug Abuse

Soviet officials long acknowledged that alcohol abuse by minors was a serious problem, although there is very little hard information to document this (Treml, 1991). But the fact that Russian youth abuse alcohol, and that this is an important factor in a range of youth problems, does not come as a surprise in a country that has a long history of alcohol abuse and alcoholism. Russia's alcohol problem is widely acknowledged to be among the worst in the world in terms of the social costs that result from drunkenness (Erlanger, 1992). These costs associated with drinking include crime, absenteeism, lost production, and sickness. It is estimated that more than a third of all crimes in Moscow are committed by drunken people; and that the proportion approaches 80 percent with such crimes as murder, rape, and robbery.

Estimates are that between 70 and 80 percent of juvenile offenders use alcohol on a regular basis. One survey of delinquents in a correctional labor colony indicated that more than half were drunk at the time they committed their offense. A quarter of these youthful offenders said they had committed their crime in order to get alcohol or to get money to buy alcohol (Levin, 1990).

Former Soviet President Gorbachev carried on a vigorous anti-alcohol campaign from 1985 to 1988. Gorbachev's campaign is acknowledged to have had an effect upon reducing the crime rate and with at least stabilizing male life expectancy at that time. Prior to 1985, the USSR was the only industrialized country in the world in which the average life expectancy for men was declining— principally as a result of alcoholism. This effort to control alcoholism had a number of negative side-effects. Vast sugar shortages developed as sugar was increasingly siphoned into the production of *samogon*, or homemade booze. The quality of some of this homebrew was such that drinking it was itself life-threatening. Even more life-threatening was the consumption of other vodka alternatives: cheap perfume, window-cleaner, bug killers, glue, and gasoline. Revenues from the sales of vodka dropped so much that budget deficits had to be covered by printing more rubles, adding to the problems of inflation. And some drinkers, particularly young ones, turned to drugs in lieu of alcohol. The latter had the effect of adding to the already increasing drug problem. Since 1991, drinking has again soared, and the life expectancy of men has further declined.

Very little is known about the problem of drug abuse among either youth or adults in the former Soviet Union. One review of illicit drug use cited 130,000 officially registered users and addicts (Lee, 1992), but also reported a Ministry of Internal Affairs estimate of 1.5 million non-medical drug users.

> [I]n a multiregional survey of 5,801 secondary school students conducted by Gabiani in 1988–1989, 597 respondents, or 10.2 percent, admitted that they had taken drugs. Gabiani estimated that the categories surveyed— which included students in professional-technical schools (PTU) and in the

84 Crime, Delinquency, and Youth Problems

top four grades of the general middle schools—included 15.2 million people nationwide. By extrapolation, the number of drug users only in these categories, which cover roughly school children between the ages of 14 and 17, could be calculated at more than 1.5 million, and the total number of Soviets who have taken drugs at least once in their lives may total more than 15 million.

Lee, 1992: 180

Another study by Gabiani found that one quarter of the addicts surveyed began using drugs before they were 16. And there is some evidence of drug use at ages 9, 10, and 11 (Lee, 1992: 181). Drug use by Russian youth still pales in comparison with drug use by American youth, but there is evidence that circumstances are changing for the worse.

Prostitution

Prostitution is another social problem that is reported to be growing in Russian cities. Sanjian (1991) concluded that the increasing amount of prostitution being practiced among young girls was best explained as resulting from a fusion of promiscuity and materialism. The promiscuity resulted, she said, from "the combined effects of boredom and thrill seeking, the lack of parental supervision, and the dismal quality of Soviet sex education, which typically avoids frank discussion of the health and other risks of indiscriminate sexual relations" (Sanjian, 1991: 279). The rampant materialism, which I have already referred to, is here simply being pursued through yet another means. Teachers report that their students have developed a tendency to view prostitution in a positive light, and to see it as a viable, lucrative, and even attractive way of making a successful living. Sanjian linked the spread of youthful prostitution with rising juvenile delinquency, gangs, and adolescent alcoholism as examples that there is too much permissiveness, and that social controls over adolescent behavior in general are weakening.

In 1993, there were estimates of large increases in child prostitution (both girls and boys) in Moscow and other Russian cities during the preceding three years. The causes of this problem in Russia are actually quite similar to the situation in certain Third World countries and in the West: runaway and throwaway children, abduction, trickery, and often just a means for children to survive.

A Concluding View

Some of the concerns and frustrations regarding crime, delinquency, and the other problems of Russian youth were illustrated in an interview with a Moscow policewoman, which was reported in the January 22, 1992 edition of *Pravda*. Her views represent particularly the longing for the old law and order that is one of the major themes underlying some of the political movements in Russia today.

As the comments reveal, the concerns expressed are not dissimilar to those often expressed in the United States. Many Russians are perplexed and fearful about how their young people are going to turn out.

> Respondent: [T]his country now has teenage black marketeers, homeless kids, newspaper sellers and youngsters living in attics and cellars . . . It used to be that the schools taught them moral and social values. Maybe they didn't do a great job of it, but at least the process went on, and the children knew what was good and what was bad, what was allowed and what was forbidden. Now everything has changed . . .
>
> Interviewer: So who rules in the teenage world these days?
>
> Respondent: The ruble rules . . . A generation with a market ideology is coming into the arena. People willing to commit crimes and murder for money are already grown up and getting stronger. Teenagers don't want to be poor. They will do anything to escape from poverty. At best, they sell newspapers and wash cars; at worst, they steal. Property crimes predominate among teenagers, and they are rising catastrophically. We now have 10- and 11-year old thieves and 14-year old prostitutes . . .
>
> Interviewer: Who should teach moral and social values?
>
> Respondent: That's the question of questions. There was a two-year struggle in this country against having the police act as pedagogues. Now various structures are being created in the Russian Federation that will assume the functions of working with "problem children" . . . [W]e . . . do not want to stand aside and close our eyes to how our children are sinking deeper and deeper into the morass of crime.

Whatever else the long-term future of Russia and the other countries of the former Soviet Union may hold, youth concerns will undoubtedly continue to be an issue and a problem.

5

CORRUPTION, THE SHADOW ECONOMY, AND ORGANIZED CRIME

An Unsavory Context for Learning Legality

Truth telling is not the forte of Soviet education . . . Indeed, hypocrisy is taught as a virtue . . . As children learn what to say regardless of what they think, they grow more responsive to outer form than to inner conviction . . . [M]any Russians with their wits about them . . . find that they must exist on disparate levels, keeping their common sense to themselves, nurturing a careful schizophrenia . . .

In the scramble for advancement and comfort, in the bending of unreasonable rules and the ignoring of impossible laws, an easy drift is attained, a state of moral weightlessness where there is no up or down, right or wrong . . .

Knowing that much of decent living depends on illegality, Russians move always in a diffuse mist of vague guilt and vulnerability, understanding that they have done many things on the dark side of the law for which they can be arrested at any moment.

Shipler, 1983: 114, 223, 224

If . . . those who carry out criminal acts in the USSR are not the minority of society but are instead the majority, then where are the boundaries and what is the nature of normal behavior? Is criminal behavior for this population the normal behavior? . . .

[T]he schizophrenic nature, the ever-changing codes in Soviet society, provide the operator with a variety of unclear signals and rationalizations. . .

[T]he value system in the Soviet Union accepts a vast amount of criminality as normal daily behavior. It encourages an ethic that turns a blind eye to stealing, certainly stealing from the state, and that permits a vast amount of daily expression of myth system, far removed from the operational code needed for survival in the system.

Rosner, 1986: 41, 42

Another aspect of describing and understanding the context—the sociolegal environment—in which legal socialization takes place requires examining those

Organized Crime **87**

grey, ambiguous areas where people's moral and legal values clash with their desires and their needs. What happens when their personal sense of right and wrong conflicts with the requirements of the institutionalized system in which they live? Moral and legal ambiguities exist in all societies. The clashes they engender create great personal moral and legal dilemmas. Because of the peculiar economic, political, social, and legal conditions in the former Soviet Union, however, people were more often and more starkly confronted with these dilemmas than are most people in most other societies.

Under the circumstances of dealing with their dilemmas, people are forced either to suppress their desires and deny their needs (and perhaps the needs of their families as well), or to act in ways that violate their own moral values and maybe society's formal rules and laws as well. Soviet peoples routinely engaged in both kinds of violations. They became "necessary" deviants, who subsequently entered into a state of what was referred to above as moral schizophrenia or moral weightlessness. That connotes a state in which personal norms and rules are suspended, at least so far as official and public behaviors are concerned—a state in which there is a necessary separation among personal beliefs, beliefs espoused for public consumption, behavior that fits with those public, outer beliefs, and finally, that behavior which is required to survive. This in part is what is meant by the institutionalization of hypocrisy, to which I referred in the previous chapter.

A personal example of the kind of hypocritical behavior that was required in Soviet Russia is that of a Russian friend and colleague. Like many ambitious Soviet young people, and despite personal beliefs that were contrary to the ideology and practices of Communism, he joined the CPSU as a young man. He did so not out of any ideological commitment, but because this was the route to the study of law at a prestigious university, to being a respected and well-paid legal scholar, to being able to travel abroad, and to all the other perquisites that were available only to Party members. This was a course of action taken by many Russians. Whether it is called suspending personal beliefs, the end justifying the means, or pure and simple opportunism—doing it demanded cynicism and hypocrisy. And it demanded justification and rationalization. Was he—and the others like him—wrong? Who is to say that they would have behaved differently given the same circumstances? Thus a dilemma.

Shipler, Rosner, Simis (1982), Lubin (1984), Shelley (1990b), Vaksberg (1991), and Timofeyev (1992)—as well as other commentators on the Soviet scene mentioned in previous chapters—have focused on some versions of the phenomenon of moral weightlessness as being characteristic of the Soviet Union. They each paint a most gloomy picture in which seemingly no area of Soviet life was exempt from pervasive corruption. They describe an environment in which either deceit or silent acquiescence was required; where public behavior demanded a kind of surrealistic distinction between "real" truth and "synthetic" truth; where it was practically impossible to know what was legal and illegal; where the normative boundaries which are needed to maintain societal order were either non-existent

88 Organized Crime

or had broken down (Rosner, 1986). If these observers—knowledgeable all—are correct in their perceptions, what does that say about the sociolegal environment in which Soviet-Russian children were socialized? It suggests yet another argument for why, at the macro-level, moral validity and congruity, and also legitimacy, might become relatively powerless in securing law-abidingness. Why, consequently, there might have to be so much dependence by the government upon the fear of sanctions.

All this bids us to ask whether any of this has changed since the demise of the USSR. Have the formal legal environmental conditions that are pertinent to legal socialization in Russia changed? The quick answer appears to be yes—but the change has not yet been for the better. Is there less corruption? Are the normative boundaries between legal and illegal behavior clearer? Is there only one kind of "truth"? Is there less need for deceit? Is criminal behavior now "abnormal"? A *New York Times* article (and it is only in the media that these issues have been considered so far) suggested that the answer to most of the above questions seems to be no:

> Some of the [current] change [in Russia] is ugly. Speculation, racketeering and corruption abound. Every starting entrepreneur has known a visit from the bulky enforcers . . . specializing in extortion. Bribery is rampant and "conflict of interest" is an alien concept to politicians who blithely market their influence.
>
> Ethnic "mafias" buy politicians and officials in the best tradition of "The Godfather." Illegal exports of capital and raw materials flow all but unimpeded.
>
> *Schmemann, 1992b*

The current conditions in Russia demonstrate aspects of what the French sociologist Emile Durkheim called "anomie." Describing people's reactions to severe economic crises, Durkheim said that the scale that normally exists in every society to balance means and needs is upset under crisis conditions. Because a new scale cannot be immediately improvised, the imbalance between needs and means continues for some indefinite period before normality can be restored. In a suggestion that is particularly appropriate to our concern with socialization, Durkheim believed that moral education must be recommended to deal with such crisis circumstances:

> Time is required for the public conscience to reclassify men and things. So long as the social forces thus freed have not regained equilibrium, their respective values are unknown and so all regulation is lacking for a time. The limits are unknown between the possible and the impossible, what is just and what is unjust, legitimate claims and hopes and those which are immoderate. Consequently, there is no restraint upon aspirations . . .

> At the very moment when traditional rules have lost their authority, the richer prize offered these appetites stimulates them and makes them more exigent and impatient of control. The state of . . . anomy is thus further heightened by passions being less disciplined, precisely when they need more disciplining.
>
> *Durkheim, 1961: 920–1*

This seems to be a rather apt description of the present circumstances in the former Soviet Union. One observer of the current scene in fact characterized the present situation in Russia as anomic. He said that the increase in crime is connected with an increase in anomie, and that as a consequence of the increasing anomie, "there will be an overlap of organized crime with youth crime" there (Kozlov, 1991: 165–6).

Another perspective that is also helpful in explaining the current events in Russia is offered by Rieber and Green (1990). These authors contend that a condition or circumstance called "the psychopathy of everyday life"—which they define as "a general trend toward a greater degree of normalized, or socially acceptable, antisocial behavior in . . . society generally"—is caused by an increase in social distress (Rieber and Green, 1990: 49). Social distress, in turn, is defined by value conflicts resulting from "widespread disorganization in the basic value systems of the populace" (Rieber and Green, 1990: 82). This reminds one of Viktor Frankl's writings, a generation earlier, in which he described a quite similar condition. Frankl called the circumstance in which social conventions, traditions, and values no longer tell people what they should do—an existential vacuum (Frankl, 1969). He said that as a result of this existential vacuum, which was created by the crumbling and vanishing of traditions and values, people suffer feelings of aimlessness and emptiness. These variations on a theme, presented by Durkheim and the others, capture rather well what the Russian people are now going through.

Certainly there is great social distress in Russia today—even more so than before when there was tighter control. But the idea of the psychopathy of everyday life appears to assume some earlier state of "normalcy," which is subsequently disrupted by social distress. What if, however, the earlier state was one in which "normalcy" was as has been previously described in the former USSR? What then are the effects of increased social distress? The current situation is not one of temporary aberration from which the society can be restored to a pre-existing condition. Except for the hardline former Communists and their sympathizers, there is little desire to return to the previous kind of normalcy. What is being recommended by people like Kozlov is a whole new moral and legal system, one built from the ground up. There are certain indications that this is already occurring, in the restoration of the role of the church, and in the various legal and constitutional reforms discussed earlier. We will come back to these questions and perspectives at the conclusion of the chapter.

90 Organized Crime

Among the grey areas where distinctions between right and wrong get blurred in every society are the kinds of crimes known as victimless or consensual crimes, which often become the province of organized crime. Crimes involving drugs, prostitution, bribery, and so on, require victim participation. They occur because of the victim's desire for forbidden goods and services. Zones of ambiguity include also acts that are not inherently wrong, but that are legally forbidden (*mala prohibita*), such as (in the case of Russia) buying and reselling goods for a profit.

Underlying each and every grey area are unmet demands. These unmet demands for goods and services, whether they be illegal or legal, give rise to moral ambiguity and moral compromises. Such demands act also, however, as an incentive to entrepreneurship. We know from the laws of the marketplace that demand stimulates supply. In the USSR, and today in post-Soviet Russia, the entrepreneurial spirit appears not only in legal markets, but also in semi-legal and illegal forms: (1) in the black market and the shadow economy; (2) in the different strains of organized crime that are all referred to by Russians generically as "mafia"; and (3) in the corruption that accompanies and surrounds each of the first two. These will be the "stuff" of our discussion in this chapter.

"Colored" Markets in the USSR

I have already made a number of references to something called the black market or the shadow economy. Let us examine the variety of legal and illegal markets in greater detail. The following table, taken from Gordon B. Smith (1992a: 248), lays out this variety in a comprehensive way.

Smith (1992a) and Shelley (1990a) describe an extensive second economy that operated in the USSR. It consisted of a wide variety of legal, illegal, and semi-legal activities, stimulated mainly by the chronic shortage of consumer goods. Particularly prevalent, they say, was the theft of state property. "Given the low salary levels of most workers and the chronic shortages of numerous items, workers often feel they are justified in stealing from their employers" (Smith, 1992a: 247). Shelley linked the illegal second economy, both inside and outside the workplace, to widespread corruption. "Corruption," she concluded, was "pervasive at all levels of the Soviet system" (Shelley, 1990a: 19).

Lubin (1984: 193) had earlier likewise described a system in which a host of party and government functionaries "frequently and regularly receive[d] sizeable bribes to exert (or not to exert) their influence in an individual's or enterprise's favour." The widespread semi-legal and illegal private production required "greasing the wheels at every level of 'parallel' private activity," in order to protect the involved individuals from discovery and punishment. The greasing included bribes, personal favors, gifts of time, and connections.

Yakovlev (1992b) argued that the state-command economy of the Soviet Union was only able to work at all because there was an illegal, but effective,

Organized Crime 91

TABLE 5.1 Colored Markets in the USSR

Nature of Market	Commodity	Source	Method of Sale	Example
White (legal)	Legal	Legal	Legal	Sale of food in a state store or farmer's market.
Grey (semi-legal)	Legal	Legal	Semi-legal	Selling Italian shoes under the counter.
	Legal	Semi-legal	Legal	Providing dental treatment on the side, using state-owned equipment and supplies.
	Legal	Semi-legal	Semi-legal	Purchase of blue jeans from a foreign tourist.
Black (illegal)	Legal	Legal	Illegal	Speculation—selling vodka for more than the mandated price.
	Legal	Semi-legal	Semi-legal	Selling blue jeans purchased from foreign tourist.
	Legal	Illegal	Illegal	Sale of stolen auto parts.
	Illegal	Illegal	Illegal	Prostitution; narcotics.

private market under the surface. "If you try to suppress a legal market," he said, "it will persist as a black market, and any attempt to quash the black market by administrative measures means more bribes will be paid. Of course, the legal entrepreneur is also often willing to pay bribes if it will produce additional profits; but the illegal capitalist must pay for his very existence, and so he pays more" (Yakovlev, 1992b: 25). Yakovlev elaborated upon the connection between the Soviet black market and corruption, and also drew the contrast with the West:

> the black market brought corruption. Underground capitalism preserved all the evils of the unbridled pursuit of private interests, without any regulation. Corruption is general. Of course, private entrepreneurs may not be above corruption in a free market economy either. They may bribe officials too; bribery is a constant feature of life in every system. But bribery occurs in a free economy for the purpose of obtaining some extra benefit, some extra profit, which a businessman would not acquire otherwise. Under a state monopoly, the underground capitalist must pay bribes for his very

92 Organized Crime

existence, and so bribery is more common in the U.S.S.R. than in the west, and the price is much higher.

In my country this underground capitalist economy, and the corruption associated with it, is what we call "organized crime."

Yakovlev, 1992b: 252

There is an observation in Yakovlev's book by one of the Canadian law students attending the lectures from which the book was taken that is relevant to the currently evolving deviance in the new Russia. The student observes that democratic forces seem to be best able to organize in ex-Soviet institutions where corruption is difficult or impossible—for example in schools as opposed to bread factories. According to this notion, in those situations where someone has his or her hand in the cash register, it is much easier to keep them in line, because of their self-interest arising from the fear of punishment and/or from their desire to continue profiting from corruption. These persons, according to this view, would not respond particularly well to democratic reforms, because they have a vested interest in maintaining the status quo. The implication is thus that corrupt structures must be dismantled before democracy can operate effectively.

We could conclude from this, as Yakovlev seemingly does, that the Russian economy must first be freed from state domination—as is now happening, albeit slowly—and that only then can the corrupt structures begin to be dismantled.

Because of the unique confluence of circumstances and characteristics, it is possible, as suggested earlier, that the USSR produced a people uniquely socialized to facilitate their involvement in widespread deviance. Their common heritage included the Soviet command economy that produced massive shortages as well as widespread bribery and thievery. As I have repeatedly stated, no area of life in the Soviet Union was exempt from universal corruption.

The black market carried a wide variety of products: Western consumer goods such as perfume, clothing, and electronic equipment, as well as stolen goods, stolen cars, drugs and bootleg liquor, cigarettes, and so on. One of the more frightening aspects of the 1990s situation was the new black market in weapons. With the breakdown of the old social controls, there came a vast increase in the number of guns in the hands of people (including especially criminals) across the country. The number of weapons and the firepower of some of these weapons, when combined with the decrease in the effectiveness of law enforcement and the brazenness of criminals and criminal groups in their use of weapons, created an extremely dangerous situation (Serio, 1992b). Weapons were bought from soldiers, and also stolen from military and police arsenals. The black market in weapons included not only small caliber arms, but also submachine and machine guns, grenade launchers, antitank weapons, and even army tanks. Organized criminal gangs obtain these weapons and so too do various ethnic and national groups engaged in interethnic skirmishes.

Russian Organized Crime

During most of the years of Soviet history, as I indicated previously, information about crime and criminals in the USSR was a closely guarded national secret. It was not until Gorbachev instituted the policy of glasnost in the mid-1980s that crime data were generally publicized. Taking account of all the usual limitations of the reporting, accuracy, and completeness of such information, these data showed that the USSR had relatively far less crime being reported than did the United States. The figures also demonstrated, however, that crime began increasing very rapidly at the end of the 1980s.

Along with information about crime in general, there began to appear in the newly enfranchised Soviet media sensationalistic reports of gangsters, racketeers, and a so-called mafia. These reports were picked up and highlighted by the Western press. There were stories about a proliferation of gangsters and racketeers who were, as one publication reported, "into every imaginable racket—from smalltime shakedowns, drugs, prostitution, and even murder for hire to infiltration of legitimate new businesses, especially restaurants and construction firms" (Gurevich, 1990: 24).

In late 1990, I met in Moscow with officials from the Soviet Ministry of Internal Affairs who were charged with investigating and prosecuting organized crime. These particular officials (who were lower-level practitioners rather than higher-level bureaucratic functionaries and politicians—and thus more likely to be frank in their discussions) admitted that there were considerable gaps in their knowledge about the true picture of organized crime in the USSR. Their estimates were that there were some 1,000 organized crime "gangs" then operating across the country; but both the numbers of organized groups and their activities were believed to be seriously underestimated. Official Soviet data later enumerated some 4,000 to 5,000 criminal groups (Serio, 1992a). These figures are misleading, however, in the sense that they included all groups of two or more individuals involved in joint criminal activity, no matter how unsophisticated and unorganized. In 1990, "organized groups" were thought to be responsible for 15–18 percent of crime. These crimes included many of those typical of organized crime anywhere: drugs, gambling, prostitution, robberies, and so on.

Organized crime in both Soviet and post-Soviet Russia has a regional character. Where there are more entrepreneurial activities, ergo more criminal opportunities—particularly in the big cities—there is more organized criminal activity. One of the major crimes of the newer crime groups is extortion. Fledgling private businesses and their employees are threatened with a variety of harms if they do not pay extortion to various criminal groups. Because police protection is inadequate, and because there is no insurance and minimal private security, these businesses have no choice but to be victimized. Much of the Russian organized crime evolves from and is related to the shortages, and thus it is linked closely to the black market.

94 Organized Crime

As sensational and frightening as the first Gorbachev-era disclosures about racketeers and mafias were for the average Russian, they were not taken (at least by knowledgeable observers) to mean that an entirely new phenomenon called organized crime was arising in the old Soviet Union for the very first time. Although it is true that some new forms of organized crime began to appear, they were neither the first nor the only forms. When criminologists, freed from the required obsequiousness toward the Soviet state, began describing the evolving organized crime at the end of the last decade, they referred to it as a menacing danger that developed because of the corruption of the Communist Party and the state apparatus (Karpets, 1990; Rumer, 1990).

In the old USSR, the most elite type of organized criminals engaged in mass corruption and illegal trafficking in what were otherwise mostly legal goods and services. Because of the failings of the economy, which we have already described, practically everything was subject to chronic shortages. Whenever there are unmet demands, supply opportunities arise, including illegal ones.

The top tier of Soviet organized crime was occupied by Communist Party officials and top-level government bureaucrats. From their positions of power, these apparatchiks and nomenklatura enriched themselves by controlling and dispensing the scarce goods and services which were in great demand. The "partocracy" abused and exploited its Party and State positions in a form of white-collar crime, which was the most sophisticated Soviet manifestation of organized crime (Vaksberg, 1991; Timofeyev, 1992). This particular brand of Soviet organized crime bore no relationship to American organized crime. "Organized crime [of the state kind] bears a resemblance only in its muscle, power, and corruption of the use of legal procedures" (Simis, 1982: 7). As a Russian colleague described it to me, the only comparable situation in the U.S. would have been if Cosa Nostra had taken over the government of the United States at every level.

Current Perspectives

The old "Soviet mafia" is now ostensibly gone—along with the other trappings of the Party. But is that really the case? In one sense at least, seemingly not, since former Communist Party officials, including perhaps some who were part of the mafia (although reborn as nationalists and democrats) are still very much in charge. Because they are in charge, and because they are the people who are the most knowledgeable about how to operate the levers of political and economic power, they can (and apparently do) exploit the present turmoil and confusion to their own best advantage. Their continued presence at the highest levels of government would seem to give good reason for the average Russian to distrust the legitimacy of the present governmental apparatus. It looks as if there has been little more than a shuffling of the cards among the same players. "Just as it was before, Russia is currently entangled in a web of secret connections, where the interests of [former] Party bureaucrats, the criminal world, the bigwigs of the military-industrial complex, and the black marketeers are strangely interwoven" (Timofeyev, 1992: 27).

Below the old elite tier of party and government organized crime, there were always clans of professional criminals. The clans are often divided along ethnic lines, and they continue to exist and to actually thrive in today's climate in Russia. Some, called "thieves in law" (*vory v zakone*), manage, organize, and maintain an ideology of professional crime—bribes and payoffs, financial and moral support for imprisoned clan members and their families, resolving clan conflicts, and so on (Shcheckochikhin, 1990). These clans of sophisticated professional criminals are most akin to Cosa Nostra in the United States. They maintain strict discipline, have certain bonding rituals, employ hired killers, and have international connections that they are seeking to expand.

Racketeers have been reported to be operating nationwide and international networks that trade in scarce luxury goods, icons, and drugs. Some of these organized criminal networks maintain contacts with Soviet émigré gangs in the United States and elsewhere in the West. Russian criminal organizations are said to be establishing affiliates and criminal franchises, and to be collaborating in new ways with major international crime syndicates like the Sicilian Mafia.

Along with the thieves in law are numerous clans of other more or less sophisticated criminal groups likewise engaging in "a much wider range of illegal activities than they did during most of the Soviet period" (Lee, 1993: 1). These activities include burglary, drug trafficking, weapons trafficking, murder for hire, pornography, prostitution, black market profiteering, trafficking in stolen cars, kidnapping, people smuggling, bank fraud, counterfeiting, and so on. Protection/extortion rackets run by several of the clans extort money from either common criminals as a form of street tax (a fee paid to be permitted to pursue their criminal activities) or from private businesses. Russian banks have been particularly hard hit by the latter form of organized crime. Bankers have been killed for refusing to pay extortion, grant loans, or illegally transfer hard currency abroad. It has been estimated by the Moscow police that organized crime groups in fact control more than 40 of Moscow's 260 banks (Celarier, 1993).

What accounts for this burgeoning criminal environment in Russia? According to the Center for Strategic and Global Studies of the Russian Academy of Sciences, there are four basic causes of this condition (Fituni, 1993). First is the economic crisis arising from the dismantling of the Communist superstructure.

> Citizens are called upon to enrich themselves virtually without any real legal possibilities to do this . . . In this situation one of the only accessible ways left even not only to get rich, but just to preserve the old standard of consumption is to join the ranks of those who assume that to ignore the law is not a big sin today.
>
> *Fituni, 1993: 3*

96 Organized Crime

The second cause of the criminalization is reputed to be the association, in people's minds, of the police with the former rulers and the repression. The "democratic propaganda of recent years has contributed a lot to such . . . perception. In order to uproot the old regime, to mobilize [the] masses to overthrow communism, [the] democratic mass media purposefully or involuntarily brainwashed the people." They did this by

> asserting that the laws that existed under communism were faulty; people are allowed not to honor laws that limit their freedom; inmates in Soviet prisons were nearly always depicted as political prisoners, rather than common criminals. In this situation judicial structures feel themselves helpless.
>
> *Fituni, 1993: 3*

Of particular interest to us is the third cause cited in the Fituni paper:

> This leads me into the third cause, which has mainly to do with subjective, rather than objective factors, viz. population's attitudes to the law, and in more general terms what is allowed and what is forbidden. The capitalist revolution in Russia has freed the consciousness of the population much in the same way like did the Bolshevik or the Great French Revolution. Many taboos disappeared.
>
> At the same time, the example of the present authorities contributed a lot to [a] general view, that if a law becomes a barrier in one's activities, then one should ignore the law . . . It is natural to expect that the population's attitudes mirror those of the authorities.
>
> *Fituni, 1993: 3–4*

The final factor in the rise of criminality is said to be the greater transparency of the borders. There is two-way trafficking of transnational crime, to and from both the East and the West. Russian organized crime is especially being transported in major ways to the West, where there are lucrative markets for sophisticated weapons, munitions, and narcotics. The West is also the most profitable market for the vast looted Siberian resources of oil, timber, diamonds, and metals.

Among the more ominous of the consequences and implications of this metastasis of criminality are the fact that people believe the government is not in charge, and is thus not supportable and due their loyalty. When combined with the absence of law and order, this acts to subvert efforts to democratize and create a liberal society. Similarly, the imposition of social control and the promotion of deviance by organized crime threatens the struggle to maintain a civil society and simultaneously corrupts social values. Finally, the privatization of the economy is subverted and comes to be seen simply as the privatization of organized crime.

Organized crime, and its old special Soviet accompaniments—corruption, the shadow economy, and the black market—arose and flourished originally because of the peculiarities of the Soviet economy and Soviet politics. Both the economy and the politics have changed markedly in recent years, and even as this is being written, changes are rapidly evolving. But so far the deviance has only gotten worse.

Effects of Organized Crime on Russian Youth

Since our focus here is on the legal socialization of children, we need to consider the possible relationships between the various phenomena just described and the attitudes and behavior of youth. Of particular interest is the connection between organized crime and juvenile delinquency.

According to Donald Cressey (1970), organized crime influenced delinquency in three ways. First, successful racketeers and corrupt politicians demonstrate to young people that crime indeed does pay. This demonstration makes it difficult for parents, teachers, adult authority figures, and other sources of moral values and beliefs (such as churches) to argue that the only or the best way to get ahead in the world is through honest labor. Second, successful organized crime requires effective corruption of law enforcement and political operatives. Organized crime traditionally immunizes itself from investigation and prosecution by corrupting the investigators and prosecutors, and their political superiors. The alliance among organized criminals, politicians, and law enforcement officials helps, according to Cressey, "to break down the respect for law and order." There is strong evidence that there were such alliances in the former USSR, and that they are even bigger today.

The third form of antisocial influence on youth that comes from their contact with sophisticated criminal networks is in the enforcing of values, social pressures, norms, and moral systems that are favorable to criminal behavior. Young people growing up in areas where there is a considerable organized crime presence may be socialized into criminality. As the American criminologist Edwin Sutherland put it, in such criminogenic environments youth learn the techniques of crime; they learn the motives, drives, rationalizations, and attitudes favorable to lawbreaking; and, they learn to define legal codes unfavorably.

Each of these influences is very much present in the cities of Russia today. For example, a version of the "crime pays" phenomenon was described to me by a Moscow school director (incidentally her school is one of the schools from which our 1992 sample of youth is drawn). She said that her school was enrolling a number of students from outside of Moscow. Some of these students came from a region of the northern Caucasus called Chechnya. The Chechens happen to be one of the dominant groups in the Moscow underworld.

The school director told me that the Chechen students at her school were presenting a problem because they brought very large sums of money to school

98 Organized Crime

to spend. This caused a great deal of resentment from their fellow (Russian) students, who had very minimal spending money. The Chechen students' money comes from their families, who are believed (by school administrators and teachers) to be racketeers and Mafiosi. If so, then there is certainly an unintended lesson being taught about how one makes it in the world. According to Serio (1992a), the Chechens are actively recruiting juveniles from the Chechen region into their criminal networks. This recruitment is facilitated by the high unemployment there.

Naglost

In my discussions with average Russians in Moscow in 1992 and again in 1994, I found considerable resentment of "millionaire" businessmen, of high government officials, and of others who could easily afford the new high prices; prices that had increased more than a hundredfold since the beginning of 1992. But beyond just the economic concerns, which admittedly are considerable, there is a feeling that whatever trust and discipline previously held the society together have now broken down. "*Naglost*," defined as impudence or brazen insolence, is believed to sum up the currently prevailing atmosphere in Russia (Bohlen, 1992b). According to that *Times* article, and reinforced by my own discussions, the widespread view is that people are just out for themselves, and that anything goes.

The old legal order based upon controlling behavior through fear and deterrence is gone. The legitimacy of the current government—and its laws and rules—is, however, still an open question. "Distrust of leaders, suspicion of hidden connections, corruption, and hypocrisy are so widespread that in and of themselves they exert a continual influence on the array of political forces and threaten the stability of government" (Timofeyev, 1992: 7). Trust and confidence that the leaders are on the right track, are doing the right thing, and that things will get better, which are prerequisites to legitimacy, are very tenuous. Depending upon acceptance of legitimacy to maintain law-abidingness under these conditions can only be partially successful at best. Assuming a lack of both desire and ability to return to a police state, social control would seemingly thus be forced to resort to reliance upon personal moral beliefs and values. Unfortunately, these too are being sorely tested by the basic survival concerns.

We might sum up the current situation in Russia as follows: as before, self-interest demands acquiescence in illegal or quasi-legal activities, but the psychological effects of this may be greater than previously because different expectations have been raised. The authorities have yet to gain legitimacy. Maybe most importantly, moral obligations with respect to the law would appear to remain ambiguous.

There is a clear division among those Russians who believe in the reforms and what they conceive to be democracy—keeping in mind that democracy is an

Organized Crime **99**

elusive concept in Russia—and those who believe that what is needed is a strong, authoritarian hand, a leader, to do something about the economic crisis, about the various ethnic/nationality conflicts, and so on. Returning to Durkheim's point about the need to discipline passions, these two contrasting views seem to offer two possible forms for such disciplining. In the first, which is the democratic form, the discipline is self-imposed. People come to believe in the social contract, and agree to become part of a regulated society. Rules and laws are legitimate because they have moral validity and because they derive from the informed consent of the governed.

In the second form, the authoritarian one, discipline is imposed from outside. This has been the traditional governmental form throughout Russian history. Rules and laws are obeyed, not out of moral obligation or because they are legitimate, but principally because of self-interest in avoiding sanctions. The debate continues.

Prologue as Precursor

Before beginning in the next chapter the presentation and discussion of the 1987 and 1992 empirical studies of legal socialization, it is useful at this point to tie together a few conceptual and theoretical loose ends. I will do this by briefly reiterating the theoretical foundations for the research, and linking these theoretical perspectives to sociolegal environmental conditions in the former Soviet Russia. This will provide us with a guide to questions regarding possible differences, pre and post the collapse of the USSR, concerning a number of issues.

These issues include, first, the legal reasoning of Russian and, by comparison, American youth. Next are the so-called mediating attitudes (mediating in the sense that they may serve as a link between reasoning and behavior)—included are perceptions of the likelihood of being caught and punished for offenses, perceptions of peer approval/disapproval of behaviors, and satisfaction with law enforcement/criminal justice performance. Third is the normative status of certain deviant behaviors—the perception of which itself is a measure of personal morality. And last to be examined is the comparative behavior of the youth as measured by a behavioral proxy that is a sort of looking glass self-view of one's own law-abidingness.

We will also look at a series of cross-cultural comparisons using the data collected from American youth in 1987. We will explore factors such as age, gender, and involvement in delinquency, which are pertinent to legal socialization. The latter may be expected, according to what we know from prior research, to interact with the across time and across country differences. Our overarching focus will be on empirical evidence of any comparative changes from the old to the new Russia. It is here that we have the rare opportunity to follow the evolution of the nature and meaning of law and deviance that transpires within a cataclysmic natural experiment.

100 Organized Crime

For the operative definition of legal socialization theory and the influence of legal culture upon socialization, we turn again to Cohn and White:

> The linkage between the processes of legal reasoning and the content of the legal culture is found in the attitudes and behaviors that are learned and sanctioned in the rule-governed environment . . . this environment defines the collective responsibilities for individuals in a society and sorts out the relative importance of communitarian and individualistic values. While rights and duties are formally defined by the law, the legal meaning of various kinds of social interactions becomes clear through individuals' encounters with authority and with the symbols, both verbal and behavioral, through which authority is expressed in a society.
>
> *Cohn and White, 1990: 22*

Legal reasoning, as an abstract cognitive process, has not been shown to be directly related to behavior. Cohn and White and others believe, however, that there is definitely a link between reasoning and behavior, and that this link is through what they call mediating attitudes and perceptions. The latter in turn are products of the legal environment in which the socialization takes place.

The approach to law and justice that predominated in Soviet Russia best coincides with the pre-conventional level of legal reasoning. So, for example, it might be expected that Soviet children and youth who reason at this level would be relatively positive toward Soviet law and its enforcement. Those who were reasoning at conventional and post-conventional levels, on the other hand, could be expected to be relatively more negative.

When we come to 1992, we are confronted with the issue of the shakeup, and the effects of that shakeup in the Russian legal climate. Anomie, social distress, existential vacuum—all are fitting terms to describe Russia today. How will the upheavals affect the legal reasoning, attitudes, and behavior of Russian youth?

Whatever the current Russian state of normlessness or valuelessness is called, it clearly requires major adaptations—adaptations in behavior, adaptations in attitudes, and seemingly adaptations in reasoning. Judgments about right and wrong have to be refined and redefined. The same is true of judgments about what is normal and what is deviant. Out of this process will ultimately develop new norms and even some old norms revisited. From these will then come rules and laws. This is a natural progression in creating a rule-of-law society. But for this evolution to complete its cycle, there must not be any catastrophic reversal of direction, such as by a return to dictatorship.

6

THE JOYS AND SORROWS OF CROSS-CULTURAL RESEARCH

The research undertaken here is a particular kind of cross-cultural research, generally referred to as being cross-national. Comparative or cross-cultural research, of whatever kind, always presents special problems of methods. Where the countries being compared have different languages, as in this case, these differences have to be dealt with through translation and back-translation of the various research instruments. If oral communication is involved, such as in interviews, then interpreters may be required. A dependence upon interpreters, however, adds considerably to the time required to do the research, and more importantly, may result in some misunderstanding or confusion over basic terms and concepts.

In all cases, cultural differences in the meaning and understanding of the concepts encompassed in the research have to be identified and handled appropriately. A difficult concept in this research, for example, was that of "due process." Due process does not have a clear, precise, universally accepted meaning. It presented major problems in thinking about how to adequately convey its meaning into words in English, let alone then into Russian. The issue was resolved simply by excluding questions that directly asked about due process. Another example is the English phrasing of one item in our questionnaire, "It is OK to take advantage of suckers." In Russian, this initially came out in back-translation as, "If a person is 'sloven,' then this can be used."

Differences between one country and another in research approaches, and in the very meaning of research, likewise have to be resolved. Something that is perfectly acceptable in one country may be unacceptable in another. Simple access to information, to officials, and to research settings can be a special problem in a country such as the former Soviet Union. Because that country is so highly bureaucratized, with the bureaucracies very jealous and protective of their

102 Cross-Cultural Research

"territories," and because entrée is so dependent upon connections, access in some cases proved to be impossible. For example, I have, over a period of years, made a number of requests of my Russian colleagues in the Academy of Sciences to arrange for me a visit to a juvenile corrections colony where delinquent offenders are confined. These colonies are under the jurisdiction of the Ministry of Internal Affairs. For various reasons, but principally because of an absence of connections between my colleagues and appropriate MVD officials, this has not yet been possible.

Differences from one country to another in the availability and forms of existing data, in general access to and requirements for studying human subjects, in adherence to the scientific method, and so on, all have to be dealt with and resolved in some mutually acceptable fashion. The more unalike the participating cultures in these regards—as, for example, with the case of the United States and the former Soviet Union—the greater are the problems to be solved.

Cross-discipline research similarly presents special methods problems. The three main collaborators at the outset of this study were a sociologist, a psychologist, and a lawyer. It happens that social science research methods are different from legal research methods. So to further complicate matters for us, the research being presented here entailed problems of this cross-disciplinary kind as well.

I believe there is heuristic value for the field of comparative research in frankly acknowledging and clarifying the difficulties faced in this joint American-Russian project, and in explaining how we went about trying to deal with these difficulties. For this reason, I have included both in this chapter and in the Appendix a detailed discussion of the research methods used. We (my Russian colleagues and myself) believe that despite the difficulties faced, the research makes a considerable contribution to theory, method, and practice.

I will begin by detailing the procedures and sources used to develop the original research approach. The differences in the survey questionnaires used in the two countries for the initial (1987–89) study, and the implications of those differences, are dealt with mostly in the Appendix. The American and Russian subjects involved in the Phase I research are profiled, and the data collection procedures and statistical analyses are briefly described.

The latter part of this discussion turns to the etiology and design of the 1992 study of Russian youth. This section describes the background, the subjects, and the procedures of the second or "post-Soviet" research.

Breaking the Ice: Designing a Joint Study

In October, 1987, a joint American-Soviet conference on legal knowledge and values clarification was held at Rutgers University. The conferees were Soviet legal scholars from the Institute of State and Law of the Soviet Academy of Sciences, and American criminologists and legal scholars from Rutgers, the University of Minnesota, the University of Toronto, and the Police Foundation. An agreement was reached at the conclusion of that conference to conduct an empirical, comparative study to focus on legal knowledge and values clarification.

Three conference participants—June Tapp, Alexander Yakovlev, and myself—were charged with designing and carrying out the research. We decided to use a survey approach, and to target youth as our research subjects. We put together the first draft of a survey questionnaire principally from items drawn from a questionnaire developed by the University of Colorado's Center for Action Research, and used by that Center with junior high and high school students in the Law-Related Education Evaluation Project to which I referred in Chapter 2 (1983).

Our questionnaire also used items from June Tapp's Tapp Rule-Law Interview and another of her research instruments entitled Your Ideas About People and Rules (Hess and Tapp, 1969), as well as items from the Tapp–Levine Rule Law Inventory (Tapp and Levine, 1974). Certain of these questionnaire items had been used in an earlier six-country, seven-culture study of legal socialization. Some knowledge of the law questions were taken from a previous survey of adolescents' knowledge of the law by Rafky and Sealy (1975). The remaining items were created especially for this research.

Because of differences in the laws and the legal systems of our two countries, it was recognized at the outset that the knowledge of the law sections of the survey instruments would have to be country-specific and thus different. We could not, for example, ask Russian children questions about the U.S. Bill of Rights, nor American children questions about the Soviet constitution. Nevertheless, initial efforts were made to make the knowledge items comparable in both content and degree of difficulty. It is in the case of the latter where we can see an example of the cross-discipline problems mentioned earlier. Dr. Yakovlev, a legal scholar, had not done previous work with children as the subjects. Consequently, the knowledge of the law items in the Russian version of the questionnaire (called Mastering Legal Values or MLV) that he created tended to be rather complex and difficult, and very "lawyerly"; particularly in view of the fact that nine- and ten-year-olds were going to be surveyed. Despite some modifications following discussion on this point, the resulting MLV items were still more difficult than the comparable items in the U.S. questionnaire (called the Internalization of Legal Values Inventory or ILVI). This, of course, has implications for interpreting the cross-national findings in this particular area.

Between October 1987 and February 1988, the ILVI was refined, pretested on small samples of children in both New Jersey and Minnesota, and was simplified. This developmental process led us through four versions of the survey questionnaire. The pretesting revealed that younger respondents were unfamiliar with concepts such as "civil suit," and did not, for example, understand the meanings of "executive," "legislative," and "judicial" branches of government. Their understanding of what they were being asked was obviously affected by their immaturity and their lack of exposure to technical ideas, as well as by their unfamiliarity with

104 Cross-Cultural Research

difficult words. Both the language and format of the ILVI were thus changed to create a more "child-friendly" version that would be more comprehensible for younger children and for those with poorer reading skills. Further, because we were using a forced-choice format, we were particularly sensitive to the need for an unverified understanding of the items. We did not want random responses to arise from simple ignorance and lack of understanding.

What is most unfortunate—and was something that arose out of a combination of communications problems and misunderstandings among and between the American and Russian researchers, delays on the American side, and a deadline that had to be met by the Russian team—is that the final version of the ILVI used in the United States (Form IV) was not used in the Soviet data collection that took place in 1987 and early 1988. Instead, the Soviet questionnaire used (the MLV) was actually the first-draft version of the ILVI that we had worked on in October.

Communications between the United States and the former Soviet Union were at that time normally difficult and time-consuming. The more complex the communications, as in this case, the more affected they tended to be by these difficulties. Nevertheless, there was communication about what we were doing to Moscow. There was no communication back to the U.S. in response, nor any indication that the survey of juveniles had already gone ahead. Therefore, it came as a great shock and surprise to the American principals when we arrived in Moscow in April, 1988 with our new ILVI-IV, to find that the Soviet data collection was already complete; and that in fact there were preliminary data analyses already done. We argued for a new data collection effort using the ILVI-IV translated into Russian. But this proved to be unavailing, largely on grounds of limited time and resources. We therefore had to resort to what might be termed a salvage operation. We think we have done that salvaging reasonably well, but nevertheless we should recognize that that is what it was.

Lest we conclude that all this is somehow unprecedented, even a brief survey of the comparative research literature clearly demonstrates that this occurrence is far from unusual. Kohn (1987), for example, referred to the need for "damage control" in such circumstances. Part of what I describe here and in the Appendix was in fact a kind of damage control effort.

Sampling American and Soviet-Russian Youth

The total sample size in the initial 1987–89 study was 288 children and youth (this phraseology is used because the ages ranged from 9 to 17). Exactly half were from the United States and half from the former Soviet Russia. The total sample included 142 non-delinquents and 141 delinquents (delinquency status inform-ation is missing in five cases). There were 142 males and 141 females (again with five cases of missing data). Excluding missing information, the sample was made

Cross-Cultural Research **105**

up of 60 9–12-year-olds (21 percent), 123 13–15-year-olds (43 percent), and 104 16–17-year-olds (36 percent).

There were no nine-year olds in either the U.S. delinquent sample nor in the entire Russian sample. This resulted from a lack of consensus on the major difficulties to be presented by attempting to include this youngest category in the latter samples. It is easy to find nine-year-olds in an elementary school in the U.S. It was apparently not so easy to include this age group in surveys in the USSR— not because they could not be found, but because there was reluctance to include children this young in the study. It is also not at all easy to find them in facilities for juvenile delinquents. These points were raised in our joint discussions, but the Minnesota researchers proceeded to survey nine-year olds anyway. Here again, we have both cross-cultural and cross-discipline differences affecting the research.

Socioeconomic classifications of the Russian sample presented particular problems because of the non-fit of parental occupations there with the most commonly used classification schemes in the U.S. For example, there were not any corporate executives of major, private corporations in the former Soviet Union. The top of the socioeconomic ladder there was occupied by top government and party officials, and by some sports and entertainment celebrities. Doctors, on the other hand, had a relatively lower socioeconomic status. This difficulty was the main reason for simply dichotomizing the two samples according to SES.

The United States non-delinquent sample (N = 72) was drawn from two elementary, two junior high, and two senior high schools in the Minneapolis–St. Paul suburban area of Minnesota. This sample is primarily white, middle to upper socioeconomic status, and 90 percent are from intact families. The 72 subjects (36 males and 36 females) were randomly chosen from an original sample of 209. One-third of the sample was taken from each of the 4th, 8th, and 11th grades.

The U.S. delinquent sample was obtained from non-random, cluster samples of subjects at juvenile justice facilities in four New Jersey locations, and from a juvenile correctional institution at a rural site in Pennsylvania that serves large numbers of urban minority youth from Philadelphia. Altogether there were six sample sites: four juvenile detention/corrections facilities (both secure and non-secure), one treatment clinic with two locations, and a juvenile court intake unit located in a probation department. In order to insure adequate representation of girls and younger subjects, we oversampled in these categories. A random selection of 72 subjects was then chosen, stratified by gender and age, from the total U.S. sample of 162 delinquents. The criminal/delinquency histories of the latter sample were not examined, but site personnel reported that offenses among the group ranged from minor/status misbehavior to serious, adjudicated delinquencies, and to criminal offenses—including homicide.

The fact that no self-report delinquency data were collected in the initial study means there is a rather arbitrary distinction between the non-delinquents and the delinquents in both the American and Russian samples. Are the "non-delinquent" public school samples truly non-delinquent? There is a considerable body of

106 Cross-Cultural Research

research that shows this to be an erroneous assumption. The true extent of variability in delinquent conduct, as opposed to officially labeled delinquent status, both within the delinquent samples and between them and their non-delinquent counterparts is unknown. In fact, the implicit definitions of delinquency used in this research may have also differed between the two countries, as will be seen; but in any event, in both countries delinquency was operationally defined by residence in the facilities from which the samples were drawn. These definitional issues raise questions about the validity of the delinquent and non-delinquent groups, and may account for certain of the findings in Phase I.

The 144 Soviet Russian subjects were chosen from 200 youth between 10 and 17 years of age who were surveyed using the MLV. From this larger group, 144 were chosen mostly on very practical grounds. Some youth refused to finish their questionnaires, and some additional (fairly large) number left major portions of their questionnaires incomplete. These were the youth who were weeded out.

As in the United States, two categories of Russian youth were questioned. First, the non-delinquents were school students in various grades of several Moscow schools in three city districts—Sokol'niki, Kiev, and Babushkin. The Moscow location means that the sample was made up almost exclusively of urban Russian subjects. This may be important in light of the point about political socialization discussed earlier.

The second group, the delinquents, was drawn from the Moscow Receiving and Distribution Center. This is an institution that I have had the opportunity to visit on two occasions. A somewhat forbidding-looking, high-rise building, it is located on the outskirts of Moscow. The facility houses both boys and girls of varying ages. Several hundred young people were held there because they had run away from home elsewhere in the former Soviet Union; because they had escaped from juvenile facilities; because they had been neglected by their parents or guardians; because they had no parents or guardians; or, because they had committed various crimes and delinquencies.

As in the U.S. sample, there was an arbitrary distinction made between the non-delinquents and the delinquents. Beyond that, one gets the impression from visiting this center that really serious juvenile offenders were in the distinct minority there. To what extent (if at all) any serious, felony-type offenders appeared in this first Russian delinquent sample we do not know, again because delinquent histories were not checked. It may be that the U.S. delinquent sample was much more "delinquent" than its Russian counterpart. This too, of course, would have a bearing on interpreting the comparative results.

Collecting and Analyzing the Initial Data

The ILVI-IV and the MLV were group administered to all subjects. Data on U.S. non-delinquents were collected exclusively by research team members having no affiliations with the schools from which the samples were drawn. Teachers or

Cross-Cultural Research **107**

other school authorities were not even present during this process. Children who volunteered to participate received both verbal and written assurances of complete anonymity and confidentiality.

In the case of the U.S. delinquent sample, the situation was a little more complicated. Initially, several juvenile facilities in New Jersey and the one in Pennsylvania were approached about participating in the study. They readily agreed. In each of these facilities, researchers introduced themselves and described the project to the potential participants. Youth were then invited to volunteer to participate. Administrations of the questionnaire generally took place in classrooms with facility teachers either present or in an adjacent classroom, but not directly participating in questionnaire administration.

When additional juvenile programs in New Jersey were contacted in order to increase the size and heterogeneity of the delinquent population, the administrative office of the New Jersey courts became involved. After some delay and required review of our procedures and materials, this office decided complete anonymity of the juvenile subjects could only be ensured by eliminating all direct contact between the researchers and the research subjects. Accordingly, questionnaires had to be hand-delivered to the additional sites that were willing to participate, and the staff in these facilities had to be trained in the administration of the questionnaire. Completed questionnaires were then returned to the research team.

Altering the data collection procedures in this manner can obviously affect the reliability and validity of the responses. In one instance, this procedure effectively resulted in more than two-thirds of the questionnaires not being completed. Regular probation or institutional staff have neither the time nor the same degree of enthusiasm for the study as the researchers themselves do. To make matters worse, this particular program with all the incompletes involved many younger and more minor offenders, and girls—categories that had been difficult to find in the other sites.

For both the delinquents and the non-delinquents in the U.S., the subjects were generally enthusiastic, being particularly intrigued by the fact that the research project was international in scope and involved participation by their counterparts in the former Soviet Union. In the case of the non-delinquents and at least the first segment of the delinquents, researchers were present to explain questions and response modes, but not the meanings of words or concepts. In several instances with the delinquents, because of severe reading problems, researchers read the entire questionnaire aloud to them. One could assume that this element of the data collection procedure suffered when it was turned over to the facility staff.

In Moscow, respondent groups of 10 to 15 juveniles were given detailed instructions on filling out the questionnaire. The goals of the study were also explained to them. Researchers reported that in the course of completing the questionnaires, it was often necessary to provide clarification in individual cases on questions that posed difficulties. The subjects, in general, filled out the

108 Cross-Cultural Research

questionnaires with care and interest. In fact, the research team reported that some juveniles reacted in such a lively manner and with such enthusiasm that they tried to discuss the questions among themselves. This was particularly the case with the delinquents at the Receiving and Distribution Center.

All the statistical analyses, with the exception of a preliminary analysis of the Russian data, were done in the United States. It was agreed from the beginning that there would be a complete exchange of raw, unaggregated data between the two countries. Getting the Russian data transferred to the U.S. in computer-readable form, however, required considerable time and effort. The U.S. data were transferred to our colleagues in Moscow, but to my knowledge nothing has ever been done with them. The kind of problems we faced are again fairly typical of comparative research. Things take longer, and require more effort and consequently more resources. Nevertheless, this kind of research can still produce rewarding results.

Studying the "New" Russian Youth

The 1992 study is not an exact replication of the 1987 study. As has been described here and in the Appendix on methods, it should be obvious that this is generally a good thing. The Phase II study actually came about for several reasons—some of which had to do with shortcomings in the original research.

First there were interminable delays in attempting to complete the write-up of the first study in order to disseminate it by way of publication. As a consequence of these delays, the research that was essentially finished in 1989 was not ready for publication as of the end of 1991. This failure to publish then got caught up in the collapse of the Soviet Union. This collapse became a major factor in stimulating the new study. It meant that not only were the original data perhaps getting stale, but that in a sense they had almost become moot. There was suddenly less interest in "Soviet" children's reactions to "Soviet" law. As a result, it seemed if there was going to be any release of the findings of the first study, and if the context of those results had any chance of being fully understood, new research had to be undertaken.

The fact that the old Soviet Russia no longer existed was not, however, the only contextual circumstance that was changed for the new research. Neither of my two earlier collaborators was able, in one case, or interested, in the other, in mounting a second study of this kind. It was essential therefore to identify and secure the cooperation of new Russian participants. This I was lucky to do. It is also most fortunate that these new collaborators turned out to be a much more diverse group than those involved earlier. In addition to a colleague from the Institute of State and Law of the Russian Academy of Sciences (who also took part in the initial study), we were joined by two faculty members from the Moscow State University law faculty (and approximately a dozen of their law students), and by school directors and a teacher from three Moscow city schools.

This new team combined a knowledge of law and law education with an in-depth knowledge of children and child development in Russia.

Further to be considered was the issue of replicating the American side of the study. The main argument against it was that no revolutionary changes affecting the context for legal socialization had occurred in the U.S. in the intervening five-year period; changes that would be in any way comparable to those taking place in the former USSR. There was thus no similar before and after situation. Second, the difficulties surrounding the failure to use similar forms of the survey questionnaire was a problem with the original Russian data, not with the American data. Third, as a practical matter, the real interest in the research was in the Russian aspect and not in American youth's perceptions of the law. Given these realities, and given the usual practical constraints of limited time and practically no resources, it was decided to focus the new research effort exclusively on Russia.

Settings and Samples

A total of 425 Russian youth, from five different settings, were surveyed between the end of October and the beginning of December 1992. The first group of 155 came from the two colonies for male juveniles located in the vicinity of Moscow. The choice of these particular colonies was designated by Russian correctional authorities. Given their close proximity to Moscow and thus to official visitors, these two colonies should not be regarded as being representative of other colonies. The 155 youth are made up of 145 16–17 year olds, and ten 13–15 year olds. The survey questionnaires were administered by law faculty students from Moscow State University under faculty supervision. Colony administrators were not present. The procedures were explained to the juveniles, questions were taken, and the respondents were assured anonymity.

These two colonies are one of two types of juvenile correctional institutions dealing with more serious juvenile offenders. The kind of colony represented here is mainly for first offenders. Some 400 juveniles on average, mostly convicted of various kinds of theft, and ranging in age basically from 15 to 18, are held for periods of up to three years. Although officially minimum security, these colonies often have double fences, barbed and electric wires, guard towers, and dogs. Recreational and educational programs are minimal, and the principal activity is work—six hours a day for six days a week. The other type of juvenile colony, the "enhanced" kind, is for serious and repeat offenders. In these latter facilities, the security is even greater. There are no concerns with this delinquent sample as there were with the earlier Russian delinquents that these particular youth are not sufficiently "deviant."

The other three sites are again Moscow city schools. These schools have students from 7 to 17 years old, in grades 1–11. Questionnaires were administered in all three schools by a senior teacher from one of the schools. This teacher had participated both in the earlier study and in the design of the new research.

110   Cross-Cultural Research

She explained the study, answered questions, and assured the young people that their participation was both voluntary and anonymous. There are 90 subjects from each of the three schools in the sample. In each case, the 90 include 30 10–12-year-olds, 30 13–15-year-olds, and 30 16–17-year-olds. Half are males and half are females in each age group. Because age and gender are significant variables with regard to legal socialization, this stratification is important.

Unhappily, age and gender variability are not similarly represented in the delinquent sample from the colonies. There are no females and no 10–12-year-olds; and the 16–17-year-olds are vastly overrepresented. These disproportionate weightings have been adjusted in our analyses. In addition to age and gender, information on socioeconomic status, national background, and family living arrangements was also collected from the youth.

As before, all analyses were done in the United States. We used a variety of statistical techniques to explore and tease out differences within and among what were now three groups—two from 1987–89 and one from 1992.

More than a year after the August 1991 coup attempt, nearly one year into the new Russian regime of Boris Yeltsin, and going into what some considered then to be Russia's second winter of discontent, we were able to look again at a whole range of issues and questions. Our hope is to learn about the effects of the shifting political and legal contexts upon what these young people now believe and feel, their views of right and wrong, what kinds of deviance they might be predisposed to undertake, and what crimes they actually commit.

7

A SOVIET AND AN AMERICAN VIEW OF THE LAW

This and the subsequent chapters that deal with the research embrace the premise that legal socialization—that package of reasoning, knowledge, attitudes, and behavior that both shapes and is shaped by rules and laws and their enforcement—is inseparably bound to both the micro and macro sociolegal environments in which it develops. With that as our premise, let us turn our attention to a comparative examination of the youthful products of two rather different legal contexts and socialization processes.

We begin the examination with a look at the results of our first joint study. And we start with an isolated snapshot of just the Soviet youth. The data and findings described were gathered in the late fall and winter of 1987–88, a time when Mikhail Gorbachev was at the zenith of his powers as the leader of the USSR. Glasnost was in full bloom. The promise of democratic and legal reform was permeating Moscow.

There was a preliminary compilation and analysis of the Soviet data by our Soviet colleagues. This produced some very intriguing findings, as well as raising a number of questions and issues. Thus, although there are not directly and specifically parallel analyses and results for the American sample on each and every point raised, the Soviet report of their findings is presented here first, because it should be particularly enlightening and informative for American readers. It should be noted, for the sake of empirical purity, that these particular findings (and only these) are offered just as they were received, without any further analysis in the U.S.

Soviet Youth and the Law

One of the agreed upon areas for comparative investigation between our two sides was that of legal knowledge. How much, both groups of investigators wanted to

112 A Soviet and an American View of the Law

know, do our young people know about the law, the legal systems, and the legal procedures of their respective countries? This was considered to be important because it would tell us something about the relative effectiveness of attempts at law-related education. Even more important is the fact that legal knowledge is a strategy to enhance legal reasoning, and is presumed to be an element in compliance.

Knowledge of Law

Our Soviet colleagues reported that the average "grade" for the 144 Soviet youth whom they questioned on their law examination was 64.5 percent. In other words, these youth got nearly two-thirds of the rather complex questions about law, law enforcement, and the Soviet legal system correct. Males, on the whole, did much better than females. The delinquent and non-delinquent males got grades of 78 percent and 77 percent respectively. Delinquent females got only 56 percent correct, whereas law-abiding females did even worse—getting only 48 percent correct. Legal knowledge thus seemed to be strongly related to gender (keeping in mind that no tests of statistical significance were done); but it seemed to be essentially unrelated to whether or not the youth were delinquents.

It was found, as could be expected from other research, that knowledge of the law increased with age. For example, 85 percent of the Soviet 15–17-year-olds knew at what age (i.e., 14 years) criminal responsibility began in the USSR; whereas only 56 percent of the 11–12-year-olds knew the correct answer to this question. The Soviet youth were the least informed about the matter of procedural rights. These are rights that pertain to the practices—and the legal limitations on those practices—of the police, prosecutors, and courts. An example of a question in the procedural area was: "Can the police, according to the law, hold a suspect under arrest without formally accusing him?" Of the 15–17-year-olds, 38 percent got this right; of 11–12-year-olds, only 8 percent did. The answer at that time, by the way, was yes, but only for ten days.

Attitudes toward the Law

Next, is an area that the Soviet researchers broadly defined as attitudes toward the law. Here there were some rather odd results. For example, asked to react to the statement, "if one takes something from a store, it's not harmful to anyone," 92 percent of the delinquent Soviet males disagreed—and in fact they had the highest rate of disagreement. On the other hand, at the other extreme, only 37 percent of the law-abiding females disagreed with this statement; meaning, apparently, that a substantial majority of them thought shoplifting was not particularly bad. There could be a number of explanations for this gender split in perceptions. One is that the girls are being more truthful than the boys; that is, they reflect more accurately a belief that stealing from state stores was not all that wrong. Asked about what would happen if you broke a rule or law, a possible indicator of their relative senses of deterrence, a quarter of the non-delinquent boys and 30 percent of the delinquent boys thought nothing would happen. Among the girls, however, more than three-quarters of the law-abiding ones and 60 percent of the delinquents thought nothing much would happen.

The Soviet girls seemed to have a lower regard for the efficacy of the Soviet legal system than did the boys. A fear of sanctions, which is one of the principles of pre-conventional legal reasoning, also did not seem to carry much weight with these young Soviet females. With the male youth, on the other hand, such fears seemingly did have some importance. In general, the cynicism of the females toward the system and their rationalization of deviancy appeared to be much greater than that of the young Soviet males.

The normative status of deviance was assessed by asking a series of questions about the wrongfulness of certain behaviors, for example, stealing something worth less than five rubles, stealing something worth more than 50 rubles, or breaking into an automobile or an apartment. It should be pointed out, in the context of the massive devaluation of the ruble which began in 1991, that when these questions were asked in 1987–88, 50 rubles was still a substantial sum of money for most Soviets. The overwhelming majority (94 percent) of the Soviet delinquent males considered all such acts to be either wrong or very wrong. The same was true of the law-abiding Soviet boys (91 percent), and also to a lesser extent, of the delinquent Russian girls (76 percent). But again, only 63 percent of the law-abiding females considered these deviant acts to be either wrong or very wrong.

Continuing in a similar vein, only 40 percent of the law-abiding girls indicated they would be disturbed by breaking the law, and only 20 percent of them would feel bad about breaking a law or rule. In contrast, 81 percent of the delinquent boys said they would be disturbed and 70 percent of them would feel bad.

These dramatic gender differences are pretty consistent with regard to attitudes toward the law and its enforcement. The young Soviet females in general, and the law-abiding schoolgirls in particular, reflect rather negative views. The Soviet researchers reported that these girls did not believe that wrongdoing was harmful, that they would not feel bad about doing wrong, and that they did not seem to be afraid of sanctions.

Legal Reasoning Levels

The initial results bearing on legal reasoning should be treated with caution because of the possible problems with the nature of the responses. Nevertheless, notwithstanding the fact that they are extremely interesting, the results are also useful because they furnish a very broad classification of this first Soviet sample. Following the Soviet researchers' own analysis scheme, if we subgroup their

114 A Soviet and an American View of the Law

sample into the four categories of delinquent males (DM), non-delinquent males (NDM), delinquent females (DF), and non-delinquent females (NDF), and then look at the general ranking of the six possible responses on each of seven legal reasoning items that were tabulated, we can then determine which responses received the most first choices. (Using only the first choices helps limit the problem of response errors.) The items and responses receiving first choices, by group, look as follows (the Legal Development Level of each response is indicated as I, II, or III):

- The law is necessary primarily in order to:
  (III) ensure the rights of all—DM, NDM, DF, NDF
- Citizens carry out the laws in order to:
  (II) maintain order in society—DM, NDM, NDF
  (I) carry out what the organs of power prescribe—DF
- One may break the law if:
  (II) I need to—NDF
  (III) the law is unjust—DF
  (I) one should never break the law—DM, NDM
- That law is just which:
  (II) ensures equal distribution of benefits—NDF
  (III) ensures equal distribution of rights and responsibilities—DM, NDM, DF
- Law should be carried out because:
  (II) it is necessary to maintain order in society—DM, NDM, DF, NDF
- Citizens ought to have rights in order:
  (II) to support their way of life—NDF, DF
  (II) to defend that which they have earned or achieved—DM
  (III) that they correspond to the main interests of all citizens—NDM
- A citizen may be right and have broken a law if:
  (III) he had kind motivations and founded interests—NDF
  (III) he was defending the rights of others—DM, NDM, DF

The aggregate responses are mainly clustered between the conventional (II) and the post-conventional (III) levels of legal reasoning. In this sense, their appreciation and understanding of the role and the rule of law was not much different—and in fact if anything it was a little more advanced—than that of other populations of youth who have been studied in this respect. Whatever other effects the macro-Soviet sociolegal environment may have had on their attitudes and behavior, one of them did not seem to have been to retard or to stultify their legal reasoning. The legal development of these youth was not fixated at a deterrence or strictly self-interest level. On the contrary, this sample of young people who had been steeped in the peculiarities of Soviet justice and law enforcement nevertheless still seemed to think of "law" mostly in terms of legitimacy, and even in terms of justice, fairness, and moral obligation.

Another related issue of concern here is any links between legal development and legal behavior. Given that there were no reported differences between Soviet delinquents and non-delinquents in their legal development levels, these preliminary findings offered no support for the proposition that legal reasoning may have some causal relationship to juvenile delinquency.

The strikingly skeptical posture of the Soviet schoolgirls that came out of the Soviet analyses presented a vexing issue. Our Russian colleagues offered several explanations for their generally negative views—a kind of negativism or contrariness that they found in almost all their analyses. The young women were said to be reflecting a particular "hedonism," and to be making a special effort to distance themselves from so-called "commonly accepted" ethical norms. They were also characterized as reflecting a certain "unprincipledness." But why this should have been so was not explained. It may be that they were the group in this particular sample of Soviet youth who most exemplified the alienated, rebellious youth population in the Soviet Union at that time. It may also be that there is something about the particular (generally inferior) status of women in the former Soviet Union that might account for their cynicism. Or, it may be that the other Russian youth (particularly the males) gave what they thought were the expected and safe answers; and only these girls were being truly honest. One other possible explanation for the results is that these girls simply did not take the survey itself seriously, and may have haphazardly responded or deliberately responded dishonestly. If so, then that too could be taken as an indication of their rebelliousness; but we have no way of knowing that. In any event, we will return to the legal reasoning of the Soviet youth in our discussion of the comparative findings with the American young people. We will also then come back to this gender issue.

Justice and Fairness

Asked to agree or disagree with a series of statements about the justice and fairness of the Soviet criminal justice system, the youth were most in agreement with general statements about justice in the broadest or most abstract sense. For example, given the statement, "for breaking the law, you are punished without regard for who you are," more than 80 percent of the boys (delinquent and law-abiding) agreed, as did 64 percent of the delinquent girls. Bringing up the rear again were the law-abiding girls, with only 54 percent agreeing.

There was much less agreement that the courts are fair, as measured by such statements as, "an innocent person is rarely punished." Only the delinquent boys, with 72 percent, gave this particular statement majority agreement; and they are the ones most likely to have had personal experience with the courts. Only four in ten of all the girls thought that innocent people were rarely punished, or that the courts related equally to everyone. Two-thirds of the boys, on the other hand, agreed that Soviet courts were fair.

116 A Soviet and an American View of the Law

Agreement that procedures are fair and just was even lower when it came to the police. This is significant because the police are the most visible representatives of law enforcement, and are the officials with whom these youth were most likely to be personally familiar. For example, the statement, "the police are similarly just to all minors," got 40 percent agreement from non-delinquent boys, 33 percent each from delinquent boys and girls, and only 11 percent from the especially skeptical schoolgirls. There was also considerably less than majority agreement that the police always have good reason when they detain someone. These responses taken together reflected considerable doubt about the fairness and justice of the Soviet legal system.

Law-Abidingness

The youth were asked how their parents, teachers, and friends see them, and specifically whether these authority figures would view them as being a bad person and as breaking the law. Both groups of boys (delinquent and non-delinquent) indicated that their parents and their friends held them in pretty high regard. They both were a little less confident of their teachers. Both groups of girls, on the other hand, indicated that their teachers held them in especially low regard. The delinquent girls also perceived their parents as thinking especially poorly of them.

Particularly conflictual situations concerning the females in the sample are evident in a few other results as well. Nearly a quarter of the schoolgirls (three times as many as any other group) said they didn't care if their parents were disenchanted with them. This might in some way help account for their generally negative attitudes. Sixty percent of this same group, and more than a third of the delinquent females, said they sometimes felt that in school nobody cared about them. Again there is evidence of their isolation from adult authority figures. The same is true of the fact that both groups of females were much less concerned than were the males about what would happen to them at home if they were caught committing a theft.

There are some indicators in the demographic information collected from the youth that might be relevant in helping to explain these gender differences. For example, only 57 percent of the schoolgirls and 48 percent of the delinquent girls lived in intact families. The corresponding male figures were 74 percent and 69 percent for schoolboys and delinquents respectively. The socioeconomic status of the males and females was also very different. For example, 49 percent of male non-delinquents and 51 percent of male delinquents had mothers who had high-status jobs requiring higher education. Conversely, the mothers of only 12 percent of the law-abiding girls and 9 percent of the delinquent girls had such jobs. The same sort of distribution was true of the social positions of the fathers as well. Despite coming from the same schools and the same institution, the family conditions and socioeconomic status of the Russian males and females

A Soviet and an American View of the Law **117**

is rather different. These differences may have been influential factors in helping to produce the differential attitudes and opinions.

Our Russian colleagues tentatively concluded from their preliminary analyses that no firm relationships had been established between legal socialization and juvenile delinquency. They did not, however, reach any conclusions about the specific issues of the instrumental, legitimacy, and moral obligation bases for legal compliance. One of the conclusions from their preliminary report does bear repeating, however, because of its relevance to the consideration of the role of legal context in shaping reasoning, attitudes, and behavior:

> One can reach the conclusion that all groups of [these] respondents with the exception of [the] legally obedient girls do not approve of dishonorable ways of achieving positive goals. True, *based on the realities of contemporary life*, some doubt may be had in the sincerity of the answers of the respond-ents. Are we not meeting here and possibly in other instances with the phenomenon of receiving instead of an expected real picture we are getting its ideal variant, that is to say, *they are telling us what ought to be and not what is.*
>
> *Emphasis added*

This implies that these researchers were doubtful about some of the positive views expressed by some of the youth in their sample.

Let us now turn to the comparative analyses of the combined American and Soviet data to see if these preliminary conclusions continue to hold, as well as what else we might find.

A First Look at Comparative Views

There were, unfortunately, some major differences in the forms of the data collection instrument used in the United States and the former Soviet Union as detailed elsewhere. As a consequence of these differences, findings pertaining to knowledge of the law, legal reasoning levels, and attitudes regarding persons having the power to punish rule/law violations are only descriptive and not directly comparative. Other sections of the two legal socialization survey forms, on the other hand, were determined to be equivalent or even identical. Thus those results can be examined and considered in a comparative manner.

The independent variables used in the analyses are country, delinquency status (delinquent or non-delinquent), sex, and age. Information was also collected on living arrangements (two parents, one parent, or other), and socioeconomic status. We additionally asked our youthful subjects for information on their ethnic or national backgrounds as well. But all this information was so confounded or of such suspect reliability that it has been dropped in these analyses.

118 A Soviet and an American View of the Law

Suggestive Findings

Knowledge of the Law

The average score or grade for the American youth was 43 percent. This compares rather unfavorably with the earlier reported 64 percent for the Soviets. Despite the fact that their knowledge of the law test was much more difficult, the Soviet youth did far better than the Americans. Perhaps that says something for their law-related educational curricula. But as we will see in a moment, it may not be only formal education that produced this result. Within the samples, the only reliable differences in knowledge of the law were by age—younger respondents (age 9–12) knew less than older ones (age 13–17) in both the U.S. and the USSR.

It is interesting that the U.S. non-delinquents had slightly more overall knowledge of the law than did their USSR counterparts, but that the reverse was true for the delinquents. The Soviet delinquents in fact had the highest average score of the four groups. These results do not allow us to conclude much of anything about the possible relationship of knowledge of the law and delinquency. What we can conclude is that age in particular, delinquency status to some degree, and country are all factors related to legal knowledge.

Legal Reasoning Levels

The mean developmental level for the American youth was 1.92, for the Soviets it was 2.00. Since these means were produced from non-comparable forms, no statistical tests were done on them. Examining the two samples separately, the only significant difference in legal level was by delinquency status ($p < .01$). Within both samples, law-abiding youth had slightly (but statistically significant) higher legal levels than did the delinquents. This supports the hypothesis derived from legal socialization and moral development theory regarding the purported relationship (and the direction of the relationship) between legal/moral reasoning and juvenile delinquency.

Contrary to previous research, there were no significant age differences in legal level. The absence of expected age differences in the Soviet sample could be attributable to a methodological artifact. The Soviet instrument used a more complex ranking procedure, which resulted in some of the USSR subjects aborting the procedure or simply responding randomly. It is a reasonable assumption that this happened more with younger than older subjects. On the other hand, using only the first choices in the analyses minimizes this threat to validity. So for example, with the U.S. sample as well, where the complexity of response problem did not exist, age was likewise not a significant source of variation in legal reasoning levels. This is an unexpected result in that cognitive development is presumed to be highly correlated with age. But to the extent that other factors, for example, intelligence/reasoning ability and socioeconomic status, play important roles in cognitive development, developmental levels may not necessarily increase with chronological age. Younger children can sometimes be found to reason at higher levels than older youth. This may help explain the findings here. The females in the U.S. sample had a significantly higher mean developmental level (X = 1.97) than the males (X = 1.87), although both were reasoning at the middle, conventional level. This particular gender difference is of special interest in light of the controversy surrounding the question of gender differences in the closely related area of moral development, and the continuing argument about the possible need for an alternative theory of feminine moral development (see, for example, Gilligan, 1982).

The legal development perspective pioneered by Tapp and her colleagues that is one of the bases for this research was closely modeled upon Kohlberg's theory of moral development. The latter has been criticized by Carol Gilligan and others because research based upon it seems to show that women achieve lower levels of moral development than men. It follows that if one were to adopt Gilligan's argument that females reason differently from males about the application of rules in resolving moral dilemmas, one might anticipate that the responses of young females to the legal development items in our legal values inventory would result in their being classified at a lower level than the males answering those same items. This was not the case here, and in fact the reverse is true. That outcome can lead to any of several possible conclusions. Either the methods of measuring legal and moral development are sufficiently different that measuring the former does not reflect a gender bias, whereas measuring the latter does. Or, the moral and legal development constructs themselves are different enough that any gender bias in the former does not appear in the latter. Or, Gilligan and her colleagues need to reconsider, and perhaps revise and expand, their explanations of gender-related differences regarding the specific area of reasoning about rules and laws. Whatever the explanation—and we will also return to this issue before we are finished—when looked at in concert with the just-reported Russian female/male differences in their own analyses, it appears that something related to gender may be going on.

Power to Punish

Asked "Can teachers punish you if you do something wrong?" in the ILVI and "Will teachers punish you if you do something wrong?" in the MLV, there were no significant differences by country. Both American and Soviet youth were clustered between sometimes and almost always. There were significant differences in this perception by status and age, however. Teachers seemed to be viewed as being more powerful by delinquents and by younger children.

Parents' power to punish was seen differently by country, age, status, and gender. American youth were significantly more likely (almost always/always) to attribute this power to parents than were Soviet youth (almost always). Younger

120 A Soviet and an American View of the Law

children, delinquents, and females were significantly more impressed with parents' power to punish than were older youth, the law-abiding, and males. Soviet law-abiding males were the least convinced that their parents would punish them if they did something wrong.

The perceived role of friends in their ability to punish was also significantly different by country. Soviet youth thought that their friends would sometimes punish them for wrongdoing; whereas Americans thought that their friends could almost never punish them. Non-delinquents in the United States sample, especially the females, were the least impressed by the ability of their friends to punish them if they did something wrong. The greater orientation of the Soviet youth to their friends in this respect is important here because it says something about the greater power of the primary group collective in influencing the views of Soviet youth.

This finding is compatible with other research attesting to the especially important rule-maintenance role of peers and of the collective in the USSR. It likewise fits with the notion that Americans are more autonomous and thus less attuned to the power of the group. We get an inkling from this difference of the potential influence of the micro-level legal context on the Soviet Russian youth. The informal rules and rule-enforcement at the primary group level of peers is shown here to be important to them.

Delinquents were more impressed with their friends' influence than were the law-abiding youth. This is consonant with explanations of delinquency that stress the negative influence of the peer group in stimulating and supporting deviant behavior. Friends' power to punish was also different for younger versus older youth. Whereas younger subjects, in both countries, believed that friends almost never have the power to punish, older subjects believed that they sometimes do have this power. This may reflect the developmental shift toward peers as more important authority figures in the eyes of older youth.

American and Soviet youth also differed significantly in their beliefs about the power of the police to punish them for doing something wrong. While the Soviet young people reported that the police *will* almost always punish wrongdoing, American youngsters maintained that they *can* punish only sometimes. Soviet males were especially impressed with the power of the police. This result is consistent with the expectation that the young Soviets might view their police as being more authoritarian and coercive than do American youth. It also lends support to the possibility that obeying the law in the USSR could have been motivated particularly by the kind of self-interest reflected by deterrence and a fear of sanctions.

Guilt

The items in the two versions of the instrument pertaining to feeling bad if you broke the teacher's rules or the orders of the police were deemed comparable. The same is not true for the questionnaire items pertaining to whether they would

A Soviet and an American View of the Law **121**

feel bad if they broke their friends' or their parents' rules; or if they broke the laws of the U.S./USSR.

Soviet and American youngsters differed significantly in whether they would feel bad if they broke the teacher's rules—even if no one knew. The USSR mean is 3.43 (sometimes/almost always), whereas the U.S. mean is 2.53 (almost never/sometimes). These findings are illustrated in Table 7.1. Keeping in mind that the Soviets did not have stronger feelings than the Americans that their teachers would punish them for wrongdoing, there nevertheless appears from this particular result a much greater orientation to the teacher as an authority figure. This again may reflect a principal difference in the two societies. As emphasized in our previous discussion, the former Soviet Union has historically been an authoritarian society. At the micro-level, for Russian schoolchildren, the teacher is the authority. This is also true to a degree in the United States as well, especially as far as younger children are concerned. At the same time, American society has a history of openly thumbing its nose at authority. Soviets who defied authority at that time usually did so privately. Publicly they were conforming and obedient. In contrast, in America there is an irreverence and a disrespect for authority, for authority figures, and specifically for teachers. Some of these differences may have been reflected in the results.

For the combined samples, concern for the teacher's rules was also significantly related to age, gender, and status. Younger subjects would almost always feel bad about breaking the teacher's rules; whereas older ones were between almost never and only sometimes. One unexpected result is that delinquents would feel more guilty than non-delinquents. American and Soviet young women combined

TABLE 7.1 Guilt About Breaking the Teacher's Rules by Country, Sex and Delinquency Status, with Age

	Mean	*F*
Country		
U.S.	2.53	25.43★★★
USSR	3.43	
Sex		
Male	2.59	12.88★★★
Female	3.24	
Status		
Non-delinquent	2.46	7.44★★
Delinquent	3.23	
Age		21.11★★★

★ $p < .05$
★★ $p < .01$
★★★ $p < .001$

122 A Soviet and an American View of the Law

(X = 3.24) would feel more guilty than the young men (X = 2.59). Contrary to what we had been led to believe from the earlier-cited preliminary reports of our Soviet colleagues, the Soviet females do not appear to have any special disregard for the rules of their teachers. In fact, just the opposite is true. The Soviet females would feel more guilty (almost always) about breaking the teacher's rules than either the American females or the males from either country. This difference in findings may be attributed to the greater sophistication in analytic techniques that we used working with the combined data sets.

The pattern here, not surprisingly, seems to be that responsiveness to the rules of the teacher is greater among younger children and among girls. Of direct pertinence to our concerns about rules and rule enforcement in disparate enforcement settings is the finding that the Russian youth of that time would feel more guilty about breaking the rules of a significant adult authority figure than would the American youth. This is certainly consistent with the views of Bronfenbrenner and others about the effects of special efforts toward socialization to conformity among Soviet youth.

The conformity pattern holds, at least in part, when we move to the level of the police as well. Soviet youth reported that they would be more likely to feel bad if they broke police orders or directions than would American youth (again even if no one knew). The difference between the U.S. and the USSR only approaches statistical significance, however. As with the teacher's rules, females and younger children would feel more guilty. Also as before, the Soviet females would feel the most guilty of all.

In sum, specifically the Soviet youth, and for the combined samples generally younger children and females, reported that they would feel more guilty about breaking the rules of two representative external authority figures than would their counterparts. These findings raise questions about the possible impact of the socializing effect of expressive (facilitative) and repressive (coercive) law. American law is of the first variety, whereas Soviet law, as demonstrated in the earlier discussion, was very much of the latter kind. While age and gender differences were evident across countries, the seemingly greater guilt expressed by the Soviet sample merits our continued attention in terms of understanding the differential impact of both the micro- and macro-level legal contexts on the legal socialization process. As we have begun to do here, further consideration needs to be given to how this context differs between the United States and the former Soviet Union.

There is certainly a suggestion here that maybe Bronfenbrenner and others were not wrong after all in their thoughts about the differences in socialization as between collective versus individual-oriented societies. This raises a tantalizing and perhaps worrisome question: What if one of the major continuing results of greater democracy in Russia is a loss of respect for external authority, which then emerges in the form of increased crime and delinquency, drug use, and various other forms of deviance—just as conservative politicians in the former Soviet Union warned, and just as has been happening so far?

Attitude and Status Correlates of Legal Socialization

Moving on in our findings, we turn next to the further comparative perceptions of teachers, parents, and peers, and to one's own law-abidingness, the wrongfulness of certain behaviors, the moral validity of the law, the fairness of the law, the efficacy of the law, and views of certain law operatives (see Box 7.1).

BOX 7.1 VARIABLE CLUSTERS

Law Efficacy:

It is rare for an innocent person to be put in jail.
Often a guilty person gets off free in the courts of this country.
People who steal things from stores usually get caught.
Most of the time you break a law, nothing much happens to you.
People who damage somebody else's property hardly ever get caught.

Law Fairness:

Judges are fair when they deal with young people.
It is rare for an innocent person to be put in jail.
The punishment for breaking the law is the same no matter who you are.
Often a guilty person gets off free in the courts of this country.
Courts give fair and equal treatment to everyone in this country.
Police always have a good reason when they stop somebody.
* Police try to give all young people an even break.

Morality of Law:

Most things that young people do to get into trouble with the law don't really hurt anyone.
I obey the law because I'm afraid of getting caught if I don't.
It's OK to lie if it keeps your friends out of trouble.
You have to be willing to break some rules if you want to be popular with your friends.
To have friends like you, sometimes you have to beat up other people.
Getting into trouble with the law would bother me a lot.
If you broke the laws of the US and no one knew, would you feel bad?

Wrongfulness:

How wrong would it be for someone your age to:
. . . steal something worth less than $5.00?
* . . . purposely damage property that is someone else's?
. . . smoke in school?

---

124 A Soviet and an American View of the Law

. . . cheat on school tests?
. . . drink alcohol?
* . . . break into a building to steal something?
. . . steal something worth more than $50.00?
People who leave things around deserve to have their things taken.
Taking things from stores doesn't hurt anyone.
It is OK to take advantage of someone who does not know any better.
Teachers who get hassled by students usually have it coming.
The worst thing about getting caught stealing is the trouble I would have at home afterwards.

Perception of One's Law Abidingness:

How much would your *parents* agree that you:
. . . are a bad kid?
. . . break rules?
. . . get into trouble?
. . . do things that are against the law?
How much would your *teachers* agree that you:
. . . are a bad kid?
. . . break rules?
. . . get into trouble?
. . . do thing that are against the law?
How much would your *friends* agree that you:
. . . are a bad kid?
. . . break rules?
. . . get into trouble?
. . . do things that are against the law?

Law Operatives:

Judges are fair when they deal with young people.
I have a lot of respect for the police in my town.
Police always have a good reason when they stop somebody.
Police try to give all young people an even break.
If your friends got into trouble with the police, would you be willing to lie to protect them?
* Can police officers punish you if you do something wrong?
Can judges punish you if you do something wrong?
If you broke the laws of the US and no one knew, would you free bad?
If you broke a police officer's orders and no one knew, would you feel bad?

AUTHORITY FIGURES:

Peers:

It's OK to lie if it keeps your friends out of trouble.
You have to be willing to break some rules if you want to be popular with your friends.
To have friends like you, sometimes you have to beat up other people.
When my parents want me to stay home and my friends want to go out, I usually stay home.
How much would your friends agree that you:
   . . . are a bad kid?
   . . . break rules?
   . . . get into trouble?
   . . . do things that are against the law?
If your friends were leading you into trouble, would you try to stop what they were doing?
If your friends got into trouble with the police, would you be willing to lie to protect them?
* Can friends punish you if you do something wrong?
If you broke your friends' rules and no one knew, would you feel bad?

Parents:

When my parents want me to stay home and my friends want to go out, I usually stay home.
At least one of my parents (or guardians) usually knows where I am and what I'm doing when I'm away from home.
I have a lot of respect for my parents (or guardians).
I would not care if my parents were a little disappointed in me.
How much would your parents agree that you:
   . . . are a bad kid?
   . . . break rules?
   . . . get into trouble?
   . . . do things that are against the law?

Teachers:

Teachers who get hassled by students usually have it coming.
My teachers care about me as a person.
I really liked some of my teachers last year.

126 A Soviet and an American View of the Law

How much would your teachers agree that you:
  . . . are a bad kid?
  . . . break rules?
  . . . get into trouble?
  . . . do things that are against the law?
*   Can teachers punish you if you do something wrong?
  If you broke the teacher's rules and no one knew, would you feel bad?

* Excluded as non-comparable in the US–USSR comparisons.

Looking first at just the U.S. sample (see Table 7.2), there are some significant correlations that are of particular interest. We see that those American youth who have a stronger sense of the moral validity of the law (believing in the necessity of law–obedience, feeling guilty about breaking the law, etc.) also have more positive views of law operatives, that is, police and judges, and a more positive orientation toward their parents and their peers. This indicates that for American youngsters, respect for laws and rules seems to go together with a respect for certain authority figures as well; but teachers are apparently not included. A similar sense comes from the normative attitudes toward deviance—called the wrongfulness of behaviors. U.S. youth who tend to view deviant acts as harmful also have more positive views of the fairness of the law, of the efficacy of the law, of law operatives, and of their parents and (this time) teachers. Those young people who have a more positive view of the fairness of the law also tend to see law operatives more positively and to think the law works better.

Turning to the Soviet data (Table 7.3), we find many more significant relationships among these various factors. Perceptions of the moral validity of the law are highly correlated with views of the fairness of the law, of the efficacy of the law, and of law operatives. Only the latter was significantly correlated in the U.S. sample. The same three factors (fairness, efficacy, and law operatives) are also strongly associated with normative judgments about the wrongfulness of certain behaviors, with perceptions of parents and peers, and with beliefs about how others view their own law–abidingness. The differences with respect to wrongfulness and law–abidingness between our two samples are most interesting. There are no such strong associations in the American sample, but in the Soviet sample, those young persons who have the higher regard for the law's moral validity also are more likely to view certain deviant behaviors as being wrong. This demonstrates a certain consistency in their attitudes since both factors contain items that measure the willingness to rationalize deviancy. Among the American youth, on the other hand, the relationship is very weak and does not demonstrate consistency.

Those Soviet young people who had a greater regard for the moral validity of the law were also more likely to think that significant others (parents, teachers,

TABLE 7.2 Correlation Matrix of Attitudes: United States

	XLFAIR	XLEFF	XLOPS	XWRNGBS	XPARENT	XPEER	XPEER6	XOLABID	XTEACHE
XMORALV	.1096	.1483	.3631***	.0886	.2886***	.2020*	-.0596	.0989	.1414
XLFAIR		.6178***	.6367***	.3728***	.2353**	.1042	-.1477	.1058	.2879***
XLEFF			.3733***	.3771***	.0772	.0798	-.1045	.0312	.2213**
XLOPS				.5386***	.4907***	.1787*	-.1186	.2565**	.3709***
XWRNGBS					.3411***	.1157	-.0774	.1608	.2701***
XPARENT						.3488***	-.0808	.6672***	.1142
XPEER							-.2281**	.7226***	-.0412
XPEER6								-.2127**	-.0957
XOLABID									.0030

* p < .05
** p < .01
*** p < .001

TABLE 7.3 Correlation Matrix of Attitudes: Soviet Union

	XLFAIR	XLEFF	XLOPS	XWRNGBS	XPARENT	XPEER	XPEER6	XOLABID	XTEACHE
XMORALV	.2991★★★	.2598★★	.5023★★★	.4414★★★	.4613★★★	.2999★★★	−.0737	.1903★	.1292
XLFAIR		.6059★★★	.6259★★★	.3335★★★	.3911★★★	.1939★	−.0985	.0925	.0123
XLEFF			.2730★★★	.3352★★★	.2518★★	.2150★★	−.1175	.1501	−.0776
XLOPS				.4039★★★	.4570★★★	−.0259	−.0772	−.0757	.3069★★★
XWRNGBS					.4735★★★	.3131★★★	−.1057	.2952★★★	.0958
XPARENT						.4196★★★	−.0948	.5694★★★	.0215
XPEER							−.2002★	.7693★★★	−.3017★★★
XPEER6								−.2624★★	−.0918
XOLABD									−.0239

★ p < .05
★★ p < .01
★★★ p < .001

A Soviet and an American View of the Law   **129**

peers) regarded them as troublemakers. This could simply be a reflection of a greater sensitivity to the views of those authority figures.

Those Soviet youth who felt most strongly about the harmfulness of the specified behaviors also had the higher regard for the fairness and efficacy of the law, and the most positive views of law operatives. They also had positive orientations toward parents and peers, although not particularly toward teachers. Finally, Soviet youth who thought the law was fair also thought it worked well, and were more positively inclined toward law operatives. We will examine all these findings in more detail as we take up each result in turn.

Authority Figures

Teachers

The variable cluster "teacher" is composed of eight items from the survey instrument. These items include assessments of liking and being liked by teachers, how teachers perceive the subject, and again, how one would feel about breaking the teacher's rules. The reliability coefficient for this variable (calculated using the items in the U.S. instrument) was a very acceptable Cronbach's alpha of .84.

The only statistically significant difference in perceptions of teachers is by country (see Table 7.4). The USSR mean (3.24) is significantly higher than the U.S. mean (2.94), indicating a more positive orientation toward teachers by the Soviet youth. Thus, the Soviet young people would not only feel more guilty about breaking the teachers' rules—which is possibly accounted for by the particular socialization in the school—but they were also more apt to like their teachers, to see themselves as

TABLE 7.4 The Teacher as an Authority Figure by Country, Sex, and Delinquency Status, with Age

	Mean	F
Country		
U.S.	2.94	34.23★★★
USSR	3.24	
Sex		
Male	3.11	1.27
Female	3.06	
Status		
Non-delinquent	3.12	2.77
Delinquent	3.06	
Age		.66

★ p < .05
★★ p < .01
★★★ p < .001

130 A Soviet and an American View of the Law

being liked by their teachers, and to think that their teachers generally think well of them. The overall difference in perceptions could again be reflective of cultural differences in our two societies. The teacher as an external authority figure was a larger presence in the eyes of these Soviet youngsters than was the case with American youth.

There are no significant differences by age, gender, or delinquency status. Apropos the previous discussion of the Soviet females, here we see that those young women are somewhat less positive toward teachers than their male counterparts in the Soviet sample, but only very slightly so. The same is true of the American females. Any especially negative attitudes on the part of Soviet girls are not apparent.

Parents

The variable cluster "parent" is made up of eight items. These items measure respecting and caring about parents, and perception by parents of the subject's propensity for getting into trouble. The reliability coefficient (Cronbach's alpha) for these items is .80, again highly acceptable. The mean score for the U.S. sample is 3.55 and for the USSR sample 3.42 (see Table 7.5). This difference is not statistically significant. The suggestion is that the American youth have a more positive orientation toward their parents than do their Soviet counterparts. This is also true of females. One might be tempted to conclude, based upon the earlier Soviet analyses of their data described at the outset, that the young Soviet females would come on as being especially negative toward their parents.

TABLE 7.5 The Parent as an Authority Figure by Country, Sex, and Delinquency Status, with Age

	Mean	*F*
Country		
U.S.	3.55	2.97
USSR	3.42	
Sex		
Male	3.42	2.30
Female	3.55	
Status		
Non-delinquent	3.15	60.98★★★
Delinquent	3.79	
Age		9.53★★

★ p < .05
★★ p < .01
★★★ p < .001

A Soviet and an American View of the Law **131**

These combined data do not show that. The average view of Soviet females toward their parents is slightly more positive than that of Soviet males; the American females in contrast have a decidedly more positive orientation. The delinquent young people in both countries have a significantly more favorable view of their parents than do the delinquent youth. The same is true of the younger children versus older youth.

Among the informal, rule-enforcement authorities in the USSR, parents seem to be less important, less influential when compared to teachers, peers, and to the police (who can have both an informal and a formal enforcement function). Let us further explore this possibility by looking again at the peer group and its influence.

Peers

The variable peers was broken into two dependent variable clusters because of differences in the scoring mode. The first cluster "peer" has eight items (see Table 7.6a). These deal with desire to be popular with friends, how friends perceive the subject, and the item "how you would feel if you broke your friends' rules?" The Cronbach's alpha for the eight items is an acceptable .67. The difference between the U.S. (X = 3.07) and USSR subjects (X = 3.35) on the eight-item cluster, showing a greater orientation toward peers by the Soviet youngsters, is statistically significant. There are also statistically significant differences by status and age, but not by gender. Examining the country-by-gender data shows that it is the Soviet males who are the most peer-oriented; conversely the U.S. males are

TABLE 7.6A Peers as Authority Figures by Country, Sex, and Delinquency Status, with Age

	Mean	F
Country		
U.S.	3.07	16.08★★★
USSR	3.35	
Sex		
Male	3.22	.27
Female	3.20	
Status		
Non-delinquent	3.04	16.22★★★
Delinquent	3.35	
Age		4.68★

★ p < .05
★★ p < .01
★★★ p < .001

132 A Soviet and an American View of the Law

TABLE 7.6B Deviant Peers as Authority Figures by Country, Sex, and Delinquency Status, with Age

	Mean	*F*
Country		
U.S.	1.82	9.92★★
USSR	2.00	
Sex		
Male	1.85	5.13★
Female	1.97	
Status		
Non-delinquent	1.88	.22
Delinquent	1.94	
Age		5.93★

★ p < .05
★★ p < .01
★★★ p < .001

the least peer-oriented. The Soviet females are more attuned to their peers than are either the American males or females.

"Peer 6" has three items measuring relationships with friends who get into trouble (see Table 7.6b). The reliability coefficient for this cluster is .63. There are again highly significant differences by country and also by age and gender on this variable. The mean score for the American subjects is 1.82; but for Soviet Russian subjects it is 2.00. In this case, the higher scores indicate greater willingness to stick with friends who are getting into trouble, and to refrain from trying to stop them. Here, as with the earlier findings, Soviet youth have a greater commitment to peers—in this case deviant peers—than do American youth.

It appears that Soviet youth see their peers as having a greater rule-maintenance (power to punish) role than do American youth, are more likely to feel guilty about breaking their rules, and have a greater commitment to them even when these peers are themselves deviant. This finding too is illustrative of the power of the collective's authority. Sticking with your friends who are in trouble with the formal authorities may, for these Soviet young people, have been a way of showing their own disdain for that formal authority. It reinforces the argument about the importance of the collective in Soviet childrearing, suggesting that it is at that level that conformity and obedience may be especially instilled and enforced.

There are also significant differences by gender here. The fact that the Soviet females are by far the most willing to go to bat for their peers and to stand by them is of interest. Since that might entail defying legal authorities, this finding could be seen as resonating with the earlier Soviet reported results.

Fairness of the Law

The variable cluster "law fairness" contains six items. These items tap dimensions of the fairness of judges and courts ("Judges are fair when they deal with young people"), of the police ("Police always have a good reason when they stop somebody"), and of punishment for breaking the law ("The punishment for breaking the law is the same no matter who you are"). Cronbach's alpha for these items is .66. There are highly significant differences by country on this variable. The U.S. mean score is 2.94, whereas the USSR mean score is 3.49 (Table 7.7). This suggests that Soviet youth perceived their law and its application to be fairer than American youth perceived American law to be. From the previous discussion of the Soviet data, we know that fairness is attributed by Soviet youth more in abstract situations than it is in concrete situations. This finding, on its face, runs counter to any expectation that compared to American views of the American legal system, the Soviet legal system would have been perceived by the Soviet youth as being unfair.

For the combined American and Soviet samples, delinquency status is also a significant source of variation in perceptions of fairness. There is a curious split here, however. Within the four groupings (Soviet delinquents/non-delinquents and American delinquents/non-delinquents) the Soviet delinquents had the highest regard for fairness, whereas the American non-delinquents had the lowest. These results are contrary to the findings of other studies, where non-delinquents were usually more likely than delinquents to see the law as fair. Those earlier findings were usually the result of the delinquents having had more experience of a negative kind with the law; and/or their engaging in a process of neutralization

TABLE 7.7 Law Fairness by Country, Sex, and Delinquency Status, with Age

	Mean	F
Country		
U.S	2.94	56.13***
USSR	3.49	
Sex		
Male	3.18	.46
Female	3.25	
Status		
Non-delinquent	2.98	21.86***
Delinquent	3.43	
Age		26.23***

* p < .05
** p < .01
*** p < .001

134 A Soviet and an American View of the Law

and rationalization (the police and courts are unfair!) in an attempt to justify their own deviant behavior. As far as the delinquents here are concerned, their relatively more positive attitudes could be an example of a different kind of reality effect arising from actual involvement with the juvenile justice process. In the dose of reality, negative stereotypes can sometimes be countered by experiences that lead to a generally more favorable impression about fair treatment. That could be what is happening here.

Another significant source of variation in perceptions of fairness is age. The 9–12-year-olds were more inclined to view the law as fair than were the 13–17-year-olds. These age effects are consistent with the results of other research that has found older youth tend to have more negative attitudes toward the law. The Soviet females were more favorably inclined toward the fairness of the law than were American females or either American or Soviet males. The American girls had the most negative attitudes regarding law fairness. The gender effects thus diverge in opposite directions. The findings from the Soviet girls are consistent with other work; the American female results are not.

Efficacy of the Law

This variable refers to how well the law works, how effective it is. It is comprised of five items, and three of the five pertain to the likelihood of getting caught and punished if you do something wrong; for example, "People who steal things from stores usually get caught," and "Often a guilty person gets off free in the courts of this country." The reliability coefficient for the cluster is .59. American (X = 3.12) and Soviet Russian (X = 3.14) youth do not differ significantly in their perceptions of law efficacy (see Table 7.8). Since efficacy could be a measure of potential deterrence, it is interesting to observe that neither country's youth, at least as represented by this sampling, have any especially strong feelings about the law's deterrent effectiveness.

There are again significant age and status differences here. Delinquents in both countries—but especially in the USSR—thought that the law worked better than non-delinquents did. Law-abiding youngsters in the Soviet Union had especially low regard for the efficacy of the law. Delinquents might be expected to see the law and law enforcement working better than would those who have not gotten caught and punished for lawbreaking. This could again be an example of the reality of experience counteracting the negative stereotypes held by those without that experience. Younger subjects in both countries also thought the law worked better than did the older ones.

Law Operatives

"Law operatives" is intended to capture subjects' views of officials in the criminal justice system. Of the five items, three in this cluster pertain to the police and one

A Soviet and an American View of the Law **135**

TABLE 7.8 Law Efficacy by Country, Sex, and Delinquency Status, with Age

	Mean	F
Country		
U.S.	3.12	.14
USSR	3.14	
Sex		
Male	3.09	.96
Female	3.17	
Status		
Non-delinquent	2.95	11.34★★★
Delinquent	3.29	
Age		23.27★★★

★ p < .05
★★ p < .01
★★★ p < .001

to judges. They include the items "judges are fair," "police usually have good reason to stop someone," and "police usually give kids a break." The other two items refer again to "guilt" feelings about breaking the laws, and breaking a police officer's orders. The reliability coefficient for these five items is .74.

The mean score for the American sample is 3.08, and for the Soviet sample it is 3.39. This difference in views of law operatives is statistically significant (see Table 7.9). The higher score for Soviet young people, reflecting a more

TABLE 7.9 Law Operatives by Country, Sex, and Delinquency Status, with Age

	Mean	F
Country		
U.S.	3.08	11.85★★★
USSR	3.39	
Sex		
Male	3.03	16.88★★★
Female	3.45	
Status		
Non-delinquent	2.95	15.16★★★
Delinquent	3.50	
Age		40.11★★★

★ p < .05
★★ p < .01
★★★ p < .001

136 A Soviet and an American View of the Law

positive attitude toward law operatives, dovetails with our earlier findings on guilt and law fairness. What accounts for this consistency? Perhaps, as was suggested earlier by our Soviet colleagues, it comes from a tendency among the Russian youth to give the socially desirable response. Or perhaps it comes from a combination of very effective law-related education in the Soviet schools—which education had as one of its primary objectives instilling respect for the Soviet legal system—combined with the suppression of any information bearing on the historical illegalities engaged in by the Soviet authorities. In any event, whichever one or combination of these influences is operating, as with the issue of fairness, the findings among Soviet youth here run contrary to expectations about any possible poisonous effects on legal attitudes from having been socialized into laws and rules under a system that operated to a great extent outside the rule of law.

Again there are significant differences by age, gender, and status. Younger children, females, and delinquents are all more impressed with the police and judges than are their opposite numbers. The Soviet females are especially impressed.

Moral Validity of the Law

This cluster of items is intended to capture the notion of the rightness and goodness of the law and of rules. Do youth obey the law only because they are afraid of getting caught? Would they be bothered by breaking the law? Is breaking the law really harmful? If they broke the laws of the U.S./USSR and no one knew, would they feel bad? The six items making up this cluster have a Cronbach's alpha of .65. There were significant differences by country on this variable. The mean score for U.S. subjects (2.98) was significantly lower than the mean score for USSR subjects (3.43). We thus see that, along with the finding that Soviet youth were more likely to perceive their law as being fair and to have a higher regard for their police and judges, Soviet youth also seemed to reflect a greater belief in what is being called the moral validity of the law. I propose that some of the same influencing factors just mentioned above could be operating here as well.

For the combined samples, status is again a significant source of variation on this variable. Delinquents (most surprisingly!) reflected a greater commitment to the law than did law-abiding youth. Younger children also had a higher regard for the moral validity of the law than did older youth. Gender, however, was not a significant source of variation (see Table 7.10).

Wrongfulness of Behaviors

This variable cluster is made up of nine items. Cronbach's alpha for these items is .74. Three items deal with kind of limited rationalizations for deviant behavior; for example, "people who leave their things around deserve to have them taken." These are limited because they deal with failures or mistakes by personal victims, of which one can take advantage. They are not rationalizations in any larger sense.

A Soviet and an American View of the Law **137**

TABLE 7.10 Moral Validity of Law by Country, Sex, and Delinquency Status, with Age

	Mean	*F*
Country		
U.S.	2.98	72.43★★★
USSR	3.43	
Sex		
Male	3.14	3.61
Female	3.26	
Status		
Non–delinquent	3.04	26.95★★★
Delinquent	3.36	
Age		9.27★★

★ p < .05
★★ p < .01
★★★ p < .001

One item deals with parental reaction to stealing. The majority of items (five) ask how wrong would it be for someone your age to do things ranging from smoking in school to stealing something worth more than $50 (or 50 rubles).

Lower scores mean a greater tendency to view the behavior as being wrong. The mean score for the U.S. youth is 3.48, and for the USSR youth it is 3.37. This difference is not statistically significant (see Table 7.11). Both groups of

TABLE 7.11 Wrongfulness of Behaviors by Country, Sex, and Delinquency Status, with Age

	Mean	*F*
Country		
U.S.	3.48	3.52
USSR	3.37	
Sex		
Male	3.38	3.72
Female	3.50	
Status		
Non–delinquent	3.19	45.20★★★
Delinquent	3.64	
Age		24.08★★★

★ p < .05
★★ p < .01
★★★ p < .001

138 A Soviet and an American View of the Law

subjects agreed that certain behaviors are wrong. As expected, there was greater agreement that the more serious behaviors are wrong.

As a possible surrogate for actual delinquent behavior, these items worked in that "official" juvenile delinquents saw less harm in the delinquent acts than did the "official" law-abiding youth. This suggests congruity between normative judgments about deviance and willingness to commit deviant acts. Once more, there are significant differences in the expected direction by age. Younger children tend to see the most harm in these acts.

Own Law-Abidingness

This cluster is intended to measure perceptions of others' views of one's own law-abidingness. There are a total of 12 items: four each for parents, teachers, and friends. The items pertain to being a bad kid, breaking rules, getting into trouble, and doing things that are against the law. The reliability analysis produced an extremely high Cronbach's alpha of .91.

Youth in the USSR sample thought that parents, teachers, and peers saw them as law-abiding. The mean scores are U.S. = 3.28, USSR = 3.18; lower scores in this instance are toward the positive end (law-abiding). The difference here, however, is not statistically significant (Table 7.12).

The only significant source of variation is delinquency status. Delinquents have a higher mean score in both countries (X = 3.40) than do the law-abiding youth (X = 3.05). Thus, we get a finding with respect to delinquency that is consistent with the labeling theory of delinquent behavior, in that the delinquents here agree that certain significant others have the opinion that they are less law-abiding.

TABLE 7.12 Own Law-Abidingness by Country, Sex, and Delinquency Status, with Age

	Mean	F
Country		
U.S.	3.28	3.22
USSR	3.18	
Sex		
Male	3.25	.25
Female	3.22	
Status		
Non-delinquent	3.05	35.97***
Delinquent	3.40	
Age		1.43

* p < .05
** p < .01
*** p < .001

One puzzle is what happened to the negative and contrary views of the Soviet females that were reported by our Soviet colleagues, and that I remarked upon rather extensively in the beginning of the chapter? There are several possible explanations for what might appear to be their disappearance. The Soviet researchers tabulated individual items by hand, and thus did not work with the variable clusters used in the foregoing analyses. Employing these variable clusters resulted in a fair amount of missing data in the combined analyses, especially with the Soviet sample. This is because their survey questionnaires were completed much more haphazardly. The greatest amount of missing data occurred on the guilt about breaking the teacher's rules item, where there were 54 missing cases in the Soviet sample; and on the wrongfulness of behaviors variable cluster, where there were 36 missing Soviet cases. The individual items tell us that the young Soviet females really had rather negative attitudes. It is the clustering that washes some of this out. In any event, we will attempt to sort that out in the later study.

In general, the above results strongly suggested the need for further research that would be both more rigorous and more comparable. This new research, it was thought, should do a number of things: (1) incorporate measures of self-reported delinquent behavior; (2) more reliably measure legal developmental levels; and (3) include more equivalent operationalizations of knowledge of the law. All of these conditions, I am pleased to say, were met in the 1992 study. Yet also needed in future research are measures of the various legal socialization strategies; having the youth themselves define wrongfulness in an open-ended way; and some measure of participation in the rule- and law-making process.

Conclusions

We can conclude from the Phase I study that Soviet and American views of the law differed in some respects but not in others. The judgment of whether the law is inherently worthy of being respected does seem to vary, but not in what might have been the expected directions. Guilt and the fear of authority played a greater role in effecting thoughts about legal compliance among the Soviet Russian youngsters than they did among the Americans. Young Soviet males were more likely than the females—and the Americans—to indicate that they would obey the law because of the fear of getting caught. Both Soviet males and females were more oriented toward maintaining law and order. The harmfulness of law-breaking (especially among the Soviet schoolgirls) seemed, on the other hand, to be of lesser import in their minds.

Our initial results tended to support suppositions about there being differential effects of different sociolegal contexts upon legal attitudes (as these are elements of legal socialization), as well as upon legal knowledge. What they did not show is that there were any differences in legal reasoning between our two samples. The findings with respect to the Soviet young people might further be taken to demonstrate the greater importance of that law and those rules that are closest

140 A Soviet and an American View of the Law

to us, as compared to those that emanate from the larger political system. On their face, the results do not show dramatic effects from being socialized under two very different legal and political state systems: one that had traditionally depended more on authority, and on coercion and force to bring about compliance; as compared to one that relied more on legitimacy and the rule of law. Before we put those issues aside, however, we will now travel in time to five years later, when Russia had moved away from its former Soviet state (albeit in fits and starts), but without yet fully achieving either legitimacy or the rule of law.

8

LAW AND DEVIANCE THROUGH THE EYES OF RUSSIAN YOUTH

As was argued at the outset of this book, one of the main purposes of undertaking an examination of legal socialization in the former Soviet Union, and one of the chief reasons for selecting that country in particular, is to explore the effects that different kinds of legal contexts have upon what young people believe and how they behave with regard to the law. Russians are the largest group of ex-Soviet peoples, and they are the ones most identified with the former USSR.[1] It is they who most influenced and in turn are most likely to have been influenced by the unique legal culture and environment of the USSR. Our concern here is thus with the legal socialization of explicitly Russian children and youth. The first focus of that concern in this chapter will be on their legal reasoning—and on what has been termed for purposes of this research their legal developmental level.

Legal reasoning, as previously explained, is a way of thinking about rules and laws. It is one way of sorting out one's relationship to the social order of the larger society in which one lives. This sorting out process, this defining of the reciprocal relationship that exists between each of us and our sociolegal environment, requires addressing a host of questions that have to do with the law: What is the purpose of law? Are laws necessary? If so, particularly when and under what circumstances are they necessary? Why should one obey the law? What should happen if one does not obey the law?

It is not being suggested that all of us, all the time, go around thinking about these kinds of questions. We all, however, consider these sorts of things from time to time. We especially think about whether we personally should follow a particular rule or law, for example obeying the speed limit when we are in a hurry, and what might be the consequences if we do not. Some legal writers and scholars, for example, Hyde (1983), believe this narrow sort of self-interest is the main reason why people obey or do not obey the law.

142 Law and Deviance

Reasoning about laws and rules further involves thinking about our rights and obligations, and about what is justice and fairness. This raises even more questions that again we may on occasion explicitly contemplate, but that generally act as implicit guides for our behavior. What is a "right"? What rights do I have? What do rights have to do with laws? What is a "fair" law? Should one always obey the law? Should one obey an unjust law? How do I decide that a law is unjust or unfair? How do I decide that law enforcement is unfair?

Legal reasoning—the consideration of these difficult kinds of issues and questions—is an abstract, cognitive process. It is not a simple matter of acting, always and exclusively, in one's self-interest. It involves reflecting on and coming to some understanding about right and wrong, and what one defines as right and wrong for oneself as well as for others. Such reasoning further involves assessing one's own self-interests in the context of and in comparison with the interests of others, of our primary groups (collectives in the Russian sense), and of the larger society.

Legal socialization theory classifies people into three levels of legal development, with particular modes and complexities of reasoning associated with each legal level. It is not assumed that anyone thinks, believes, and behaves exclusively at any one of these levels; but rather that our predominate legal perspective falls into one of these three categories. The first, or so-called pre-conventional level of reasoning, is the most egocentric form. Persons who reason principally at this level do view obeying the law as largely a matter of self-interest. They believe that people are deterred from law violations mostly by their fear of sanctions. At the same time, they themselves would not be constrained from breaking the law if it suited them and they thought they could get away with it. The making of laws and rules is seen as an exercise in power; that is, laws are made, are enforced, and changed only by those who have enough power to enforce their will. This is a worldview most commonly associated with younger children who are at an early and incomplete stage of socialization, and who are therefore legally immature.

Legal immaturity might also be thought to be the product of the kind of legal system that dominated in the Soviet Union. The prevailing legal environment throughout Soviet history, as described earlier, was one in which lawmaking was very much an exercise in power politics. The rules were made and enforced in a partocracy of the Communist Party, rather than in a democracy governed by mutual consent. That context was also one in which you would expect that obeying the law would have been motivated primarily by fear and deterrence, perhaps resulting in a kind of enforced pre-conventional level of legal reasoning. But in addition, there was also the official ideology put forward by a vast apparatus of Party and State organizations and intended to build acceptance of the legitimacy of the State.

The conventional Level IIs, according to the theory of legal development, are oriented to the maintenance of law and order. Rules and laws are believed to be necessary to a well-ordered society because they help prevent antisocial behavior. At the same time, laws are judged to be more or less legitimate if the system from which they emanate is believed to be legitimate. Perceptions of legitimacy are a complex matter, however, and laws may have to meet rather demanding criteria in order to meet the test of legitimacy. The following definition of legitimacy is an example of just how rigorous that test can be: "[To be effective, laws] must be seen as emanating from legitimate authority; that is, the law-making body must be regarded as credible, as worthy of respect and veneration, as authentically concerned with the welfare of its constituency, as an exemplar of probity and integrity" (Hogan and Mills, 1976: 273). The issue of legitimacy is important for our concerns, because it raises the question of the extent to which the Soviet system was viewed by the Soviet people as being legitimate—as an "exemplar of probity and integrity."

This question sets up a possible inherent contradiction, which complicates the relation between the legitimacy of laws and the legal system on the one hand, and public support for and compliance with those laws on the other. It might be, and in fact it seems quite possible, that people could simultaneously question the legitimacy of a political system, but still believe in and support that system's control of disorder and lawlessness. Many people with whom I have spoken in the former USSR seem to hold these competing views. This contradiction (if in fact it is a contradiction) does not impugn the validity of the conventional legal reasoning typology, but simply re-emphasizes the complexity of the reasoning process. An illustration of the support for control among the Russian populace can be found in the results of a public opinion survey carried out in the European part of Russia in September–October 1992 (the same time as our legal socialization study). In a description of the survey results it was reported that "[a] consensus appeared to be growing that the best form of government was one that strove toward the security and protection of the population rather than protection of individual liberties" (Rhodes, 1993: 43). The proportion of the Russians sampled holding this view increased from 35 percent in April–May 1991, to 39 percent in September 1991, to 63 percent in the fall of 1992. Maintenance of law and order had become an overriding concern.

Generally, Level IIs believe laws are to be obeyed, although they may be broken in certain emergency situations. Because they profess a basic belief in the need to be law-abiding, persons who reason mainly at this level may be forced (more so than the Level Is) into rationalizing any lawbreaking on their part. This is because they have to reconcile what would otherwise be a cognitively dissonant situation. If you do not try to rationalize and neutralize your deviance, how else do you reconcile breaking the law with your professed belief that laws are necessary and that people ought to be law-abiding? Blasi addressed this idea of reconciliation in indicating that some students of moral reasoning and moral behavior in fact believe that moral reasoning is really nothing more than rationalization: "Moral reasoning is viewed [by some] as rationalization, that is, as

144 Law and Deviance

a result of rather than as a preparation for one's action and as an expression of the human need for a coherent account of what we are doing" (Blasi, 1980: 3). Reasoning about our actions (whether past or contemplated) would certainly seem to have to incorporate elements of rationalization. If we have done something, we try to justify it in our own eyes as well as in the eyes of others. If we are considering doing something, it makes sense that we would weigh our potential ability to explain and justify it. Saying that, however, is different from saying that rationalization is the only element of reasoning; that moral reasoning is rationalization and nothing else.

Those who reason at the conventional level present a relatively conservative worldview. It is one that is very much oriented toward maintaining the status quo. And it is this conservative, status quo orientation that may help explain why one still falls into accord with laws and law enforcement despite questioning their legitimacy. Persons holding this kind of conventional view of the law would not be expected to condone lawlessness, but on the other hand they would not be expected to be in the forefront of legal dissent and reform either.

Thus, the picture with respect to the Russians is rather complex. There is, on the one hand, reason to doubt full and complete acceptance by the Russian people of the legitimacy of the Soviet system, and of Soviet law and its enforcement. On the other hand, Russians are basically a conservative people who dislike disorder, and who find strong authoritarian rule to be attractive. As a result, there may be mixed motives influencing the legal reasoning process.

The last group, the Level IIIs, are the most principled thinkers about the law. Post-conventional reasoning incorporates a much greater role for personal moral values, and for a sense of moral obligation, than does either the pre-conventional or the conventional levels. Moral obligation may include a felt obligation to obey or disobey a particular law that is adjudged to be unfair or unjust. Such persons see the purpose of law to be the gaining of rights and benefits for all, but also the sharing of burdens by all. Previous research has identified only a few people who reason pretty consistently in this upper range. Persons espousing strong moral views, openly challenging the legitimacy of the Soviet state, and criticizing the injustice of Soviet law and its enforcement would have been in a minority and would most likely have been found in the various dissident groups that developed in the USSR.

Let us turn now to the first generation of post-Soviet Russian youth, and see what they think and feel about law in contemporary Russia. We will also learn from their own reports something about their personal involvement in deviant acts.

Legal Reasoning among Today's Russian Youth

The Russian youth at the four sites in and around Moscow were shown, as part of the ILVI-V survey questionnaire, 11 statements drawn from previous research intended to reflect and to operationalize levels of legal development. The youth were asked to rank order three possible responses to each of these statements in accordance with their own views about the statements. In each instance, the three responses represented each of a Level I-, a Level II-, and a Level III-type response. The subjects' "scores" on legal reasoning are the means of the sum of the responses that they ranked first (what is called the first-choice method of scoring). This average score can range from a low of 1 (which would correspond to a pure Level I) to a high of 3 (corresponding to a pure Level III).

Where did our young Russians come out? Again squarely in the conventional middle! The average score for legal reasoning for the sample as a whole was 2.03. In general, these youth are very much in the mainstream—in the middle of the cognitive spectrum—in their reasoning about the law. As was true of the earlier Soviet sample, they do not look much different from other youth who have been studied at other times in other places. For example, the Hess, Minturn, and Tapp cross-cultural study in Greece, India, Italy, Japan, Denmark, and the United States nearly three decades ago found that the legal developmental level (LDL) of the 10–14-year-olds they studied was similarly centered in the conventional range (Tapp, 1970). More recently, Cohn and White (1986) found LDLs of 2.10 and 2.13 respectively, for their male and female university student subjects.

The Russian females in our sample, all of whom came from the Moscow city schools, have the highest average legal reasoning score (2.10). This LDL is up there with Cohn and White's university students. Because the Americans were both older and ostensibly represented an above average intellectual capacity given that they were university students, the fact that the Russian schoolgirls are on a par with them is testimony to these girls' reasoning capacities. Our next highest reasoning score is that of the boys from the city schools, who are classified as non-delinquents in terms of status. Their LDL is 2.03. The lowest level, 1.94, is that for the delinquent males from the juvenile colony.

For our contemporary Russians, these results suggest again that whatever the effects of the unique Soviet-Russian legal context might be on legal development, the legal history and current events that serve to define that context at the macro-level do not seem to have particularly repressed, or in some way distorted downward, the legal reasoning of this sample of Russian young people. Having made that overall observation, let us first go through the survey results that have a bearing on (either affecting or being affected by) legal reasoning and legal development, and then come back to consider all the various implications.

Attitudinal Correlates

Legal reasoning is significantly correlated with views about the moral validity of the law; with perceptions of the fairness of the law; with perceptions of the efficacy of the law and law enforcement; with judgments about the wrongfulness

146   Law and Deviance

of certain deviant behaviors; with views of parents, peers, and teachers; and with perceptions of how others view one's own law-abidingness. The only non-significant correlation with any of these variable clusters is with the young people's views of law operatives (see Table 8.1).

What do these particular results mean? Taken together, they present a most interesting and intriguing picture. First, with respect to moral validity, the implication is that Russian youth who reason at higher legal levels seem to be more likely than those at lower levels to believe that breaking the law is harmful, and that they would be bothered by breaking the law. This finding is very much in the direction predicted by legal socialization theory, and it fits with other research findings on moral and legal development. It is also consistent with the premise that higher-order legal reasoning is more likely to have moral content. Moral content in this case refers to seeing lawbreaking as harmful to the society, and to feeling guilty about breaking the law.

There is further sense of the importance and influence of legal reasoning in the foregoing results from the significant association shown between legal reasoning and wrongfulness. This too is an important result because it speaks to the relationship between reasoning and normative criteria for behavior. The items in the questionnaire asking about how wrong it would be to do various things are intended to assess normative standards regarding certain deviant behaviors. This finding demonstrates that higher-level reasoners are more likely to view certain behaviors as being wrong. Those youth who reason in a more sophisticated fashion about the need for law, the purpose of law, and so on, have a higher regard for and belief in the moral validity of the law; and, they also exercise more moral judgment about the harmfulness of deviant conduct.

There is also the suggestion that those Russian young people who reason at higher levels are less likely to see certain victims (people who leave things around for example) as being deserving of their victimization. Since such beliefs would be one way of rationalizing and attempting to neutralize wrongdoing, we can conclude that more sophisticated legal reasoners here are less likely to engage in these kinds of rationalizations and neutralizations. This has a bearing on the earlier point made by Blasi about the overlapping meaning of reasoning and rationalization. Contrary to the position that moral reasoning is synonymous with rationalization, higher-order reasoning here is the antithesis of rationalization.

Third in our trilogy of support for legal reasoning is law-abidingness as viewed by others—the sort of looking-glass self-phenomenon. In this case, as with wrongfulness, the negative correlation is in the direction that the theory would predict. Lower scores on law-abidingness are in the direction of the youth perceiving that others believe them to be more law-abiding. Therefore, higher-level legal reasoners tend to think that certain others (parents, teachers, and peers) see them as not getting into trouble, breaking the rules, or doing things that are against the law. Those reasoning at the lower levels, on the other hand, are more likely to think that these significant others see them as deviants. Since lower reasoning is

TABLE 8.1 Attitudinal Correlates of Legal Reasoning (LDL)

	MORALV	LFAIR	LEFF	LOPS	WRONGBS	PARENT	PEER	OLABIDE	TEACHER
LDL	.1659**	−.1039*	−.1144*	.0811	−.2144***	−.1761***	−.1129	−.1760***	−.2378***
MORALV		−.1356**	−.1775***	.5554***	−.4559***	.2571***	−.0589	−.3133***	−.3749***
LFAIR			.5530***	.0946	.2980***	.2875***	.1417**	.2397***	.2953***
LEFF				−.1488**	.3159***	.2295***	.1018*	.2058***	.2264***
LOPS					−.3874***	−.0696	−.0195	−.1216*	−.1641***
WRONGBS						.3369***	.2190***	.4534***	.5438***
PARENT							.4979***	.8088***	.6132***
PEER								.7072***	.4023***
OLABIDE									.7906***

* p < .05
** p < .01
*** p < .001

148 Law and Deviance

more likely to be associated with being delinquent than non-delinquent, this perception fits very well with the reality of the makeup of our samples.

The remainder of the relationships can be viewed from a number of different angles. The fact that they are negative means that the Russian young people whose legal reasoning is in that upper range, where they can be expected to be most concerned about the legitimacy of laws and their enforcement, and about the morality and justice of rules and laws, tend to have a lower regard for the fairness of Russian law and its enforcement. They also tend to see the law enforcement system as less effective—particularly with regard to the likelihood of getting caught and punished if you do something wrong. The more pre-conventional thinkers, in contrast, tend to believe the reverse. They have a higher regard for both fairness and deterrence. Because the lower level of reasoning is more prevalent among the delinquent boys confined to the institution for juvenile offenders, it means that these law violators who have obviously had more direct experience with the law and its enforcement are more favorably impressed with the law's operational aspects. As we saw before, there may be an interaction effect of experience and reasoning operating here to produce this result. If so, it would support the idea that behavior can be a stimulus to both attitudes and reasoning.

The higher-reasoning youth also have pretty negative orientations toward all three groups of authority figures. In each instance, albeit most strongly for teachers, our higher-order-reasoning young Russians seem to think that the authority figures have rather negative views of them. They do not think that their teachers like them; nor would they feel bad about breaking either the teachers', or their parents', or their friends' informal rules. The negative orientations toward teachers of the upper-level reasoners include even seeing teachers as deserving of getting hassled, and seeing teachers as not caring about them—and vice versa.

At least one of the factors that seems to be driving this last result arises from the fact that the Russian schoolgirls sampled have the highest LDL. It is these non-delinquent females in particular, and the school sample in general (both males and females) who demonstrate the most negative attitudes toward their teachers. It is the colony juveniles, on the other hand, who have relatively more positive views of teachers. Why this should be so is open only to speculation, since this research cannot provide any definitive answers.

It does not necessarily mean that the colony residents have particularly fond memories of their former teachers. It simply means that the current students are still in the throes (as they view it) of the authoritarian school environment, which many of them may regard as being incompatible with their interests—remember the earlier reported comments about the desire for early marriage and some sense of the irrelevance of school among certain of these students. It is probably also pertinent that practically all of the teachers and administrators in the schools surveyed are women. Our preadolescent and adolescent Russian girls may be especially negative toward and be chafing under the authority of older (in some

Law and Deviance **149**

cases old), and rather conservative female teachers. The girls could be rejecting as role models some of the older teachers who represent the old ways. They may also be expressing their resentment against the double standard that they see being applied to them. It is reasonable to expect that they have been imbued with the hypocritical stance of Soviet and now Russian society concerning the supposed equality of men and women. All of this of course would not be an issue for the boys.

Status Correlates

There are four of what will be called status variables, which we can look at with respect to their correlation with legal reasoning. These four are age, sex, knowledge of the law, and delinquency status (again defined as whether the youth comes from the colony or the school). It was mentioned previously that there are differences in reasoning scores by sex and by delinquency status. Tables 8.2 and 8.3 show that if we treat legal reasoning (the average score for legal development) as a dependent variable, and seek to determine the explanatory effects upon legal reasoning of age, sex, and so on, it is delinquency status and knowledge of the law that seem to have the greatest effects. Although sex alone is significantly correlated with legal reasoning, as we saw above, when looked at in combination with status and legal knowledge it becomes less of a factor.

Age, as we found before, is not significant at all here. This is again surprising because legal reasoning is considered to be a developmental concept. That means that it is a characteristic or attribute that supposedly changes and develops with age and maturity. As children advance developmentally, as they become more socialized—according to the theory—they are expected to reason at higher levels.

TABLE 8.2 Legal Developmental Level by Delinquency Status and Sex, with Age and Knowledge of the Law

	Mean	*F*
Status		
Non-delinquent	2.07	6.82**
Delinquent	1.94	
Sex		
Male	1.99	3.59
Female	2.10	
Age		1.35
KOL		9.25**

* $p < .05$
** $p < .01$
*** $p < .001$

150 Law and Deviance

TABLE 8.3 Status Correlates of Legal Reasoning (LDL)

	Age	Sex	KOL	Status
LDL	−.047	.187★★★	.149★★	−.208★★★
AGE		−.261★★★	.072	.559★★★
SEX			.036	−.508★★★
KOL				−.102★

★ p < .05
★★ p < .01
★★★ p < .001

Or at least they are expected to advance from a more prohibitive to a more prescriptive view of the law. The greater learning and experience of older children and youth are thought to increase the complexity of their cognitive processes. The latter in turn is supposed to lead them to think in a less self-centered, self-interested fashion, and more in terms of moral obligation and the larger moral good of society. Be that as it may, not only is age not significant with this sample, but there is even a slight negative correlation. It should be observed, however, that delinquency status here is highly correlated with both age and sex. This is because the official delinquents are all older males. They are also the ones who are reasoning at the lower levels. It may be that the younger school children simply have greater cognitive skills than do the older colony residents.

Given its prominent effects, we should look a little more closely at the knowledge of the law factor. This variable was defined by means of a 21-item test of legal knowledge. The items used a true/false/don't know response mode. These same items had been used in the ILVI-IV for the earlier American sample; and they were translated for use with only very slight alterations here. This test, unlike the country-specific versions of our 1987 knowledge of the law tests, contains generic, universally applicable items.

The test was graded as a test of legal knowledge. Results show one Russian youth getting a zero, and one getting the highest "grade," which was an 86 percent. The bulk of the scores were between 48 and 71 percent, with the mean being 55 and the mode 57 percent. Girls (57 percent) did slightly but not significantly better than boys (55 percent). Knowledge of the law is not associated with either sex or age in this sample. The young Russian females may think about the law in the abstract, in a more complex and sophisticated fashion than do their male counterparts, as witness their higher legal developmental level, but they do not necessarily know more about the law.

The finding regarding age is again an unexpected result in that it is generally assumed that knowledge about law and the legal system increases with age. For some reason, that is not the case with this population. The answer could again be that when the sample is treated as a whole, the delinquents are all older. It is also the delinquents who have less knowledge of the law, as reflected in the correlation matrix. That official delinquents would know less law than comparable non-delinquents may come as a surprise to some who believe that involvement with the juvenile and criminal justice systems is one source of legal knowledge. It may be—but in this case that is not demonstrated on a test of legal knowledge. Most important for our purposes is the fact that legal knowledge has a significant positive correlation with legal reasoning (.15; $p = .002$). It appears that, as legal socialization theory assumes, legal knowledge is a significant component of legal development—more knowledge is associated with higher-order and more complex reasoning. This has several possible implications. First, persons with greater cognitive skills, more complex thinkers, have relatively more knowledge of some substantive areas of knowledge, such as law. Second, again perhaps not unexpectedly, it suggests that you need to know something about something in order to reason about it. This is a kind of cultural literacy factor. Third, the finding offers some support as well for the kinds of law-related education initiatives described earlier, on the grounds that more information is associated with higher-order reasoning. Coupled with a finding that higher-level reasoning is associated with less deviant behavior, this result could offer some ammunition to those who support giving children training in the law.

In an effort to discern more how these status factors might be influencing legal development, we further manipulated (statistically) several of the factors. Because age is skewed, meaning not normally distributed here, as a result of the colony delinquents being mostly 16–17 years old, a logarithm of age was created to compensate for this. Making this correction does not alter the result that age is not significantly correlated with legal development. When this log of age is combined with sex to create an interaction term, however, that interaction term has a highly significant correlation with LDL (.19; $p = .001$). Thus, although age has no major independent effects upon legal reasoning, it does interact with sex to produce a significant effect. This is because the younger schoolboys reason at a higher level than the older institutionalized boys, whereas the older schoolgirls reason at a higher level than the younger schoolgirls.

We will now turn to look in more detail at what is arguably one of the most important items of interest in all of this, namely the connection between legal reasoning and delinquent behavior. We will not attempt global explanations of current Russian delinquency, but only consider the narrower issue of the role of legal development.

Reasoning and Behavior

A finding that Russian delinquents reason at a lower level than Russian non-delinquents is consistent with other research findings from studies of both moral and legal development (see, for example, Blasi, 1980; Sagi and Eisikovits, 1981). The theory of legal socialization seems to clearly assume there to be a connection

152 Law and Deviance

between a cognitive orientation that is self-centered, that views rules and laws pretty much in terms of the risks of getting caught versus the personal benefits of lawbreaking, and that does not view breaking the law as being particularly harmful, as being stimulative of a greater propensity to break rules and laws. Any number of theories of criminal behavior in fact also adopt the premises that offenders are generally self-centered, have little or no regard for their victims, and tend to regard the law as something to be gotten around. Thus, finding a linkage would not only lend support to the behavioral implications of legal and perhaps moral development as well. It would likewise very much fit with criminological theory.

The first indication of any relationship between legal reasoning and delinquency comes from the fact that the young delinquent males from the Russian juvenile correctional colony have a lower reasoning score than their counterparts, male as well as female, in the schools. Simply finding that a known population of delinquents reasons at a lower level than a population of youth who are ostensibly non-delinquent does not, however, allow one to conclude that lower legal reasoning *causes* juvenile delinquency. For many reasons—the representativeness of the samples, the mutual exclusiveness of the samples (meaning there are no delinquents in the non-delinquent sample), the definition and measurement of the reasoning and behavioral variables, the control of other factors that might affect both reasoning and behavior, and so on—one cannot reach any conclusions about causation from just this result.

As emphasized previously, there is a problem with defining delinquency and who is or is not a delinquent in a simple dichotomous fashion. The official status or label of "delinquent" is in part a measure of the criminal justice system's response to delinquent behavior rather than a measure of the behavior itself. This is just as true in Russia as it is in the United States and elsewhere. For many reasons, only some delinquents get caught and punished, and thus become officially labeled. This kind of artificial dichotomy also erroneously assumes that those in the schools are really "non-delinquent." Evidence from U.S. studies indicates that most juveniles commit delinquent acts during the course of their adolescence, and sometimes even earlier, for which they do not get arrested, much less incarcerated in a juvenile institution.

One way to deal with these definitional problems is to employ what is called a self-report measure of delinquency. We wanted to do this in the earlier Russian study in 1987, but our Soviet colleagues would not agree at that time to asking their youth about their behavior.

Given the various controversies about links (or lack of links) between legal reasoning and law-abiding behavior, let us begin to tackle this issue then by looking to see if there is any association; but this time doing so with an actual behavioral measure. When we do that, we find that reasoning level among the Russian youth is indeed negatively correlated with self-reported delinquent behavior. The behavior in this case is measured by the number of 28 possible

Law and Deviance **153**

delinquent acts reportedly engaged in by the Russian young people in the preceding 12 months. This we called a delinquency index.

The correlation coefficient between reasoning and behavior (–.20) is significant at the .001 level. It means that taking our sample as a whole, present-day Russian youth who reason at higher legal levels are less likely to report having engaged in deviant behaviors in the past 12 months, and vice versa. This finding not only supports the notion of there being a possible connection between legal reasoning and deviant behavior, but it also is in the direction predicted by legal socialization theory.

We must be cautious and immediately temper our enthusiasm in interpreting this result, however, because further examination, introducing other factors, demonstrates that legal reasoning is far from being the most powerful predictor of delinquent behavior in this sample. Table 8.4 in fact shows that when legal development (LDL) is introduced into a regression equation that examines the effects of a combination of factors upon the delinquency index, the influence of reasoning is sharply diminished. Considered along with age, sex, knowledge of the law, own law-abidingness, moral validity of the law, and fairness of the law (the latter three having been determined to be the attitude variables with the greatest independent effects and with minimal overlap or multicollinearity), legal reasoning is less important than age, sex, and own law-abidingness. The latter are significant predictors of the Russian youth's delinquent involvement, whereas legal level is not significant. The model as a whole, however, is very powerful, predicting 50 percent of the variance in the delinquency index. The power in this case is being exerted by the age and sex factors.

Overall, the delinquency index offers quite a range of potential involvement in delinquent acts. The acts themselves vary in seriousness from cheating on a

TABLE 8.4 Delinquency Index by Age, KOL, LDL, OLABIDE, MORALV, Sex, and LFAIR

	B	$Beta$	$T\ Ratio$
AGE	.850	.296	6.61★★★
KOL	–.032	–.063	–1.58
LDL	–1.469	–.061	–1.51
OLABIDE	3.477	.366	8.40★★★
MORALV	–.931	–.056	–1.32
SEX	–2.790	–.194	–4.46★★★
LFAIR	.980	.060	1.37

$R^2 = .50$; F = 47.63★★★
★ $p < .05$
★★ $p < .01$
★★★ $p < .001$

154 Law and Deviance

school test to using force to get money or things from people. Of the 425 Russian youth who responded, 35 indicated that they had done none of the 28 acts in the previous year. Twenty-one of the "real" non-delinquents were females. At the other end of the spectrum, two subjects (both residents of the juvenile colony) reported committing 27 of the 28 offenses. The average number of offenses was 7.8, but the mode was only two. As would be expected from other self-report studies on other national populations, the majority of the Russian youth reported doing only a few and only the more minor of the acts listed. The average number of offenses for the females was 3.3; for the "non-delinquent" males it was 6.2. For the official delinquents it was 13.12. This means that young Russian males, like young males elsewhere, are more deviant than young Russian females. It further suggests that the right juveniles are being incarcerated there. The distribution of offenses for the females was highly concentrated around none, one, and two, with one being the mode. The mode for the high school boys was seven. The Russian males here are much more delinquent than the females, and that is clearly and expectedly so in the case of those delinquent males who are in confinement. A second measure, called delinquency level, was also created out of the self-report data. Four delinquency levels were defined as (1) no offenses; (2) offenses unique to the status of being a juvenile (such as truancy, running away, drinking underage, etc.); (3) minor offenses (avoiding paying for movies, food, etc.); and (4) serious, felony-type offenses (such as hitting parents, selling hard drugs, and robbery). Unlike the index, which is a simpler indicator of the magnitude of delinquent involvement, level is an indicator of the nature and seriousness of deviancy. It takes account of the fact that seriously attacking someone or stealing a car is more serious than cheating on a school test or being drunk in a public place.

The correlation between legal developmental level and this delinquency level variable is again significant ($-.16$; $p = .003$). Higher-level reasoning is associated with less serious deviancy; lower-level reasoning is associated with more serious deviancy. This negative relationship duplicates but also extends that with the delinquency index. Delinquency level indicates that those Russian youth reasoning toward the pre-conventional end of the spectrum are more likely to report having committed more serious delinquent acts. Those in the conventional/post-conventional ranges, in contrast, are more likely to report no offenses or only status or more minor offenses.

Before concluding the chapter with an attempt to explain this behavior, let us deal briefly with the various attitudes and perceptions that were examined in the first study as well, and see how our contemporary Russians come out on these.

Status Factors as Determinants of Russian Attitudes

We need to consider attitudes for several reasons. First, because they are important ends of the legal socialization process in and of themselves. It is important to know what is the degree of respect and support for various legal institutions, and for the law itself. Attitudes are indicators of perceptions of legitimacy. They also tell us something about these Russian youths' fear of sanctions and their estimates of risk. Attitudes are also important because it may be, as Cohn and White suggested, that they are influential mediators between reasoning and behavior.

Attitudes are formed and taught by the legal culture and context (both formal and informal) in which one is socialized. Given the present environment of anomie and social distress in Russia, there is reason to suspect that this particular sociolegal environment has had especially strong effects upon the attitudes of Russian children and youth with respect to law and legality.

The before and after comparisons of Russian attitudes and reasoning will be examined in the next chapter. Suffice it to say here that there is reason to expect differences—perhaps considerable differences—in attitudes given the current legal environment. There is, however, less reason to expect substantial differences in legal reasoning. This is simply because LDL has been fairly stable from early adolescence on in all societies studied.

Moral Validity of the Law

We look first at a factor on which we found significant differences between the American and Soviet-Russian samples in the earlier study. You will recall that this factor—called belief in the moral validity of the law—is intended to capture perceptions of the essence, the rightness and goodness, of law. There are significant effects for sex and delinquency status on views of moral validity in the present Russian sample. Girls have a much higher mean score (3.50) than boys (3.30) overall, and over just the non-delinquent boys as well (3.36). The non-delinquents (males and females) have a higher mean score (3.43) than the colony delinquents (3.25).

A statistical technique called analysis of variance was used to examine the effects of all of the status variables on attitudes about moral validity. It shows that sex, delinquency status, and age are the main sources of variation in these attitudes, with legal reasoning only approaching statistical significance (Table 8.5). This means that LDL, which is significant in a simple pairwise correlation with moral validity, is not quite significant when looked at in simultaneous combination with other factors. Knowledge of the law is also not a significant source of variation. It is the Russian girls, the non-delinquents, and the younger children who have the greatest concerns about breaking the law, who would feel guilty, and so on.

Fairness of the Law

Fairness of judges and courts, police, and of punishments for breaking the law is the next attitude for consideration. Here again, sex, status, and age are significant, as well as knowledge of the law. Legal reasoning, however, again is not. Males (X = 3.94) are more likely to see Russian law and law enforcement as fair than

156 Law and Deviance

TABLE 8.5 Moral Validity by Sex and Delinquency Status, with KOL, Age, and LDL

	Mean	*F*
Sex		
Male	3.30	8.79**
Female	3.50	
Status		
Non-delinquent	3.43	4.55*
Delinquent	3.25	
KOL		.71
Age		21.55***
LDL		3.54

* p < .05
** p < .01
*** p < .001

are females (X = 3.69). This attitude about unfairness again may reflect a much more critical posture toward authority and toward the macro-level legal system by the Russian girls. The colony youth, as did the delinquents in the earlier study, have a higher regard for the law's fairness (X = 4.06) than do the non-delinquents (X = 3.74). Here as before, one could speculate that it may be their experience with the reality of the law that gives them a somewhat more sanguine view, as contrasted with the somewhat more abstract, hypothetical view that is more negative. Or, it could be that their simpler and more concrete reasoning about the law makes them less sensitive to some of its nuances, such as with regard to fairness, for example.

More knowledge correlates only slightly with more perceived fairness. Table 8.6 portrays the simultaneous effects of all of the status variables on perceptions of the fairness of law.

Efficacy of the Law

Law efficacy, how well the law works, is seen differently by sex and age, but not by status, knowledge of the law, or legal developmental level (Table 8.7). Young Russian males (X = 3.47) think the law and its enforcement work better than do young Russian females (X = 3.28); once more the opposing view for the latter. Older youth see the law as being more efficacious than do younger children. Although the result is not statistically significant, the colony youth think the law works better than do the school youth. The results here may be a product of the items that compose this variable. Three of the five items pertain to the likelihood of getting caught and punished if you do something wrong. If we assume that there is a greater likelihood that the males, the older youth, and the colony youth

Law and Deviance **157**

TABLE 8.6 Law Fairness by Sex and Delinquency Status, with KOL, Age, and LDL

	Mean	F
Sex		
Male	3.94	5.16*
Female	3.69	
Status		
Non-delinquent	3.74	31.46***
Delinquent	4.06	
KOL		7.18**
Age		21.27***
LDL		.38

* p < .05
** p < .01
*** p < .001

are the ones to have actually experienced the criminal justice process, then we can assume that this greater respect for effectiveness is a product of the reality of experience. Those Russian youth who have been caught and punished by the law enforcement system know for a fact that it can happen.

Law Operatives

Russian youth's attitudes toward officials (police and judges) in the criminal justice system are principally a function of whether they are male or female, how

TABLE 8.7 Law Efficacy by Sex and Delinquency Status, with KOL, Age, and LDL

	Mean	F
Sex		
Male	3.47	5.69*
Female	3.28	
Status		
Non-delinquent	3.34	2.48
Delinquent	3.51	
KOL		1.11
Age		21.39***
LDL		3.15

* p < .05
** p < .01
*** p < .001

158 Law and Deviance

TABLE 8.8 Law Operatives by Sex and Delinquency Status, with KOL, Age, and LDL

	Mean	*F*
Sex		
Male	3.39	6.36★★
Female	3.53	
Status		
Non-delinquent	3.45	.55
Delinquent	3.41	
KOL		6.31★★
Age		82.84★★★
LDL		2.36

★ p < .05
★★ p < .01
★★★ p < .001

much they know about the law, and how old they are. They do not seem to be much influenced by whether the youth are delinquents or non-delinquents, nor by their legal reasoning levels (see Table 8.8). In contrast to the previous results, females this time (X = 3.53) have a higher regard for these officials than do the males (X = 3.39); youth more knowledgeable about the law have a higher regard than less-knowledgeable youth; and younger children have a higher regard than older youth.

Wrongfulness of Behaviors

We saw earlier that legal reasoning was significantly correlated with views about the wrongfulness of certain deviant behaviors, with rationalizations for certain behaviors, and with concerns about parental reactions to stealing. Here we can examine the effects of legal reasoning in the context of the other status variables (see Table 8.9). It seems to be the case that each of the other status factors (sex, delinquency status, knowledge of the law, and age) has a significant effect upon these normative attitudes regarding wrongdoing. It is in fact only legal developmental level that has no significant effect. It is simply not powerful enough to compete with those other variables.

We might for a moment recall the results of the first Soviet study with regard to the young females in that sample. Looking at some of the tabulations for just the individual questionnaire items that the Soviets compiled, there are indications that those girls (especially the law-abiding girls) were rather negative in many respects. A similar kind of female skepticism has appeared in some of the current results as well. But contrary to those earlier Soviet results, our current Russian females make the most principled judgments about harm and wrongdoing, and to

TABLE 8.9 Wrongfulness of Behaviors by Sex and Delinquency Status, with KOL, Age, and LDL

	Mean	*F*
Sex		
Male	2.82	15.03★★★
Female	2.28	
Status		
Non-delinquent	2.41	56.26★★★
Delinquent	3.06	
KOL		7.72★★
Age		75.29★★★
LDL		.38

★ p < .05
★★ p < .01
★★★ p < .001

some extent about feelings of guilt as well (X = 2.28). These girls are the most likely of the subjects here to view the behaviors and the rationalizations as being wrong—and this is coupled with the fact that they also have the highest legal reasoning. The "official" delinquents in the colony, in contrast, view the behaviors as less wrong than does the school sample (both male and female). And they have the lowest legal reasoning.

Own Law-Abidingness

This variable cluster is intended to measure perceptions of others' views of one's own law-abidingness. The others in this case include parents, teachers, and peers. Our youthful Russian subjects were asked whether each of these groups of authority figures would view them as being a bad kid, as breaking the rules, as getting into trouble, and as doing things that are against the law. The girls and the non-delinquents think that others tend to see them as being law-abiding. As evident in Table 8.10, it is only sex and delinquency status that are significant sources of variation in this perception.

Authority Figures

Parents

As before, the Russian youth were asked about respecting and caring about their parents, along with how their parents saw their law-abidingness. Sex and delinquency status again are significant sources of variation here. Girls have the

160 Law and Deviance

TABLE 8.10 Own Law-Abidingness by Sex and Delinquency Status, with KOL, Age, and LDL

	Mean	F
Sex		
Male	2.85	7.76**
Female	2.31	
Status		
Non-delinquent	2.41	55.29***
Delinquent	3.15	
KOL		.21
Age		.22
LDL		.003

* p < .05
** p < .01
*** p < .001

lowest mean score (X = 2.90), schoolboys are next (X = 3.07), and the colony residents have the highest (X = 3.45). This means that the latter have the most positive orientation toward their parents. The more negative view of their parents is a combination of rejection of authority and a sort of general disillusionment with the way the system is working that seems to persist among the Russian girls.

Peers

Peers as authority figures should be regarded as being in a different class than parents and teachers. Responsiveness to the adult authority figures has certain implications about the sources of influence and direction upon a youngster. Responsiveness to peers has rather different implications. The only significant source of variation in perceptions of peers among the Russian youngsters is delinquency status. The colony sample (X = 3.25) has a more positive orientation toward peers than does the non-delinquent school sample (X = 3.00) (see Table 8.11). The females (again rejecting authority) have the least respect and regard for the influence of peers. It is of interest to note that the items comprising this variable cluster include such things as a desire to be popular with friends, being concerned about how your friends see you, being concerned if you broke your friends' rules, and possibly having to beat up people in order to have your friends like you. The fact that the Russian delinquents are more likely to be peer-oriented than the non-delinquents is a finding very much consistent with a number of delinquency theories. That the delinquents are more concerned about their peers, and would be more responsive to peer pressures is possibly one explanation of their delinquency.

TABLE 8.11 Peers by Sex and Delinquency Status, with KOL, Age, and LDL

	Mean	F
Sex		
Male	3.14	.18
Female	2.99	
Status		
Non-delinquent	3.00	17.90★★★
Delinquent	3.25	
KOL		.02
Age		.99
LDL		1.28

★ $p < .05$
★★ $p < .01$
★★★ $p < .001$

Teacher

Finally, we come back to the view of teachers. Reference was made earlier to the negative views of teachers held by the young Russian females. This is reflected in their having the lowest mean score on the items measuring perceptions of teachers ($X = 2.78$). These girls' views of teachers are even more negative than their views of either parents or peers. On the other side, the resident males in the juvenile colony have relatively more positive views of teachers ($X = 3.40$). Neither age, knowledge of the law, nor legal developmental level is a significant source of variation in these perceptions (Table 8.12). We can conclude that the Russian females are the least oriented toward and the least responsive to all three authority groups. The delinquents, in contrast, are the most oriented and responsive in all three cases.

Explaining Delinquency

Reference was made earlier in this chapter to the significant relationships between legal developmental level and the delinquency index, and between LDL and delinquency level. The correlation matrix (Table 8.13) shows both the index of involvement in delinquency, and the nature and seriousness of that involvement to be strongly associated with each of legal developmental level, sex, the age/sex interaction term referred to earlier, and the log of age.

We can further explore what factors are explaining the delinquency index by using various multivariate analytic techniques. Table 8.14 shows that when legal developmental level is entered into a regression equation along with age, knowledge of the law, and an interaction term composed of status and knowledge

TABLE 8.12 Teachers by Sex and Delinquency Status, with KOL, Age, and LDL

	Mean	F
Sex		
Male	3.19	8.01**
Female	2.78	
Status		
Non-delinquent	2.87	43.96***
Delinquent	3.40	
KOL		.01
Age		.36
LDL		.25

* p < .05
** p < .01
*** p < .001

TABLE 8.13 Status Correlates of Delinquent Behavior

	Sex	AGESEX	Age	DLLEVEL	DLINDEX
LDL	.1873***	.1941***	−.0387	−.1560**	−.2002***
SEX		.9797***	−.2860***	−.4394***	−.4587***
AGESEX			−.0992*	−.3576***	−.3881***
AGE				.4685***	.4882***
DLLEVEL					.7191***

* p < .05
** p < .01
*** p < .001

TABLE 8.14 Delinquency Index by LDL, Age, KOL, and Status/KOL

	B	Beta	T Ratio
LDL	−2.061	−.085	−2.04*
AGE	.853	.297	6.50***
KOL	−.085	−.167	−4.02***
STATUS/KOL	.284	.418	8.85***

R^2 = .41; F = 63.35***
* p < .05
** p < .01
*** p < .001

TABLE 8.15 Delinquency Index by Sex, KOL, LDL, and Age

	B	Beta	T Ratio
SEX	−4.517	−.314	−7.09★★★
KOL	−.039	−.076	−1.81
LDL	−2.694	−.111	−2.61★★
AGE	1.138	.396	9.10★★★

R^2 = .37; F = 53.59★★★
★ p < .05
★★ p < .01
★★★ p < .001

of the law, LDL is a statistically significant source of variation in the delinquency index. It should be noted, nevertheless, that each of the other variables is a more powerful predictor of amount of involvement in delinquent acts. The entire statistical model composed of these particular variables explains 40 percent of the variance in delinquency involvement. If we adjust the variables entered into the equation, and use legal developmental level along with sex, knowledge of the law, and age, LDL is again a significant predictor, although once more not as powerful as sex and age (see Table 8.15).

Finally, employing a logistic probability model, using age, sex, knowledge of the law, own law-abidingness, law fairness, moral validity, and LDL in a statistical model to predict the allocation of the Russian subjects among the four different levels of delinquency, produces the result illustrated in Table 8.16. The model does pretty well in predicting which cases will be more minor criminal offenders

TABLE 8.16 Predicting Seriousness of Delinquency

Levels of Delinquewncy					
	None	Status Offenses	Minor Criminality	Major Criminality	Actual Totals
None	3	0	22	5	30
Status Offenses	2	0	25	2	29
Minor Criminality	4	0	106	30	140
Major Criminality	1	0	28	101	130
Predicted Totals	10	0	181	138	329

x^2 = 167.16★★★
This model uses Age, Sex, KOL, LDL, OLABIDE, LFAIR, and MORALV to predict into which delinquency level the Russian youth will fall.
★ p < .05
★★ p < .01
★★★ p < .001

164 Law and Deviance

and more serious offenders (categories 2 and 3). It does rather poorly in predicting no offenses (category 0) and only juvenile status offenses (category 1). Age, sex, and own law-abidingness are powerful predictors in this model, perceptions of law fairness and moral validity have no power, and legal developmental level has only moderate power, but nevertheless an influence.

We can conclude from this that the universally powerful factors of age and sex exert their influence when it comes to understanding and explaining delinquency in the former Soviet Union as well. The degree of involvement in delinquency by Russian girls is like the degree of involvement in delinquency by girls anywhere else—low. Boys commit more and more serious deviant acts. Similarly, older Russian youth are more delinquent than their younger counterparts.

Legal reasoning obviously does not compete with these factors. Nevertheless, there is reason from these Russian data to believe that legal reasoning/legal development is very much related to behavior. The findings do not challenge outright the principal conclusions of those who argue to the contrary, but they do open the door to the possibilities of a connection.

Cohn and White (1990) looked at legal socialization among university students. That study was the most recent prior empirical work on legal social-ization and hence a good benchmark. They found no relationship between legal developmental level and whether a student was a rule-follower or a rule-violator. Given that finding, they concluded that it is not the case that people at lower levels of reasoning are more inclined to violate rules than are people at higher levels of reasoning. Cohn and White concluded that the frequency of engaging in rule-violating behaviors could *not* be predicted by legal develop-mental level. "We believe," they wrote, "this finding is significant because it tends to undercut the developmental import of legal development theory (Cohn and White, 1990: 150). These current Russian data, on the contrary, clearly demon-strate support for the role of legal development in influencing delinquency. The Russian youth at lower, more pre-conventional legal developmental levels are more inclined to violate the law—and to commit more serious violations—than are the youth at the higher legal levels.

The most dramatic contrast in this is between the delinquent males and the non-delinquent females. I hasten to add that I am not claiming that it is legal reasoning that explains the behavior differences between the two. What I am arguing is that the girls reflect a pattern in which their higher-order reasoning, which we can assume is associated with more sophisticated cognitive abilities, is coupled with more independent thinking, more self-direction, and less dependence upon either adult or peer influences. This pattern is consistent with one of the arguments made by Kohlberg and his followers about the relationship of moral reasoning and behavior, to wit: "Higher reasoning makes one a more reliable moral agent and thus better able to withstand some incentives to illegal conduct" (Jennings et al., 1983: 311). The Russian females would appear to be more reliable moral agents.

Law and Deviance **165**

The colony residents stand in diametric opposition. They are more pre-conventional legal thinkers, are much more reactive to authorities (especially their peers), and they have a much more accepting view that the law and law enforcement work to provide control and deterrence. Just as they do not explain the male/female differences, these contrasting images also do not permit us to conclude that legal reasoning causes either law-abiding or law-violating behavior, but they certainly do encourage the conclusion that such reasoning is a vital part of the mix that explains that behavior.

Note

1 The Soviet Union was made up of a tremendously diverse collection of nationalities. Besides the 14 non-Russian republics that became independent in 1991, Russia itself has numerous nationalities. These include the Tatars, Chechens, Bashkirs, Yakuts, and literally hundreds of others.

9

THREE PERSPECTIVES: AMERICAN, SOVIET, AND RUSSIAN

In the last two chapters, we have considered in some detail the comparative differences in perspectives on law and deviance between American and Soviet youth, circa 1987 and 1988; then we took a look at the more recent views of Russian youth on these same issues. Now we want to in effect combine those three perspectives, and take up as our final major topic comparisons before and after the fall of the Soviet Union. Because we do not have information on actual deviance for the two earlier samples, our three-way comparisons will focus on legal knowledge and legal reasoning, and on attitudes about law and its enforcement.

So what should we expect to find out of all of this? There have been some pretty dramatic shifts in the sociolegal environment in the former Soviet Union since the beginning of 1992—actually beginning with the August coup of 1991. As of the late fall of 1992, when the last data were collected, Russia was an independent country with its first democratically elected president. The all-powerful Communist Party was gone, as was the heavy hand of the totalitarian state. Freedom and independence of thought and communication and action were in ascendance, and centralized authoritarian control had decreased to some degree. A Constitutional Court, with more authority than any previous Soviet court, had been created. A new constitution to limit the powers of government and protect the rights of the people was being drafted and discussed.

Along with all of these pluses, however, were a not inconsiderable number of minuses. These included first and foremost the economic woes that severely undermined the standard of living for most Russian citizens. Monetary inflation and the steeply declining value of the ruble put the cost of many goods and services out of the reach of ordinary people. There were many more things for sale on the market, but only for hard currency. This was causing a great deal of resentment.

Continuing power struggles between the president and the legislature—with the Constitutional Court often in the middle—and continuing ethnic unrest were also sources of instability.

Additional negatives included the continued spiraling-up of crime, which had begun under Gorbachev—especially including organized crime and profiteering. President Yeltsin called organized crime the most serious domestic problem facing Russia. There was no longer just the "main" Soviet mafia to worry about. Now there were numerous "mafias" engaged in exploitation and extortion. There was likewise the disorder and the incivility represented by increased drug-dealing, prostitution, pornography, and the increases in the numbers of street people—youth gangs, runaways, the homeless, former members of the military, and so on. The vast array of social problems that had come into the public consciousness in the late 1980s became even more evident and more pressing. All of this was very hard to take for a populace that had long been accustomed to order and control.

There certainly seem to be good reasons to assume that these various developments—both beneficial and destructive—would weigh heavily on the perceptions that Russian youth would have of the efficacy of law enforcement, of the officials charged with enforcing the law, and of the fairness of the law and the legal system. It is equally plausible that such developments would also influence how youth would view the moral underpinnings of the law and its enforcement, as well as their normative judgments about what is normal and what is deviant. It thus follows that one would be led to expect rather considerable differences in the views of law and deviance between 1987 and 1992.

Having said that, there is, on the other hand, basis for an argument that one should really anticipate little if any change in legal attitudes and perceptions in the Russia of 1992 as compared to the Soviet Russia of 1987. This is because the various changes that have taken place in Russia have been mostly at the macro-level of the sociolegal environment. At the same time, the informal micro-level structures of rules and rule enforcement within the various collectives in which Russian children are principally being socialized have changed relatively little. If our previous conjecture about what our data seem to show is on target, and if, as some argue, the micro-level is really more consequential than the macro-level in shaping reasoning and attitudes (and perhaps behavior as well), then the absence of fundamental change in Russian child development and socialization may loom very large in explaining our findings.

The question of attitudes aside, there is likewise no reason to expect that the legal developmental levels of Russian youth will look much different in 1992 than they did in 1987. This is because of the inherent stability of legal reasoning and its universality across cultures. That leaves knowledge of the law. But here too there are few grounds for believing that such knowledge will have either gone up or down markedly during this period. There have been changes in the school curricula. There is no longer any mandatory study of the fundamental principles of Soviet law; but law and law-related subjects are still required.

168 Three Perspectives

The consequence of the foregoing seems to be tantamount to being prepared to accept the null hypothesis. But let us see.

Legal Knowledge and Legal Development

The findings in Chapter 7 showed that overall the 144 Soviet youth from Moscow schools and from the Redistribution Center knew more about law and its enforcement than the 144 American youth from Minneapolis schools and from various facilities for juvenile delinquents in New Jersey and Pennsylvania. This despite our belief that the Soviet test of legal knowledge was more difficult than the American one. The average score for the U.S. was only 43 percent. For the Soviet youth, the average score was 57 percent.

In order to correct for the earlier incomparability between the two tests of knowledge of the law, the true/false, "culture-free" test that had been used in the U.S. was translated with some modifications into Russian for administration in Moscow in 1992. Our 425 Russian youth, again from Moscow schools, and from a colony for juvenile offenders, scored an average of 55 percent on that test, with a standard deviation of 13 percent. This average is again significantly higher than the American average. It is not, however, significantly different from the Soviet mean score of five years earlier. Without claiming that any of the three samples are representative samples, nor that the results are generalizable across the two countries, we can nevertheless conclude that over two testing cycles, two groups of Russian young people demonstrated a significantly greater knowledge of law than did American youth. This may say something about the emphasis given to law-related education in the schools in the former Soviet Union, and the comparable lack of such emphasis in U.S. schools. Given that providing legal knowledge is one of the strategies for the socialization of children into the legal system, the results indicate that the Russians have been doing a better job at this than we have been in the United States.

Turning to legal developmental level, the average developmental scores place each of the three samples in the conventional range. The 1987 Soviet youth are slightly higher; followed by the 1992 Russians, and then the Americans. The latter are only slightly lower, and the statistical differences here are not significant. What is interesting, however, is that the ordering is the same as for the knowledge of the law scores. It is also the case that the Soviet youth achieved both the highest legal levels and the highest legal knowledge scores despite having the most complex and difficult assessments in both areas. By comparison, the American youth's legal knowledge and legal reasoning both suffer. We can further examine legal reasoning by looking at the range and distribution of legal developmental levels for each of the three groups.

For the U.S., the lowest legal developmental level was a score of 1.36, and the highest was a 2.45. For the Soviets the range is .22 to 2.89; for the Russians it is .09 to 2.73. The range of deviations among both the Soviets and the Russians

Three Perspectives **169**

TABLE 9.1 Comparative Legal Socialization Levels

	Pre-conventional	Conventional	Post-conventional
United States	5.8%	86.9%	7.3%
Soviet Union	10.4%	75.4%	14.1%
Russia	9.6%	76.3%	14.2%

indicates that they are much more heterogeneous than the Americans in their legal reasoning. Using the mean and standard deviation for the combined samples (1.94 and .42) to develop rough cutting points to divide the samples into pre-conventional, conventional, and post-conventional reasoners produces the results shown in Table 9.1.

Several things strike one about these figures. One is the fact that the conventional reasoning category is the dominant grouping, by far, for all three samples. Second, the American youth are nevertheless more heavily represented in the conventional category and consequently comprise a smaller proportion of both the pre-conventional and the post-conventional developmental levels. The third observation to be made has to do with the remarkable similarity in the distribution patterns for both the Soviet and the Russian youth. Stability of legal reasoning across legal contexts (albeit very different legal contexts), and across changes in sociolegal environments is clearly demonstrated by these findings.

Comparing Attitudes toward Law and Justice

If one compares the correlations among the various attitudinal indicators for the Americans and the Soviets (shown in Chapter 7) with those for the Russians in Chapter 8, one will find some remarkable differences. The same is true when one looks at an analysis of the variance in these attitudes by country—United States, Soviet Union, and Russia. We will begin with law fairness.

Law Fairness

The across-country and across-time differences in attitudes about the fairness of the law and of the criminal justice system are all highly significant (F = 154.96; p < .001). American youth had the poorest sense of fairness—significantly lower than that of either the Soviet youth or the later Russian youth. The Soviet youngsters in turn had a significantly lower regard for fairness than did the ex-Soviet Russians.

Why do young people in the United States have a relatively poor regard for the law's fairness? Perhaps because they have a heightened awareness of and sensitivity to the discrimination that goes on in the American criminal justice

170 Three Perspectives

process? And perhaps this is coupled with a lesser awareness by their Soviet/ Russian counterparts of their own unfair discrimination?

Looking at things from the other direction, how to explain why the latter have the relatively affirmative view of law fairness that they have? One possibility is suggested in the writings by Berman, Rigby, Smith, and others. It could be that the peculiarly paternal nature of Soviet law gave it a certain added aura of legitimacy. If so, that characteristic would have helped to instill respect and to encourage acceptance of Soviet law and the legal system. This aura and the ideology surrounding it, in turn, has been conveyed rather effectively to Soviet youth through the heavy emphasis upon law-related education in the schools. We have empirical evidence of the success of the system's emphasis upon legal education.

The children who were the passive recipients of this educational indoctrination would have had little direct experience or personal involvement with the law. Thus, a combination of (1) focused law-related education, as well as aggressive public relations and propagandizing; (2) pre-glasnost suppression of information about the illegalities and law violations committed by the Soviet regime; and (3) an absence of direct personal knowledge and experience would have given school students small basis for challenging the favorable information and image being presented to them.

Another possible line of explanation involves those youth who did have direct contact with Soviet law enforcement (and perhaps those young people who knew personally youth who had had such contact as well). It is likely that such experiences would not have been perceived as being unduly harsh or unfair. The Soviet system for handling juvenile offenders was, after all, not especially punitive. It was with adult "criminals" accused of political crimes that the legal system engaged in its greatest departures from due process and the rule of law. Although some youthful offenders were committed to juvenile colonies, most of them were dealt with rather leniently in their communities. That too could have helped instill in them a certain sense of fairness. The perceptions of the Russian delinquents can be interpreted as supporting that conclusion.

A third possibility, which might have worked in conjunction with the first two, is that there is a kind of carry-over effect coming from the micro-level legal context. If the rules and the rule enforcement emanating from the youth's collectives are seen to be generally fair, that should have considerable influence in shaping their attitudes about the law in general. It would certainly have been the case that their experiences at the primary level would have been much more direct, personal, and pertinent to them.

Finally, there is of course the possibility, as was raised by our Soviet colleagues, that what we are witnessing here may be a kind of idealized response set. The youth in the 1987–88 survey in particular may have given what they thought were the expected answers, playing it safe and putting on their public faces. The fact that I have referred to this possibility several times in evaluating the responses of the

Soviet youth does not mean that lying is not also a possibility with both the American and the Russian youth as well. The differences are that the Soviet researchers themselves clearly thought that this was a possibility with the 1987 group, and it is that group that would have the greatest motivation of the three to distort their answers.

But what about the Russian youth's particularly positive views? Could these not also be attributed to a kind of idealized portrait? This possibility cannot be dismissed because the colony youth made the most glowing appraisals. But at the same time, in order to minimize any response bias, the teacher and the law professor who worked with me were fully versed on the scientific methods to be followed. The procedures for administering the surveys insured that no one in authority over the subjects was involved. The participants were all volunteers. They were all assured anonymity. I am as confident as one can be under the circumstances that the views reported are not dishonest. An alternative explanation is that the hopeful views were outcomes of improvements in the macro-sociolegal context in the former Soviet Union. Before we move too far down the road of that interpretation, however, we should look at the other attitudes to see if there are any consistent patterns.

Law Efficacy/Law Operatives

The analysis of variance in perceptions of law efficacy by country is significant (F = 19.35; p < .001). All the difference here is accounted for by the Russians, who differ significantly from both the Americans and their Soviet predecessors. Russian youth (mainly the delinquents) have a greater estimate of the efficacy of law enforcement than do the others. The delinquents believe that the law works—perhaps because they know it works.

Regarding perceptions of the police and judges, the by-country differences here again are highly significant (F = 14.20; p = < .001). But this time the Soviet and Russian youth are together in their greater regard for the law operatives, whereas the American youth are significantly lower.

Moral Validity

Looking at the three samples, we find important differences between them in how perceptions of the moral validity of the law are associated with each of the other attitude variables. Table 9.2 shows each of the correlation coefficients for each variable for each sample of youth. Two of these relationships seem to call for discussion—own law-abidingness and wrongfulness of behaviors.

Among the Minnesota and New Jersey and Pennsylvania youth there was no significant correlation between their sense of the law's moral validity and how they thought others saw them. Among the Moscow youth who made up the 1987 Soviet group, those who had the greater regard for the moral validity of law were

TABLE 9.2 American, Soviet, and Russian Attitudinal Correlates of Moral Validity

	XLFAIR	XLEFF	XLOPS	XWRNGBS	XPARENT	XPEER	XPEER6	XOLABID	XTEACHE
Moral Validity									
US	.1096	.1483	.3631★★★	.0886	.2886★★★	.2020★	−.0596	.0989	.1414
USSR	.2991★★★	.2598★★	.5023★★★	.4414★★★	.4613★★★	.2999★★★	−.0737	.1903★	.1292
Russia	−.1351★★	−.1517★★	.5467★★★	−.4414★★★	−.2584★★★	−.0876	−.0200	−.3099★★★	−.3590★★★

★ p < .05
★★ p < .01
★★★ p < .001

Three Perspectives **173**

also more likely to believe that others saw them as being troublemakers and delinquents. The earlier explanations that I offered for this seemingly odd result focused on varying definitions of the terms "bad" and "trouble"; and on the possibilities that there was a greater sensitivity to the views of others among the Soviets, and maybe greater feelings of guilt.

Now we come to the new generation of Russian youth. They see things differently from either of their American or their Soviet antecedents. Those who would be bothered by breaking the law, who see harm in lawbreaking, who view rules as being more important than popularity, and so on, are also more likely to believe that their parents, teachers, and peers regard them as being law-abiding. This result is the most fitting and consistent of the three in terms of theory.

Moving on, the next results help us to get at the essence of the differences among these three groups of young people. Among the Americans, there is apparently no connection between their views about the moral validity of the law and its enforcement, and their normative judgments about the harm in committing certain deviant acts. Conversely, among the Russian youth there was very much such a connection. Those with the greater sense of moral validity (especially the Russian females) were more likely to see harm, which makes sense conceptually. But then there are the Soviet youth. The highly significant correlation between moral validity and wrongfulness of behaviors among the Soviet Russians suggests that those with the greatest moral sensitivity regarding law were the least likely to see harm in such acts as stealing and damaging property, or smoking, drinking, and cheating in school. The latter could be taken as evidence of the kind of moral weightlessness, necessary criminality, and the rationalization of deviance discussed earlier. When these Soviet youth were asked to judge how wrong it would be for someone their age to do certain things, and whether certain victims deserved their victimization, they were being asked to make normative judgments. Making such judgments under "normal" conditions is one thing, but making them in a kind of culture of deviance is quite another. The Soviet youth were responding under conditions of normative deviance. Their relatively strong sense of the moral validity of the law did not lead them to see harm in everyday acts of deviance—which had become normalized. Given that many of the pre-existing rules to guide judgments about what is normal and what is abnormal or deviant in Russia are now off, the latest result seems to be a certain correction of this aberration.

Once more, the across-country differences here are highly significant. The across-time differences in the former Soviet Union, on the other hand, are not significant. Soviet youth had the highest regard for the moral validity of the law; both Soviets and Russians are significantly higher than the Americans, but do not differ significantly from each other ($F = 51.61$; $p < .001$).

In a sense, the findings with regard to moral validity go to the heart of our research. Certainly differences in beliefs in the moral validity of the law would be expected—given the differences in the legal foundations and legal histories of our

174 Three Perspectives

two countries. And we do have differences—significant differences, it is just that they are not in the direction that might be expected given the history of Soviet law and justice.

The micro-level sociolegal context—the collectives' influence—again could be one plausible explanation for this result. The main characteristics of the legal environment that bear on legal socialization are fair enforcement of laws and rules, the role of authority, and the legitimacy of both the rules themselves and the promulgators of the rules. We already know that Soviet and Russian youth (taken together) tend, more so than the American youth, to think that their legal system is fair, and also that they accord greater respect to the power and influence of certain authority figures. That leaves legitimacy. Beyond the education and indoctrination effects, I think that a principal element of the belief in legitimacy accrues from involvement in making rules and enforcing rules at school, for example; and that this sense of legitimacy is then generalized from the micro-level to the macro-level.

American youth would of course have had many of these same experiences of rule-making and enforcement in their primary groups. As with both the Soviet and the Russian youth, they too would have much less direct experience (as a source of information) with the formal legal system. The difference, or *a* difference, is that the Americans would have been exposed to much more material (especially critical and negative information) about the American legal system practices than the Soviets were. Even the 1992 group would have experienced the same kinds of information restrictions as did their Soviet predecessors during most of their school years.

What we may be seeing here, therefore, is empirical evidence among the Soviet youth especially, not so much of an informed acquiescence in and a commitment to the laws made by the old Soviet regime, but rather an acceptance and commitment to the rule environment made up of the various primary groups in which these youth were socialized. Assuming the truthfulness of their responses, the fact that these young people were socialized under a cynical and duplicitous formal legal system that operated outside the rule of law does not seem to have retarded their legal reasoning nor their sense of the purpose of law. The best accounting for that lack of effect rests in the overarching power of the Soviet collective (and over and above that in the communal nature of Russian society) in shaping legal socialization. These youth did not know for a certainty and from personal experience that the legal system was unlawful and corrupt, but the informal systems (the collectives) that they did know were none of these things.

Authority Figures

Teachers

The across-country differences in attitudes toward teachers are highly significant ($F = 12.64$; $p < .001$). The Soviets were the most positive, followed by the

Russians, and then the Americans—all differences being statistically significant. The Soviet youth support Bronfenbrenner's view that there was a generally positive attitude on the part of Soviet children, "and indeed the entire society, toward teachers of the young. This positive orientation is maintained throughout the school years. The teacher is generally regarded and treated as a friend" (Bronfenbrenner, 1970: 23). But that may not be so true anymore! The findings here do illustrate yet again the earlier point about the contrasting views of Americans, Soviets, and now Russians toward authority figures. But they also intimate a possible shift in views toward authority and authority figures in the former Soviet Union. The Russians, for better or worse, may be coming to look more like Americans in this respect.

Parents

Views of parents and teachers were not correlated in either of the two earlier samples; but in the latest sample there is a very strong positive correlation between the perceptions of these two authority figures. Negative views of teachers go together with negative views of their parents among the Russians. The by-country differences in the youth's views of their parents are again significant ($F = 27.74$; $p < .001$).

Peers

With regard to peers, the earlier Soviet youth were significantly more peer-oriented than were either the Americans or now the Russians ($F = 11.77$; $p < .001$). The perceptions of the latter two groups do not differ significantly. As was the case with both teachers and parents, the Russian young people are less attuned to an authority figure than were the Soviet youth before them. Put together, these three results (or at least the first two) show evidence of a possible breakdown of the old, traditional respect for authority in the former Soviet Russia. Teachers and parents are not now seen with the respect and deference that they were seen before. But the slack has seemingly not been taken up by a greater tie to the peer group. All three sources of authority are being rejected, mostly and particularly by the Russian girls.

Own Law-Abidingness

Some fascinating results come from the by-country analyses. Keeping in mind that own law-abidingness was originally intended to be a surrogate for real behavior, we again find statistically significant differences across time and across country ($F = 57.82$; $p < .001$). Today's Russian youth regard themselves as being the most law-abiding in the eyes of others. They are followed by the Soviet youth and then the Americans. The latter two do not differ significantly from each other.

176 Three Perspectives

Putting these results together with the earlier ones, and before going to our last comparison, we can discern some clear and consistent patterns in the responses of the Russian young people that distance them from the 1987 group and from the young Americans. In addition to the shifts in views concerning authorities that I already remarked on, the 1992 sample has the most positive attitudes toward the fairness and the efficacy of law, and toward legal operatives. They see themselves as being the most law-abiding. And as with their Soviet forerunners, they have a high regard for the moral validity of the law. Taken together, and excepting the argument about the possible loss of respect for authority being a problem, these results present a rather more optimistic picture than one might have been led to expect from the contemporary media coverage of events in Russia.

What is Deviance?

With respect to measures of attitudes toward macro-level legal environmental factors, the Russian juveniles as a whole are consistently most favorable. With respect to micro-level factors—parents, peers, and teachers—they are considerably (but nevertheless consistently) less favorable. Consonant with my objective stated at the beginning of the book that I would be emphasizing the Soviet and Russian pictures here, I will do the same in the matter of normative judgments of deviancy.

As with each of the previous attitudes, there are statistically significant by-country differences on these normative judgments ($F = 125.02$; $p < .001$). All of the significant difference in this case is being accounted for by the views of the Russian youth. They have a much higher estimate of or regard for the wrong, for the harm, entailed in these behaviors. In this respect, they look very different from their predecessors of just a few years before. Let me add that the Soviets were somewhat higher in their assessments of wrongfulness than the American youth of 1987, but not significantly so. Thus we will focus on the Soviet and Russian contrast.

The minimization of harm or rationalization of deviance is illustrated most clearly among the Soviet females. Their views in particular suggest that there is merit to the observations by Shipler and others (made in the old Soviet context) regarding the presence of a kind of moral ambiguity in the former USSR. The girls in the 1987 group were less apt to recognize the inherent wrong in doing certain things. A possible consequence of the undercurrent of anomalies that this seems to present could be a considerable reliance upon the kind of justification, neutralization, and rationalization of deviant behavior raised earlier, and discussed particularly by Yakovlev (1988).

Russian colleagues and university students in Moscow with whom I have discussed this finding explain it by observing that there were so many restrictions in the old Soviet Union that one had to violate them in order to live. One had

Three Perspectives   **177**

to buy on the black market. One had to use *"blat"* or deal *"na levo"* in order to get an apartment, to get into university, to get a car, to go abroad, and so on. Segal for one summed up this phenomenon when he wrote: "[m]illions of people, practically all the Soviet adult population, continue to violate the law in one way of another" (Segal, 1990: 277). If so, it would follow that particular deviant acts might not be viewed as being all that harmful.

Previously we considered what Rosner (1986) and others, such as Simis (1982), characterized as the amoral situation regarding the law in the USSR. These writers attributed this amorality to the widespread shortages on the legal market. Rosner, in particular, said that crime was an essential ingredient of the way of life of nearly all Soviet citizens. They nearly all became "necessary criminals," she believed. Both Simis and Rosner pointed out the moral dilemmas and double standards that were consequently operating in Soviet society. The result of honesty was deprivation, not only for oneself but for one's family as well. Citing Simis in part, Rosner wrote:

> He [Simis] believes that Soviet citizens are no better and no worse in terms of personal morality than those from elsewhere . . . However . . . Soviet citizens are aware of the fact that there is a dual system in operation in the USSR . . . the quality of Soviet crime is such that the normative boundaries—which need to be maintained for the preservation of order in a society—have broken down. Corruption, secrecy, and theft are now very much a part of the daily life of the Soviet citizen. The ordinary citizen of the USSR is quite aware that the norms vocalized by society are far different from the norms adhered to by that same society.
>
> [O]rdinary citizens in the USSR know that to be honest and truthful, not to participate in the underground economy, and to avoid involvement in the system of corruption, is to create a situation tantamount to total deprivation of both goods and services. They exist in a moral standard that permits morality in private dealings with members of primary groups while excluding morality in dealings with members of secondary groups.
>
> *Rosner, 1986: 38*

The dual moral standard mentioned by Rosner speaks also to the contrast we have drawn between the micro- and macro-level legal contexts. Especially the Soviet females in our study may be reflecting the kind of schizoid environment that existed in the closing days of the USSR—and to some extent are present still. They recognized and accepted the need for rules and enforcement, and also for law and order in the abstract. At the same time, they may have had to routinely condone numerous law violations because other circumstances (the need for basic goods and services) required it. Economic conditions demanded that people commit deviant acts. Everyone did it. The "crimes" were often seen as acts against the state, not against "real" victims. The fact that the legal reasoning of both the

178 Three Perspectives

Soviet and the Russian youth (especially the females) is in the upper ranges of the conventional level would seem to especially require them to reconcile and justify deviant acts. One way of doing that, of course, would be to deny or at least downplay the harm done by particular acts. Why is the same sort of normalized deviance not reflected in the normative judgments of the later Russian young people? After all, they were socialized pretty much under the same conditions. I think the answer lies in the shifts in the ideological climate that have taken place in Russia. As bad as many things are today in Russia (including crime and corruption), there is less of a sense of the kind of self-justifying ideology of neutralization and rationalization for breaking the law. There is developing a sense of a new equilibrium between individuals and their legal environment. The old equilibrium had remained pretty much static for three-quarters of a century. There were informal norms and rules governing what was permissible and what was not permissible. For example, as just mentioned, stealing from the state or from one's workplace was permissible, whereas stealing from individuals was not. Stealing from the state is no longer seen to be OK by most Russians. Now, beginning in 1992, the equilibrium has been upset; the normative climate has been altered, but it has very obviously not yet settled down.

We are fortunate to have information on the actual amount of participation in deviant acts by our young Russians. Accordingly, we can look at the relationship between their normative judgments of deviance and their doing deviant things. Analyzing views of wrongfulness by delinquency levels (none, status offenses, minor offenses, and felony offenses), sex, and age produces the results shown in Table 9.3. Both delinquency level and sex are significant sources of variation. Even though the females report the lower delinquency levels, there is not a significant interaction between sex and delinquency level because of the

TABLE 9.3 Normative Views of Deviance by Delinquency Level and Sex, with Age

	Mean	F
Delinquency Level		
None	2.16	5.60★★★
Status Offenses	2.09	
Minor Criminal Offenses	2.51	
Felonies	2.99	
Sex		
Male	2.82	10.75★★★
Female	2.29	
Age		201.83★★★

★ p < .05
★★ p < .01
★★★ p < .001

Three Perspectives **179**

views of the female versus male non-delinquents and status offenders. Those Russian youth who report committing more serious crimes are less likely to evaluate the behaviors listed as being wrong. This is especially true of stealing something of considerable value, smoking in school, and stealing something of minor value.

Apart from the cross-cultural findings, the difference in results between the delinquent and the non-delinquent youngsters is one of the major outcomes of this research. Their differing views toward fairness, how well the system works, the harm in certain deviant acts, and so on demonstrate the effects that actual experiences with the law can have in modifying stereotypes that arise out of knowledge based only upon secondary information and vicarious experience.

The females are significantly more likely than the males to believe these behaviors are wrong. In fact, those girls who report engaging in no delinquent acts are also the most likely to see harm in the various acts listed. The greatest differences by gender (always in the direction of the girls and young women seeing the behavior as more wrong) are with stealing something of minor value, drinking alcohol, and stealing something of considerable value.

Their higher normative standards are a likely product of a combination of the girls' legal reasoning, of their minimal involvement in actual delinquency that relieves them of need to rationalize, of their more independent stance toward peers in particular, and of their greater respect for the moral validity of the law. The results lead me to believe that these girls may be the best equipped morally to survive the kind of psychosocial distress of life in the new Russia.

The current sociolegal environment in Russia, or at least in the Russia experienced by our sample of Moscow youth (and I would hasten to add that these particular conditions are especially, and maybe even uniquely, characteristic of Moscow and perhaps St. Petersburg, or other big Russian cities), is characterized by anomie—by an existential vacuum. To go back to Rieber and Green (1990), the social distress resulting from the ending of the Soviet Union—from the breakdown of the cherished authority and the economic deprivations—is leading to a redefinition of "antisocial" behavior. The contemporary beliefs about law and deviance of Russian youth that have been captured here give reason for hope about the ultimate outcome.

10

VOICES OF A NEW RUSSIA

Where and how might the results of this effort fit in any larger scheme of things? With the acknowledged limitations of the surveys, what do the findings tell us about comparative differences in legal socialization between the United States, the former Soviet Union, and now Russia? This final chapter will present some concluding thoughts that address these questions on several levels.

On one level are the implications that this research has in view of the contrasting legal contexts, and the changes in legal context that have taken place in the former USSR. There continues to be considerable ambiguity about the future status of Russia. The direction of economic and political developments in this distressed country is very unclear. Likewise unclear is the specific impact of unfolding developments on crime and deviance, and on the continued progress and direction of legal reform.

It was at least partly to enhance the legitimacy of law enforcement, and to instill a belief in the moral validity of Soviet justice, that Soviet President Mikhail Gorbachev first began his rule-of-law quest. That very undertaking was an acknowledgment that there were serious inadequacies that demanded correction. The Soviet central government, like the tsarist regimes before it, had always employed law as an instrument of the state. Laws were enacted and enforced without the consent of the Soviet people and with little regard for their individual rights and freedoms. There was no mechanism, such as the U.S. Constitution and the Supreme Court, to judge laws and procedures and to declare them unconstitutional if they violated rights and freedoms protected by the Constitution. This should not be taken to mean that there have never been any bad laws or illegal incursions upon individual liberties in the United States. On the contrary, certainly there are numerous examples of bad law throughout our history. The import of review of constitutionality, however, is that there is a corrective mechanism, a way of achieving redress for these transgressions.

Voices of a New Russia

David Shipler, in his description of some of the early meetings of the then newly elected Soviet Congress of People's Deputies (which itself was also a Gorbachev initiative), alluded to this critical distinction between the legal foundations of our two countries in a 1990 article in *The New Yorker*. The following excerpt effectively and succinctly captures the essence of the differences in the formal contexts for legal socialization that exist in the United States, and that existed in the Soviet Union.

According to Shipler's report, a Soviet People's Deputy was drafting a bill in 1990 that would guarantee to people the freedom of association. In the process, this lawmaker was having to turn upside-down some of the basic assumptions of Soviet law. His proposed bill was intended to establish the right of citizens to unite around their interests and to form social or political organizations. Concurrently, the Soviet central government also had a version of this same bill—and the differences between them are enlightening. The government's version was based on what the Deputy called the "traditional Soviet assumption that whatever was not permitted was prohibited." In contrast, the Deputy's reform bill was intended to introduce what he said was the

> peculiarly American concept of the origins of rights: in Soviet legal thinking, rights are granted and defined by the state; in the American Constitution, rights exist naturally, and the state is enjoined from trespassing on them, except as the people expressly permit.

"How was it possible," he asked, "to imbue the citizenry with such a radical idea, and then shrink government's scope and create a culture in which people believed in their rights and respected the law?" How was it possible, he was asking in other words, to significantly change and enhance legal socialization? For this to happen, the Soviet legislator said,

> we need to change the upbringing of people, first of all. This people, in the course of hundreds of years, has been raised in a psychological paternalism. In the beginning was a czar, then a leader, the Party, which was the main source of rights and obligations. Everything came from above. Here people never felt the idea of natural rights. In the rest of the world, hundreds of years were required for the idea of natural rights to penetrate human psychology. If a person receives his rights and freedom from nature, from birth, he also begins to understand that he must use these rights and freedoms so they do not violate the same rights of others. And from here a feeling of lawfulness arises. But we do not have this. We live not under the Constitution and not by law but by directives or by instructions from ministries.
>
> *Shipler, 1990: 67–8*

Here was posed the disparate core of the historical and philosophical contexts in which both our Soviet and our later Russian youth, on the one hand, and our

182 Voices of a New Russia

American youth on the other, were asked to judge the justice, fairness, efficacy, and moral validity of Soviet/Russian and American law.

Assuming that the differences in sociolegal environments that have been drawn are valid, our research results seem to be all the more remarkable. Contrary to what might have been expected—given these differences, given the reported disillusionment of Soviet (and Russian) youth, given the prevalence of deviant attitudes and behavior—we have not found that Moscow youth had a lesser regard for Soviet law and the Soviet legal system than their American counterparts. We did not even find that American and Soviet youth were alike in these respects. What we did find was that Soviet young people (taken as a whole) were significantly more positive in most of our comparisons. When we surveyed a larger sample of Russian youth five years later, the contrasts in many respects are even greater. Russian youth in 1992—again looking at them over all—view their legal system even more favorably than either the Americans or their Soviet predecessors did. Assuming that our youthful subjects were not simply lying to us, these results leave us searching for other explanations. And those explanations must try to account for the gender differences that jump out at us.

As suggested several times already, the most plausible accounting or set of reasons encompasses a combination of macro-level and micro-level influences that appear to affect the reasoning, attitudes, and behavior of the youth studied here. It is reasonable to believe further that they would similarly affect children growing up in other places in the world as well.

Legal socialization is a kind of social learning. As such, it is a product of both knowledge and experience. That knowledge and experience, and the resulting socialization, are a consequence of the various means (or strategies) for enhancing legal development that we saw in Chapter 2. Included are acquiring legal knowledge, participating in rule and lawmaking experiences, resolving ethical and legal dilemmas, and understanding the relationships between different informal and formal legal systems. These approaches are carried out in a variety of ways: (1) through formal legal education of the kind typified by law-related education programs; (2) through legal indoctrination, which differs from education in that it is more directed and ideologically driven; (3) with information from the media—television, newspapers, magazines, books, and so on; (4) through personal experience with the formal justice system such as being arrested by the police and going to court; and (5) by means of participation in informal social control settings at the face-to-face level—the family, peer groups, in the classroom, and so on.

All three groups—Americans, Soviets, and Russians—have been socialized by means of these various forms. All three have, more or less, participated in and gotten knowledge and experience through each of these means. What is important is that it is precisely in the more or less, in the nature of the participation and experience, where we find the best accounting for the profoundly unanticipated differences among the three.

As far as the formal legal system is concerned, up until the last five years or so, the Soviets had a rather effective program of law-related education, but especially of legal indoctrination. As Kornai (1992) points out, the Soviet bureaucracy worked to convince the Soviet people to support their policy with an arsenal of education and modern political propaganda. The official ideology was "put forward by a vast apparatus of party, state, and mass organizations, served by the press, the other media, and educational, scientific, and cultural activity" (Kornai, 1992: 49). All this officially approved dissemination of legal information operated in conjunction with the pre-glasnost suppression of negative or critical materials that would have otherwise come from the media. In comparison, the American contemporaries of these young people received much less systematic teaching about American law because our law-related education is much more of a hit-and-miss proposition. U.S. youth also receive much less legal indoctrination, and, most importantly, much more critical information about the failings of the American criminal justice system. That is especially true for the young blacks in the U.S. delinquent sample. There is thus considerable difference in the balance of knowledge that would have come to our three groups from these various sources.

In all three cases, and excepting the officially certified delinquents, it is reasonable to suppose that there would have been relatively little direct personal experience with the legal process. This simply—but most importantly for our argument—means a greater dependence by most of them upon other sources of information such as what is taught in school, reported in the media, and experienced informally. All of which emphasizes the differences in balance just outlined.

Beyond the school, the most important formal institution in stimulating legal development is the legal system itself. In the case of those who did have personal contact with the justice system, it is interesting that the effect on the Soviet and Russian delinquents seems to have been to make them somewhat more favorably disposed toward the law and its enforcement. That same effect is not true as far as the American delinquents are concerned. I suspect that some of this contrast is due to the Soviet/Russian offenders being more likely to play it safe and give the party line. But the result may also be accounted for by the differential handling of juvenile offenders between the two justice systems. That in turn may reflect the fact that the great majority of the American delinquents were black. Treatment of blacks by the U.S. justice system is not unrelated to their perceptions of justice and fairness, and that is something to be considered in interpreting our findings.

The current Russian youth, with less mandated instruction in the law, and less indoctrination (or at least less recent indoctrination), but much more inform-ation from newspapers and television (some positive but a lot that is critical in its assessment of current conditions in Russia), were even more favorably inclined toward the law. How to explain this? Keeping in mind the gender and status

184 Voices of a New Russia

differences, it could be that having been made aware of the sordid aspects of some of their legal history, the present (at least in the abstract) looks relatively better to them. It could also be that they are responding to the potential of the numerous legal reforms and improvements that have been enacted over the past several years. Whatever the reason, the views of these young Russians are not nearly as gloomy as a lot of the American and Russian media would have us believe. One instance of that kind of portrayal is an article in one American newspaper (*The Washington Post*) that referred to current Russian youth as "a generation of cynics who regard the state as a hostile, utterly alien body and are interested only in their own private happiness." Russian young people are said to be obsessed with making money and thus very willing to engage in what were referred to as "semi-criminal activities." The *Post* article concluded by quoting a Moscow-based sociologist as saying that "there is no set of strict moral codes any more" (Dobbs, 1993: 12–13). An editorial in *The Dallas Morning News* for August 15, 1993, included this quote from a Russian police officer: "All the social and law enforcement structures that were used to restrain people were liquidated by democracy." These kinds of blanket portrayals seem to be incompatible with our results.

Which brings us then to the micro-level bases of knowledge and experience— to the primary groups. We know that all three samples of young people would, in the course of their growing-up, have participated in a number of informal rule-making and rule-enforcement systems—at home, at school, in youth clubs, and so on. They would have all been exposed to the continuities and discontinuities among the various rule systems (parents have one set of rules and peers have another, for example), and between the informal, primary group systems and the formal, state systems. But because of the greater role and weight of the collective in the socialization of Russian children, it seems reasonable that the Russians' transcendent communal experience would have had vastly more carry-over effect in shaping their views of the law overall. It is, I believe, participation in the communal groups that are so important for children in Russian society that is one of the primary factors moving Russian youth toward more mature and principled legal reasoning.

By way of conclusion on this point then, I suggest that it is the differential combination of education, indoctrination, access to information, and especially primary group socialization that best explains our findings here. The Soviets more effectively educated and indoctrinated their children with the legitimacy of the state, and they controlled their children's access to information that was critical of the state. At the same time, these children were being ingrained with the importance of compliance with the rules of the collective.

In his book, *The Moral Sense*, James Q. Wilson refers to this uniquely Russian framework for moral and legal socialization; a framework he credits for the survival of civil society in the USSR. The elemental building blocks of that society, says Wilson, "were families, friends, and intimate groupings in which sentiments of sympathy, reciprocity, and fairness survived and struggled to shape behavior" (Wilson, 1993: 251). So quite apart from what the state was doing and perhaps is doing now—good, bad, or indifferent—the primary groups of the society continued to do their job. And what is that job? To teach children right and wrong, and to give them a sense of moral values and a set of non-native judgments.

That takes us to a second set of conclusions. There are clear implications for theory, for cross-cultural or comparative research methods, and for legal education and socialization practices that can be drawn from this research. In addition to the observations already offered with regard to delinquency theory (most particularly the neutralization theory of delinquency), there are also implications for moral conflict theory, for deterrence theory, for theories of political socialization, theories about legitimacy, and theories about the role of normative values and legal compliance. Of most concern here are the implications for legal socialization theory.

The most notable of these is that legal reasoning is a strong factor in explaining deviant behavior. There were consistently significant differences in legal development between our officially delinquent and non-delinquent samples. But beyond that, legal reasoning was also a significant factor in the self-reported involvement in deviancy. Higher-level reasoners reported less involvement whereas those reasoning at lower levels indicated more involvement.

The legal reasoning and delinquency connection here is in direct contrast to the findings of the only other major study that looked directly at this issue— that of Morash (1978) nearly two decades ago. Concluding that there was little support for the proposition that legal reasoning affected delinquency in her results, Morash suggested that earlier researchers of moral development and delinquency had erred in limiting their definition of who was delinquent to only those officially so classified. Using the self-report method of determining who is and is not delinquent, she argued, eliminates spuriousness between measures of reasoning and behavior—but at the same time wipes out the connection. Not so here! Granted that I am assuming that a delinquent is a delinquent is a delinquent, whether American or Soviet or Russian. But we obviously cannot dismiss legal reasoning as being unrelated to legal behavior.

The other finding concerning legal reasoning and legal socialization that ranks among the most important is that regarding the young Russian females. They reflected the highest legal developmental levels, the greatest sense of the moral validity of the law, the most concern for the wrongfulness of certain deviant behaviors, and the lowest actual involvement in delinquency; all operating in tandem with some of the most negative attitudes toward authority figures. Their attitudes are very much like those offered by girls in Moscow five years earlier—with the distinct exception of their views of deviance.

The Russian girl's legal levels (along with those of the American girls, and some of the Soviet girls as well) challenge any notions about females being

186 Voices of a New Russia

disadvantaged by a measurement of legal reasoning, which is derived from Kohlberg's principles of moral development. The criticism that Tapp's scale—which was used to assess legal developmental level—is biased against females because it (like Kohlberg's scale) emphasizes cognitive abilities to the exclusion of empathetic capacity receives no support here. When combined with their judgments about moral validity, the legal reasoning of the young Russian women in particular suggests that they have a greater (rather than a lesser) appreciation for the moral content and justice of laws and rules when compared with their male contemporaries.

In Kohlberg's view, although he probably would not have anticipated concluding this about females, the Russian girls are "superior moral agents." They reflect the ability of certain individuals to resist those influential forces that are exerted on them by what must seem to be a heavy weight of amorality.

This result would not, however, particularly surprise Urie Bronfenbrenner. He observed more than 20 years ago that Soviet girls showed the highest level of commitment to adult standards and that "it is Soviet girls in particular who support society's values, and—both as individuals and in their collectives—exert pressure on others to conform to standards of good behavior" (Bronfenbrenner, 1970: 80). The Russian girls who provide the basis for our conclusions here have really gone beyond what Bronfenbrenner observed. They are not simply committed to adult—that is parents' and teachers'—standards, nor are they just supporting "society's values." Because of the present circumstances in Moscow, it is difficult to know exactly what the society's values are. Instead, these young women may be reflecting a greater sensitivity to the totality of their moral surroundings. They are exercising their moral judgment in an evolving environment that is seeking new standards, but that is still a long way from finding them. That is also why, I believe, they are among the least committed to parents, peers, and teachers as authority figures. They may be in the front ranks of those who, if we mark Durkheim's words, are trying to reclassify things and to create a new equilibrium.

Recent research on gender in Russia may also help us to understand the attitudes of both groups of young Russian females. For example, in a study of the gender base of institutional support in Lithuania, Ukraine and Russia, Hesli and Miller (1993) found Russian women at the end of the Soviet era to be basically supportive of the established political and economic institutions. They were also, however, more opposed to reforms of these institutions. This was not because women were more anti-reformist or apolitical than men, according to the authors.

> [R]ather, when they manifest orientations which appear to be conservative in nature it is because they are desperately seeking to maintain the few advances they see themselves as having made within the structure of the Soviet state and they are realistically assessing the possibility of future deterioration in their economic, social and political position.
>
> *Hesli and Miller, 1993: 526.*

Such things as unassisted childcare and household chores, low pay and low-status jobs, various discriminatory practices toward women generally, and low levels of self-esteem were offered by Hesli and Miller as factors surrounding Russian women's socialization into subordinate roles. "A period of transition [such as has been occurring for the past five years] can be worse than the status quo when there is no safety net and no clear expectation of improving conditions" (Hesli and Miller, 1993: 526). This may account for some of the negative attitudes of our young women in both groups.

Given the proscribed role of women in Russian society, it is especially surprising that the girls in this study should have rated so highly in legal reasoning. One of the bases for the supposed deficiencies in female moral reasoning in the Kohlberg model is the relative lack of role-taking opportunities available to women. If Russian women have an especially inferior societal position, then their role-taking opportunities would be expected to be even fewer than those of, say, American women. Why then are the Russian girls not morally deficient? The collective may again provide the answer. If sufficient opportunities to assume significant roles are available to these girls in their primary groups, this would stimulate their moral and legal reasoning. That could then counteract the proscriptions of the larger society.

Another lens for looking at the above results is provided by what is called a power-control theory of gender and delinquency (Hagan, 1989). This theory addresses the universal question of why male adolescents are freer than female adolescents to be delinquent. The answer is said to begin with the fact that in most families daughters are subject to more relational controls than sons. Relational controls are those derived from or related to affiliation and caring, such as attachment to parents, feelings of alienation toward the home, parental communication, and so on. They involve such things as feeling guilty about breaking parental rules, and caring that parents think badly of you, the kinds of things asked about in our research. Here we should recall the reports of the Soviet and Russian girls.

Relational controls differ from instrumental controls, which are more concrete —involving the use of sanctions to control behavior, for example. And, what is especially interesting, they are imposed mostly by mothers. Because of the disproportionate use of relational controls, the kind of risk-taking that leads to delinquency is allowed more for males than females. Thus, according to the theory, daughters become more "risk-averse" than sons because parental (read, mother) control reduces their willingness to take risks. As a result, they are less delinquent than sons.

Beyond the possibility that this may help explain why the Russian girls are much less delinquent than the boys—given that their relational controls would be expected to be particularly strong in view of their collective socialization—there is nothing about this so far that would furnish any peculiar or unique insights into the special situations of Soviet/Russian daughters and sons. What does move us in that direction is the further assumption of power-control theory "that the

188 Voices of a New Russia

presence of power and the absence of control both exercise . . . influence through cognitive processes in which actors evaluate courses of action" (Hagan, 1989: 159); this evaluation includes both risk assessment and moral reasoning. Our Russian girls are higher-level reasoners and more concerned with moral validity. So both their greater aversion to risk and their higher sense of morality would shield them from delinquent behavior.

Delinquency (meaning behavior that is sanctioned by the criminal law) is not, however, the only form of deviance. Hagan says that deviation from the social control imposed upon girls and young women is more likely to be recognized in expressions of psychosocial distress than in criminal behavior. Evidence of distress include running away and suicide or attempted suicide—actions which are also called "deviant role exits" (Hagan, 1989: 239). Power-control theory presumes that there are gender differences in psychosocial distress and in the search for deviant role exits. Women's social roles are said to be more stress-provoking and less fulfilling than those of men; at the same time, the opportunities and, most important, the power to challenge the sexual stratification of social control are much more limited for females. A result is that women are much more likely than men to "consider" deviant role exits. Consider them, but not actually take them. Why? Again because of their relative powerlessness and control: "relational and instrumental controls imposed by mothers on daughters act to suppress the inclinations of daughters to search for deviant role exits" (Hagan, 1989: 254). "Don't even think about it!" is passed on much more to daughters than to sons; nevertheless daughters do think about it—they just don't do it.

We know that Russian women, as witness the Hesli and Miller study reported above, apparently see themselves as both less powerful and less controlling of their life situations than men. If we couple this with the proposition that Russian women, as with women in Western society, are similarly (or under their circumstances even more so) likely to experience much greater psychosocial distress than men, we begin to get a clearer understanding of what may be happening with gender in Russia. Greater relational controls on deviant behavior, added to the higher levels of psychosocial distress among Soviet/Russian females, results in the suppression of deviance, but with attendant negative attitudes, and with cynicism and disillusionment.

As noted earlier, there was a blurring of the distinctions between what was legal and what was illegal in the old Soviet Russia. There was a kind of moral duplicity, and a sort of norm of psychopathology. At least the officially imposed ideological duplicity is now gone. But there is still very much a climate of crime, corruption, and lawlessness, and especially an environment that has the kind of high social distress associated with rapid change. It might seem extraordinary therefore to find that there are youth in Russia today who nevertheless have the greatest sense of moral obligation regarding obeying the law. And who, although they have to be sensitive to this distress, react in part by rejecting normative pressures supporting harm and deviance. This picture fits, however, with reports by the Russian Center for Public Opinion Research of an extraordinary revival of religious faith in Russia. All is not lost!

These then are what I think are the major contributions of this work. Beyond these are a number of lesser implications as well. One is what we can learn about the methods of comparative and cross-discipline research from these two studies. The importance of linguistic and conceptual comparability in data collection instruments is clearly demonstrated; as are the difficulties in achieving such comparability. The measurement of the variable "delinquency" and the absence of any direct behavioral measures were limitations imposed on the first study by the restrictions in the choices of methods. The use of self-report behavior methods in the second study shows them to be much recommended. More generally, selection bias in all the samples limits the generalizability of the results, as it would in any research. On the other hand, achieving truly random samples from a population as diverse and polyglot as that of the USSR or even of just Russia is totally unrealistic. It is safe to say that the research purist should probably avoid cross-cultural, comparative studies. Each of these considerations are nevertheless factors to be taken account of in planning any future research.

Finally, on the practical level, from both the study of the literature upon which the project was grounded, and from the research itself, there is little to recommend law-related education for children as a panacea for preventing or reducing juvenile delinquency. Such education has other values and purposes to recommend it, but there do not appear to be any direct simple connections between legal knowledge and law-abiding behavior.

The true value of this work, it is firmly believed, rests in its "firstness," and in its heuristic effects. Thus, the ultimate conclusions and implications are yet to be drawn.

APPENDIX

Questionnaire Development and Data Analyses ILVI-IV and MLV: Comparability and Equivalency

Here I want to deal in some detail with how the central concepts advanced earlier were operationalized into variables and then measures. Needless to say, theories have to be reduced to measures in this way in order to be empirically tested. Knowing specifically what was done, and how and why it was done is important to our understanding of any contributions of this work to legal socialization theory, and to any other theories of why people obey the law.

The Internalization of Legal Values Inventory, Form IV, consisted of 117 substantive items and 11 demographic items. Sections 1 (22 items) and 2 (20 items) focus on knowledge of criminal and civil law and procedures, as well as constitutional law. Our intent here was to find out just how much young people in the two countries knew about their respective laws. This is in keeping with the premise that legal knowledge is one of the elements in legal socialization. All items in both ILVI-IV knowledge of the law sections have correct answers—that is, in contrast to being measures of attitude and opinion. There was no section comparable to this Section 1 in the Soviet MLV; there is, however, a section in the latter that is comparable to ILVI-IV's Section 2. Section 3 of ILVI-IV has 32 items asking about attitudes toward the law and legal institutions, fairness, moral validity of the law, authority figures, and peers; for example: "Most things that young people do to get into trouble with the law don't really hurt anyone." It employs a five-point Likert scale ranging from strongly agree to strongly disagree. The MLV had identical items, with three exceptions. This section produced the measures of mediating attitudes that were expected to link legal reasoning with behavior.

Section 4 has 12 questions divided into three sets of four. Each set asks identical questions about subject's beliefs about how his or her parents, teachers, and friends perceive the subject's law-abidingness; for example: "How much would your parents agree that you . . . are a bad kid? . . . break rules? . . . get into trouble? . . .

Appendix **191**

do things that are against the law?" MLV had the same items. This is the looking-glass behavioral proxy to which I referred. It is a measure of normative status regarding deviance. It is also a perspective of oneself as you think you are seen through the eyes of others.

Section 5 assesses the youth's own normative judgments about deviance. It asks seven questions related to the subject's beliefs about the wrongfulness of specific law- or rule-breaking behaviors. For example, on a scale ranging from very wrong to not wrong or don't know: "How wrong would it be for someone your age to . . . purposely damage property that is someone else's?" We expected these judgments to be correlated with legal reasoning, as well as with actual involvement in delinquent behavior. Normative judgments might mediate between reasoning and behavior in the sense that, for instance, a youth who reasons at a higher level might think it OK to engage in a deviant behavior that he or she believes is not so very wrong.

Section 6 (with just three items) then deals with the influence of friends on the subject's willingness to break rules or laws; for example: "If your friends were leading you into trouble, would you still spend time with them?" These measures were intended to get at the peer pressures on adolescents that sometimes override their legal reasoning and moral judgments.

These last three sections served in part as surrogates for a true measure of behavior in the initial study. There was a lack of consensus between the American and the Russian principals in 1987 on including a self-reported delinquency component in the questionnaire. Russian researchers objected to the asking of what were regarded as personal and intimate questions about the children's own behavior that, although common and thus generally unobjectionable to Americans, might prove to be offensive to Russian children. It was also felt that there would be a high level of dishonest underreporting among the Russian children, in part because of the authoritarian school settings of the surveys and because of the presence of adults. Whatever the merits of these concerns, here again we see reflected a cultural difference that had significant ramifications for the results of the study. Self-report delinquency surveys were unknown in the Soviet Union at that time.

More generally, the concern about the honesty of the responses of the Russian sample came up a number of times in our discussions. Given the cultural and historical differences between the two countries, one could expect differences in the credence attached to assurances of anonymity and confidentiality. Soviet research subjects had in the past been much more likely to distrust such assurances. This distrust could, of course, lead to dishonest or misleading answers.

Section 7 of ILVI-IV, based on the Tapp–Levine Rule Law Interview, measures subject's conceptions of rules, laws, rights, and responsibilities. These defined the legal reasoning variable. Each of the available choices (three in the ILVI-IV format and six in the MLV format) is associated with one of the three

192 Appendix

levels of legal reasoning; example: "People should follow law . . . to maintain order for society . . . to gain benefits for all . . . to avoid being punished."

Finally, Section 8 (ten items) assesses beliefs about the power of authority figures to punish misbehavior, and feelings about breaking laws established by authority figures; example: "If you broke your parents' rules and no one knew, would you feel bad?" These measures of guilt are indicators of normative values regarding rules and laws and their enforcement.

Reliability and validity information was obtained for 52 of the 67 items taken from the Law-Related Education Evaluation Project study (Hunter, personal communication, 1989). The other 15 items were either knowledge of the law items, for which no reliability computations had been made, or they had been dropped by the Center for Action Research which conducted the aforementioned study. Available reliability coefficients for 47 items ranged from .458 to .915 (X = .715). Further, the Center indicated that 35 of our 67 items had been found to be significantly correlated with the frequency of committing nine types of delinquent acts in their own junior high school samples. These acts ranged from school rule infractions to index offenses. See Table A.1, which explicates these data.

Both the rule-law interview items and the YIAPR items from Tapp's research had demonstrated reliability coefficients in excess of .70 in earlier research. Taken

TABLE A.1 Reliability/Validity of ILVI

Variables from LREE Project (Colorado)	Equivalent Section: Item #s	Reliability: Cronbach's Alpha	Validity: Relationship With Frequency of Committing 9 Types of Delinquent Acts (Junior High Level)
1. Fairness of judges	3:1	NA*	Signif. neg. correl. with 3 types (r = .17–.30)**
2. Fairness of justice system	3:2 3:3 3:5 3:7	.458	Signif. neg. correl. with 2 types (r = .20–.27) DROPPED
3. Rationalizations for deviance	3:4 3:6 3:8 3:9 3:10	.704	Signif. pos. correl. with 9 types (r = .24–.34)
4. Altitudes toward police	3:11 3:17 3:18	.675	Signif. neg. correl. with 9 types (r = .21–.36)
5. Certainty/severity (deterrence)	3:12 3:19 3:23 3:26	.472	Signif. neg. correl. with 7 types (r = .19–.36)
6. Delinquency peer influence	3:13 3:14 3:15	.774	Signif. pos. correl. with 9 types (r = .14–.34)
7. Attachment to home	3:20 3:22 3:27	.471	Not calculated; DROPPED
8. Commitment to home	3:21 3:24	NA	Not calculated; DROPPED

Variables from LREE Project (Colorado)	Equivalent Section: Item #s	Reliability: Cronbach's Alpha	Validity: Relationship With Frequency of Committing 9 Types of Delinquent Acts (Junior High Level)
9. Isolation from school	3:28 3:29 3:30	.765	Signif. neg. correl. with 3 types (r = .14–.16) DROPPED
10. Attachment to teachers	3:31 3:32	NA	Signif. neg. correl. with 9 types (r = .17–.22)
11. Neg. labeling by parents	4:1 4:2 4:3 4:4	.872	Signif. pos. correl. with 9 types (r = .26–.33)
12. Neg. labeling by teachers	4:5 4:6 4:7 4:8	.915	Signif. pos. correl. with 9 types (r = .27–.35)
13. Neg. labeling by peers	4:9 4:10 4:11 4:12	.891	Signif. pos. correl. with 9 type (r = .31–.44)
14. Attitudes against deviance	5:1 – 5:7	.831	Signif. neg. correl. with 9 types (r = .32–.52)
15. Commitment to delinquent peers	6:1 6:2 6:3	.748	Signif. pos. correl. with 7 type (r = .14–.22)

* Alpha nor computed for one- and two-item measures.
** Significance level of .025 or better on sample size of 600+.

as a whole, this information gave us confidence in both the reliability and validity of ILVI-IV—and also in MLV where the items were identical.

The original Russian form, Mastering of Legal Values, had 86 substantive items and 12 demographic items. The smaller overall number of items was mainly a result of the absence of the true/false knowledge section, as explained earlier. Part I (Knowledge of the Law) had 15 multiple-choice items. These items dealt with criminal, procedural, constitutional, and civil law; for example: "Who can order the punishment for a specific crime? The Prosecutor-General . . . The agencies of the Ministry of Internal Affairs . . . Agencies of the Department of Justice . . . The Court."

Part II was equivalent to Section 3 in ILVI-IV—with the exception of three items (the procedure for determining equivalency will be explained shortly). Equivalency is also characteristic of Parts III, IV, and V, and their respective counterpart sections of ILVI-IV, that is Sections 4, 5, and 6.

The other major differences in the two forms occur in their last two sections. The items assessing level of legal reasoning were simplified in ILVI-IV so that respondents were required to rank only three "child-friendly" responses. The MLV form, on the other hand, required Russian children to rank-order six more complex responses, which had originally been derived from adult respondents. The fault for the discrepancy here rested mainly on the American side in that these items were originally presented as being ready and suitable for

194 Appendix

this research, when in fact this was not the case. The Russian researchers subsequently reported (not surprisingly) that some of the youth in their sample had difficulties with this harder task. One result was that there were a large number of random responses and a large amount of missing data on this part for the Russian subjects. This not only required various compensations in the statistical analyses, but effectively eliminated the possibility of making any meaningful cross-country comparisons on legal levels in Phase I.

The other major difference in the two instruments was in the counterpart sections assessing beliefs about authorities' power to punish and feelings of guilt. ILVI-IV asks respondents to react to such statements as "Can _____ punish you if you do something wrong?" MLV asks "Will _____ punish you if you do something wrong?" This critical difference between measuring ability to versus willingness to, and the fact that there are no items pertaining to parents in this section in MLV for some inexplicable reason, resulted in six of these items being eliminated in the comparative analyses. Part of this discrepancy resulted from language differences, and part from a disagreement over what the Russian researchers considered to be a given, that is that of course parents and the police have the power to punish. The issue and the more important point they argued is whether parents and the police will in fact punish wrongdoing of which they become aware. This disagreement, at least to some extent, again reflects a cultural difference.

As indicated at the outset, problems of comparability and equivalency are common in comparative, cross-cultural research. This study is therefore certainly no exception. In order to defend against these problems, as well as to counter the special difficulties just outlined above, a number of steps were taken. This brings us to damage control.

The initial ILVI items were translated from English to Russian by Professor Yakovlev. The Russian was then translated back into English by staff of the International Research and Exchanges Board (IREX), which agency was sponsoring the research, and independently by another member of the Russian research team. These two back-translations were then carefully compared with the original English version. The back-translations and comparisons were admittedly done after the first Russian data had already been collected.

The aim of translation and back-translation is to achieve cross-cultural equivalency and to preserve cross-national comparability of content. This means considering both the cultural and linguistic relevance in meaning and wording. Five research assistants in the U.S. independently reviewed the three versions. Their analyses were then reviewed by Finckenauer, Tapp, and Yakovlev. Following this exhaustive process, 11 items were excluded from the comparative analyses. Because the knowledge of the law sections and the legal levels sections were known or were judged to be non-comparable and non-equivalent, responses in these sections were transformed into z-scores in a normal distribution for analyses.

Appendix **195**

Creating an ILVI-V

The Internalization of Legal Values Inventory adapted for use with Russian subjects in 1992 was developed in collaboration with Alexander Nikiforov of the Russian Academy of Sciences. Nikiforov, a legal researcher and scholar, had participated in the earlier Russian study. The goal here was to use the original American survey questionnaire with minimal changes (in fact none at all if possible), so as to maximize comparability. Certain changes, nevertheless, had to be made. Adaptations that we concluded were necessary included eliminating from the Russian version a knowledge of the law question pertaining to grand juries, which do not exist in Russia. Questions dealing with trial by jury, bail, the Bill of Rights, and being sued (none of which are applicable to the Russian legal system) were slightly revised to seek equivalent information. The use of basically the same knowledge of the law questions, with these minimal changes, permitted more direct comparisons with the results from the earlier American sample.

Section 2 of ILVI-IV, which was specific to U.S. law, was eliminated. In Sections 3 and 4 there were no changes. In Section 5, two questions pertaining to the wrongfulness of stealing something of specified dollar values were reworded to indicate theft of things of "low" and "high" value. This was done because it was decided that American dollar values and their convertibility to rubles was meaningless under the conditions of raging inflation in Russia. Finally, there were also no changes in ILVI-IV Sections 6, 7, and 8.

In addition to the minor revisions in the existing questionnaire, a new Section 8 was added to the Russian instrument. This section, comprised of 28 items, asked the Russian youth to report on their own personal behavior during the past 12 months. These items were taken from the self-report delinquency form used in the U.S. National Youth Survey. This addition was intended to deal with the earlier described concerns about there being an artificial division of delinquents and non-delinquents, and about there being no direct measures of actual behavior. To our knowledge, this is the first time that self-report delinquency data have been collected in the former Soviet Union. These data obviously cannot be used in any comparative analyses with our earlier samples, but they furnish us a far superior indicator of law-abidingness. The availability of this information is of special importance because it can be correlated with legal reasoning, attitudes, and views about the normative status of deviant behaviors.

Comparative Analyses

A complex set of analyses was performed on the data. These included univariate and multivariate analysis of variance, multiple regression analysis, and Cohen's power analysis. Several data transformations were needed to compare data from the two different instruments in Phase I, and then to compare Phase I data with Phase II data.

196 Appendix

As already indicated, data on knowledge of the law and on legal reasoning levels were not comparable across countries. In order to use this information in other analyses, the raw scores for these sections were normalized by converting them into z-scores within each country. This means that Russian youth could be compared with each other on their knowledge of Soviet law and could be located in the distribution of knowledge scores among their mates. The same could be done with the American youth. Thus, although the scores are not directly comparable across countries, the percentile rankings of the individual youth within their respective countries are comparable.

Raw scores for the knowledge of the law sections were computed by dividing the number of questions answered correctly by the total number of questions. It is this percent correct figure that was normalized.

Legal reasoning scores were computed using the first-choice method. This method used information from all the legal reasoning questions in each of the respective sections of the ILVI and the MLV. The first-choice method simply used the first choice of each of these rankings as the legal level for that question. The first choices for all questions were then averaged to compute the subject's overall legal reasoning score.

The legal reasoning scores for both countries were based on the same scale, that of the Tapp legal levels. But because they were computed using different schemes, it was decided that they too should be normalized by converting them into z-scores. It is these scores that were used in the first analyses.

The remainder of the analyses were done by performing straightforward analysis of variance using all items deemed equivalent and comparable in various variable clusters.

BIBLIOGRAPHY

Adelson, J. (1971) "The Political Imagination of the Young Adolescent." *Daedalus*, Fall, pp. 1013–49.

Adler, N. and S. Gluzman (1992) "Soviet Special Psychiatric Hospitals: Where the System Was Criminal and the Inmates Were Sane." Unpublished paper.

Antonian, I. U. (1976) "The Sociopsychological Consequences of Urbanization and Their Influence on Crime." *Soviet Law and Government*, Fall, pp. 51–65.

Arshayskii, A. I. and A. I. Vilks (1990) "Antisocial Manifestations in the Youth Environment: An Attempt at Regional Prognosis." *Soviet Sociology*, pp. 88–98.

Åslund, A. and M. B. Olcott (1999) *Russia after Communism*. Washington, DC: Carnegie.

Babaev, M. M. and A. S. Shliapochnikov (1979) "Economic Factors in the Mechanism of Criminal Behavior." *Soviet Law and Government*, Fall, pp. 69–83.

Bargman, G. F. (1974) *A Study of Knowledge and Attitudes Toward the Bill of Rights in Selected Iowa School Districts*. Ph.D. Dissertation, University of Iowa.

Bassiouni, M. C. and V. M. Savitski (eds.) (1979) *The Criminal Justice System of the USSR*. Springfield, IL: Charles C. Thomas.

Belikova, G. and A. Shokin (1989) "The Black Market: People, Things, and Facts." *Soviet Review*, Vol. 30, No. 3, pp. 26–39.

Berdyaev, N. (1992) *The Russian Idea*. Hudson, NY: Lindisfarne Press.

Berman, H. J. (1963) *Justice in the USSR*. Cambridge, MA: Harvard University Press.

Berman, H. J. (1977) "The Use of Law to Guide People to Virtue: A Comparison of Soviet and U. S. Perspectives." In J. L. Tapp and F. J. Levine (eds.) *Law, Justice and the Individual in Society*. New York: Holt, Rinehart, and Winston.

Berman, H. J. (1980) "The Presumption of Innocence: Another Reply." *The American Journal of Comparative Law*, Vol. 28, pp. 615–23.

Blasi, A. (1980) "Bridging Moral Cognition and Moral Action: A Critical Review of the Literature." *Psychological Bulletin*, Vol. 88, No. 1, pp. 1–45.

Bohlen, C. (1992a) "Russians Ask, 'What Country Do I Live In?'" *The New York Times*. June 14.

Bohlen, C. (1992b) "The Russians' New Code: If It Pays, Anything Goes." *The New York Times*. August 30.

198 Bibliography

Bouma, D. (1969) *Kids and Cops: A Study in Mutual Hostility*. Grand Rapids, MI: William B. Erdman.

Bowlus, D. et al. (1974) *A Study of Youth Attitudes Toward Authority and Their Relationship to School Adjustment Patterns*. ERIC Document Reproduction Service, No. ED 096 088.

Bronfenbrenner, U. (1970) *Two Worlds of Childhood*. New York: Russell Sage Foundation.

Brown, D. W. (1974) "Cognitive Development and Willingness to Comply with Law." *American Journal of Political Science*, Vol. 18, No. 3, pp. 583–94.

Brown, J. F. (1992) "Toward the Rule of Law: Introduction." *RFE/RL Research Report*, Vol. 1, No. 27, pp. 1–3.

Butler, W. E. (1990) "Towards the Rule of Law?" In A. Brumberg (ed.). *Chronicle of a Revolution*. New York: Pantheon Books, pp. 72–89.

Butler, W. E. (ed.) (1991) *Perestroika and the Rule of Law*. London: I. B. Tauris & Co.

Butler, W. E. (1992) "Crime in the Soviet Union." *British Journal of Criminology*, Vol. 32, No. 2, pp. 144–59.

Cary, C. D. (1974) "Peer Groups in the Political Socialization of Soviet School-Children." *Social Science Quarterly*, Vol. 55, pp. 451–61.

Celarier, M. (1993) "Gangster Economics." *Global Finance*, September, pp. 51–4.

Chapman, A. (1955–56) "Attitudes Toward Legal Authorities Of Juveniles: A Comparative Study of Delinquents and Non-Delinquent Boys." *Sociology and Social Research*, Vol. 40, pp. 170–5.

Chesnokova, V., V. Parfenov, and A. Andreev (1990) "Reforming the Soviet Penal System for Juvenile Delinquents." Unpublished paper for the Center for Humanization of the Penal System, Moscow.

Clawson, R. W. (1973) "Political Socialization of Children in the USSR." *Political Science Quarterly*, Vol. 27, No. 2, pp. 187–203.

Clines, F. X. (1989) "There's a Crime Wave, Or a Perception Wave, In the Soviet Union." *The New York Times*, September 17, E2.

Cloward, R. A. and L. E. Ohlin (1960) *Delinquency and Opportunity: A Theory of Delinquent Gangs*. Glencoe, IL: The Free Press.

Cohn, E. S. and S. O. White (1986) "Cognitive Development Versus Social Learning Approaches to Studying Legal Socialization." *Basic and Applied Social Psychology*, Vol. 7, No. 3, pp. 195–209.

Cohn, E. S. and S. O. White (1990) *Legal Socialization*. New York: Springer-Verlag.

Cohn, E. S. and S. O. White (1992) "Taking Reasoning Seriously." In Joan McCord (ed.) *Facts, Frameworks, and Forecasts*. New Brunswick, NJ: Transaction Publishers, pp. 95–114.

Cohn, E. S., R. J. Trinkner, C. J. Rebellon, K. T. Van Gundy, and Lindsey M. Cole (2012) "Legal Attitudes and Legitimacy: Extending the Integrated Legal Socialization Model." *Victims and Offenders*, Vol. 7, No. 4, pp. 385–406.

Connor, W. (1972) *Deviance in Soviet Society*. New York: Columbia University Press.

Connor, W. (1991) "Equality of Opportunity." In A. Jones et al. (eds.) *Soviet Social Problems*. Boulder, CO: Westview Press, pp. 137–53.

Cressey, D. R. (1970) "Organized Crime and Inner City Youth." *Crime and Delinquency*, pp. 129–38.

Damon, W. (1988) *The Moral Child*. New York: The Free Press.

Dashkov, G. V. (1992) "Quantitative and Qualitative Changes in Crime in the USSR." *British Journal of Criminology*, Vol. 32, No. 2, pp. 160–6.

Bibliography 199

Dobbs, M. (1993) "An Explosion in the Soviet Lab." *The Washington Post National Weekly Edition*. September 27–October 3, pp. 12–13.

Dobson, R. B. (1991) "Youth Problems in the Soviet Union." In A. Jones, W. D. Connor, and D. E. Powell (eds.) *Soviet Social Problems*. Boulder, CO: Westview Press, pp. 227–51.

Durkheim, E. (1961) "Anomic Suicide." In T. Parsons, et al. (eds.) *Theories of Society: Foundations of Modern Sociological Theory*, Volume II. New York: The Free Press of Glencoe, Inc., pp. 916–29.

Elliott, D. (1992) "Russia's Goodfellas: The Mafia on the Neva." *Newsweek*. October 12, pp. 50, 52.

Emler, N. P., N. Heather, and M. Winton (1978) "Delinquency and the Development of Moral Reasoning." *British Journal of Clinical Psychology*, Vol. 17, pp. 325–31.

Erlanger, S. (1992) "Vodka, Scourge and Balm At Center of Russian Life." *The New York Times*, October 23.

Fagan, J. and A. R. Piquero (2007) "Rational Choice and Developmental Influences on Recidivism among Adolescent Felony Offenders." *Journal of Empirical Legal Studies*, Vol. 4, pp. 715–48.

Fagan, J. and T. R. Tyler (2005) "Legal Socialization of Children and Adolescents." *Social Justice Research*, Vol. 18, pp. 217–42.

Faraone, S. (1982) "Psychiatry and Political Repression in the Soviet Union." *American Psychologist*, Vol. 37, No. 10, pp. 1105–12.

Finckenauer, J. O. (1987) "Education in Law and Values Clarification as Correctional Treatment for Juvenile Offenders." Unpublished paper presented at Rutgers, September.

Finckenauer, J. O. (1988) "Juvenile Delinquency in the USSR: Social Structural Explanations." *International Journal of Comparative and Applied Criminal Justice*, Vol. 12, No. 1, pp. 73–80.

Finckenauer, J. O. and L. Kelly (1992) "Juvenile Delinquency and Youth Subcultures in the Former Soviet Union." *International Journal of Comparative and Applied Criminal Justice*, Vol. 16, No. 2, pp. 247–61.

Fituni, L. L. (1993) *CIS: Organized Crime and Its International Activities*. Moscow: Center for Strategic and Global Studies, Russian Academy of Sciences.

Fletcher, G. P. (1968) "The Presumption of Innocence in the Soviet Union." *UCLA Law Review*, Vol. 15, pp. 1203–25.

Fletcher, G. P. (1989) "On Trial in Gorbachev's Court." *The New York Review of Books*, May 18.

Fodor, E. M. (1972) "Delinquency and Susceptibility to Social Influence Among Adolescents as a Function of Level of Moral Development." *The Journal of Social Psychology*, Vol. 86, pp. 257–60.

Fodor, E. M. (1973) "Moral Development and Parent Behavior Antecedents in Adolescent Psychopaths." *The Journal of Genetic Psychology*, Vol. 122, pp. 37–43.

Fomin, N. S. (1978) "Factors in Legalistic Education and the Methods Used to Determine the Results of Their Influence." *Soviet Education*, August, pp. 46–59.

Fox, K. A. (1974) *Law and Justice: Adolescents' Perceptions of Policemen*. ERIC Document Reproduction Service No. ED 095 033.

Frankl, V. E. (1969) *The Will to Meaning: Foundations and Applications of Logotherapy*. New York: The World Publishing Co.

Fraser, B. J. and D. L. Smith (1980) "Assessment of Law-Related Attitudes." *Social Education*, May, pp. 406–9.

200 Bibliography

Friedrichs, D. O. (1986) "The Concept of Legitimation and the Legal Order: A Response to Hyde's Critique." *Justice Quarterly*, Vol. 3, No. 1, pp. 33–50.

Frisby, T. (1989) "Soviet Youth Culture." In J. Riordan (ed.), *Soviet Youth Culture* Bloomington, IN: Indiana University Press, pp. 1–15.

Fuller, L. L. (1969a) "Human Interaction and the Law." *The American Journal of Jurisprudence*, Vol. 14, pp. 1–36.

Fuller, L. L. (1969b) *The Morality of Law* (revised edn). New Haven, CT: Yale University Press.

Fuller, L. L. (1977) "Some Presuppositions Shaping the Concept of 'Socialization'." In J. L. Tapp and F. J. Levine (eds.) *Law, Justice and the Individual in Society*. New York: Holt, Rinehart, & Winston.

Gallatin, J. and J. Adelson (1977) "Legal Guarantees of Individual Freedom: A Cross-National Study of the Development of Political Thought." In J. L. Tapp and F. J. Levine (eds.) *Law, Justice and the Individual in Society*. New York: Holt, Rinehart, & Winston.

Gerbich, A. I. (1978) "Experience Gained in the Legalistic Education of School Pupils." *Soviet Education*, August, pp. 60–9.

Gibson, J. L. (1989) "Understandings of Justice: Institutional Legitimacy, Procedural Justice, and Political Tolerance." *Law & Society Review*, Vol. 23, No. 3, pp. 469–96.

Gibson, J. L. (1991) "Institutional Legitimacy, Procedural Justice, and Compliance with Supreme Court Decisions: A Question of Causality." *Law & Society Review*, Vol. 25, No. 3, pp. 631–5.

Gilligan, C. (1982) *In a Different Voice: Psychological Theory and Women's Development*. Cambridge, MA: Harvard University Press.

Gluzman, S. (1989) *On Soviet Totalitarian Psychiatry*. Amsterdam: International Association on the Political Use of Psychiatry.

Godson, R. (2000) "Guide to Developing a Culture of Lawfulness." Unpublished paper for the Symposium on the Role of Civil Society in Countering Organized Crime: Global Implications of the Palermo, Sicily Renaissance, December.

Golik, Y. (1990) "The Danger Is in Delusions." *The Literary Gazette International*, August, No. 2, p. 16.

Golov, A. (1991) "Can You Live Here and Not Break the Law?" *Nezavisimaya Gazeta*, Vol. 2, No. 10–11, November, p. 7.

Gray, F. du P. (1989) *Soviet Women: Walking the Tightrope*. New York: Doubleday.

Gurevich, D. (1990) "Moscow Gangland." *Details*, October, pp. 23–8.

Hagan, J. (1989) *Structural Criminology*. New Brunswick, NJ: Rutgers University Press.

Hahn, J. W. (1969) "The Komosomol Kollektiv as an Agency of Political Socialization." *Youth & Society*, Vol. 1, pp. 219–39.

Hains, A. A. (1984) "Variables in Social Cognitive Development: Moral Judgment, Role-taking, Cognitive Processes, and Self-concept in Delinquents and Nondelinquents." *Journal of Early Adolescence*, Vol. 4, No. 1, pp. 65–74.

Hazard, J. N. (1990) "Where Are the Peril Points?" *Law & Social Inquiry*, Vol. 15, No. 3, pp. 521–6.

Hendley, K. (2012) "Who Are the Legal Nihilists in Russia?" *Post-Soviet Affairs*, Vol. 28, No. 2, pp. 149–186.

Hesli, V. L. and A. H. Miller (1993) "The Gender Base of Institutional Support in Lithuania, Ukraine and Russia." *Europe-Asia Studies*, Vol. 45, No. 3, pp. 505–32.

Hess, R. D. and J. L. Tapp (1969) *Authority, Rules, and Aggression: A Cross-National Study of the Socialization of Children into Compliance Systems: Part I*. Washington, DC: United States Department of Health, Education, and Welfare.

Bibliography **201**

Hirschi, T. (1969) *Causes of Delinquency*. Berkeley, CA: University of California Press.

Hogan, R. and C.Mills (1976) "Legal Socialization." *Human Development*, Vol. 19, pp. 261–76.

Hollander, P. (1991) "Politics and Social Problems." In A. Jones et al. (eds.) *Soviet Social Problems*. Boulder, CO: Westview Press, pp. 9–23.

Horton, S. (2011) "A Culture of Legal Nihilism." *The Harper's Blog for Harper's Magazine*. Posted March 17.

Hraba, J., M. G. Miller, and V. J. Webb (1975) "Mutability and Delinquency: The Relative Effects of Structural, Associational, and Attitudinal Variables on Juvenile Delinquency." *Criminal Justice and Behavior*, Vol. 2, No. 4, pp. 408–20.

Huba, G. J. and P. M. Bentler (1983) "Causal Models of the Development of Law Abidance and Its Relationship to Psycho-Social Factors and Drug Use." In W. S. Laufer and J. M. Day (eds.) *Personality Theory, Moral Development, and Criminal Behavior*. Lexington, MA: Heath.

Hyde, A. (1983) "The Concept of Legitimation in the Sociology of Law." *Wisconsin Law Review*, pp. 379–426.

Il'Inskii, I. M. (1988) "Our Young Contemporary: Questions of a General Philosophical Upbringing." *Soviet Sociology*, Vol. 26, No. 4, pp. 18–28.

Ioffe, M. G. (1978) "Nurturing Respect for the Law." *Soviet Education*, August, pp. 37–45.

Irving, K. and M. Siegal (1983) "Mitigating Circumstances in Children's Perceptions of Criminal Justice: The Case of an Inability to Control Events." *British Journal of Developmental Psychology*, Vol. 1, pp. 179–88.

Ivanov, L. O. (1988) "Study of the Legal Consciousness of Minors: A Review." Unpublished paper.

Jacobson, M. G. and S. B. Palonsky (1981) "Effects of A Law-Related Education Program." *The Elementary School Journal*, Vol. 82, No. 1, pp. 49–57.

Jennings, W. S., R. Kilkenny and L. Kohlberg (1983) "Moral-Development Theory and Practice for Youthful Offenders." In W. S. Laufer and J. M. Day (eds.) *Personality Theory, Moral Development, and Criminal Behavior*. Lexington, MA: Heath.

Jurkovic, G. J. (1980) "The Juvenile Delinquent as a Moral Philosopher: A Structural-Developmental Perspective." *Psychological Bulletin*, Vol. 88, No. 3, pp. 709–27.

Jurkovic, G. J. and N. M. Prentice (1977) "Relation of Moral and Cognitive Dimensions of Juvenile Delinquency." *Journal of Abnormal Psychology*, Vol. 86, No. 4, pp. 414–20.

Juviler, P. (1991) "No End of a Problem: Perestroika for the Family?" In A. Jones, et al. (eds.) *Soviet Social Problems*. Boulder, CO: Westview Press, pp. 194–212.

Juviler, P. and B. E. Forschner (1978) "Juvenile Delinquency in the Soviet Union." *The Prison Journal*, Vol. 58, pp. 18–30.

Karpets, I. I. (1990) "The Reality of Crime." *Soviet Sociology*, May–June, pp. 63–80.

Keller, B. (1987) "Russia's Restless Youth." *The New York Times Magazine*. July 26, pp. 14–53.

Keller, B. (1990) "Russian Nationalists—Yearning for an Iron Hand." *The New York Times Magazine*. January 28, pp. 18–21, 46–50.

Klar, W. H. (1974) *An Inquiry into the Knowledge of an Attitude Toward the Law on the Part of Public School Students in Connecticut*. Ph.D. Dissertation, University of Connecticut.

Kogan, V. M. (1987) "Punishment Under Criminal Law and the Public Consciousness." Translated by S. P. Dunn and E. Dunn, Unpublished abstract presented at Rutgers, September.

Kogan, V. M. (1989) "The Place of Law Consciousness in the Struggle Against Crime." Paper presented to American Society of Criminology, November.

202 Bibliography

Kohlberg, L. (1958) *The Development of Modes of Moral Thinking and Choice in the Years Ten to Sixteen*. Ph.D. Dissertation, University of Chicago.

Kohlberg, L. (1963) "The Development of Children's Orientations Toward a Moral Order. I. Sequence of Moral Thought." *Vita Humana*, Vol. 6, pp. 11–33.

Kohlberg, L. (1964) "Development of Moral Character and Moral Ideology." In M. I. Hoffman (ed.) *Review of Child Development Research, Vol 1*. New York: Russell Sage Foundation.

Kohlberg, L. (1968a) "The Child as a Moral Philosopher." *Psychology Today*, Vol. 2, No. 4, pp. 24–31.

Kohlberg, L. (1968b) "Moral Development." In *International Encyclopedia of the Social Sciences*. New York: Macmillan.

Kohlberg, L. (1969) "Stage and Sequence: The Cognitive-Developmental Approach to Socialization." In D. A. Goslin (ed.) *Handbook of Socialization Theory and Research*. Chicago: Rand McNally.

Kohlberg L. and D. Elfenbein (1975) "The Development of Moral Judgment Concerning Capital Punishment." *American Journal of Orthopsychiatry*, Vol. 45, pp. 614–40.

Kohn, M. L. (1987) "Cross-National Research as an Analytic Strategy." *American Sociological Review*, Vol. 52, pp. 713–31.

Kornai, J. (1992) *The Socialist System*. Princeton, NJ: Princeton University Press.

Kozlov, A. (1991) "Metacorruption." In L. Timofeyev (ed.) *Russia's Secret Rulers*. New York: Alfred A. Knopf, pp. 147–71.

Kutsev, G. F. (1992) "Youth and Society." *Russian Education and Society*, Vol. 34, No. 7, pp. 6–55.

Lampert, N. (1988) "Criminal Justice and Legal Reform in the Soviet Union." *Soviet Union*, Vol. 15, No. 1, pp. 1–29.

Lapsley, D. K., M. R. Harwell, L. M. Olson, D. Flannery, and S. M. Quintana (1984) "Moral Judgment, Personality, and Attitude to Authority in Early and Late Adolescence." *Journal of Youth and Adolescence*, Vol. 13, No. 6, pp. 527–42.

Law-Related Education Evaluation Project (1983) *Social Science Education Consortium*. Boulder, CO: Center for Action Research.

Law: Studies by Soviet Scholars (1984) *Constitutional Foundations of Justice in the USSR*. Moscow: USSR Academy of Sciences.

Lebedev, Y. (1991) "The Final and Decisive Congress of the All-Union Lenin Young Communist League." *The Current Digest of the Soviet Press*, Vol. 43, No. 39, pp. 16–17.

Lee, R. W. III. (1992) "Dynamics of the Soviet Illicit Drug Market." *Crime, Law and Social Change*, Vol. 17, pp. 177–233.

Lee, R. W. III. (1993) *Foreign Policy Implications of Post-Soviet Organized Crime*. Testimony submitted to the Subcommittee on International Security, Committee on Foreign Affairs, U.S. House of Representatives, November 4.

Lempert, D. (1992) "Russians Still Can't Get Much Justice." Letters to the Editor, *The New York Times*. June 6.

Levin, M. B. (1990) "A Youngster's Fate." *Soviet Education*, Vol. 32, pp. 1–19.

Levine, F. J. (1979) *The Legal Reasoning of Youth: Dimensions and Correlates*. Ph.D. Dissertation, University of Chicago.

Levine, F. J. and J. L. Tapp (1977) "The Dialectic of Legal Socialization in Community and School." In J. L. Tapp and F. J. Levine, *Law, Justice and the Individual in Society*. New York: Holt, Rinehart, and Winston.

Liebshultz, S. F. and R. C. Niemi (1974) "Political Attitudes Among Black Children." In R.C. Niemi (ed.) *The Politics of Future Citizens*. San Francisco: Jossey–Bass Inc.

Lipman, M. (2016) "Twenty-Five Years After the Failed Soviet Coup." *The New Yorker.* August 19.

Lubin, N. (1984) *Labour & Nationality in Soviet Central Asia.* Princeton, NJ: Princeton University Press.

Lukasheva, E. A. (1987) "The Social-Psychological Mechanism of Internalization of Legal Norms and Values by the Individual." Translated by S. P. Dunn and E. Dunn. Unpublished abstract presented at Rutgers, September.

Makarenko, A. S. (1967) *The Collective Family,* ed. U. Bronfenbrenner. New York: Doubleday.

Markovits, I. (1989) "Law and Glasnost: Some Thoughts About the Future of Judicial Review Under Socialism." *Law & Society Review,* Vol. 23, No. 3, pp. 399–447.

Markowitz, A. (1986) "The Impact of Law Related Education on Elementary Children in Reducing Deviant Behavior." Ph.D. Dissertation, Rutgers University.

Markwood, J. M. (1975) *Knowledge and Attitudes Regarding the Juvenile Justice System Among Delinquent and Non-Delinquent Youth.* Ph.D. Dissertation, University of Virginia.

Marshall, G. (1977) "Due Process in England." In J. Roland Pennock and John W. Chapman (eds.) *Due Process.* New York: New York University Press.

McClellan, D. S. (1987) "Soviet Youth: A View from the Inside." *Crime and Social Justice,* Vol. 29, pp. 1–25.

Mickiewicz, E. (1990) "Ethnicity and Support: Findings from a Soviet-American Public Opinion Poll." *Journal of Soviet Nationalities,* Vol. 1, No. 1, pp. 140–7.

Miller, A. H., W. M. Reisinger, and V. L. Hesli (1990–91) "Public Support for New Political Institutions in Russia, the Ukraine, and Lithuania." *Journal of Soviet Nationalities,* Vol. 1, No. 4, pp. 82–107.

Minturn, L. and J. L. Tapp (1970) *Authority, Rules, and Aggression: A Cross-National Study of Children's Judgments of the Justice of Aggressive Confrontations: Part II.* Washington, D.C.: United States Department of Health, Education, and Welfare.

Morash, M. A. (1978) *Implications of the Theory of Legal Socialization for Understanding the Effect of Juvenile Justice Procedures on Youths.* Ph.D. Dissertation, University of Maryland.

Morash, M. A. (1981) "Cognitive Developmental Theory: A Basis for Juvenile Correctional Reform?" *Criminology,* Vol. 19, No. 3, pp. 360–71.

Morash, M. A. (1982) "Relationships of Legal Reasoning to Social Class, Closeness to Parents, and Exposure to a High Level of Reasoning Among Adolescents Varying in Seriousness of Delinquency." *Psychology Reports,* Vol. 50, pp. 755–60.

Motivans, A. and E. Teague (1992) "Capital Punishment in the Former USSR." *RFE/RL Research Report,* Vol. 1, No. 26, pp. 67–73.

Mussen, P., L. Sullivan, and N. Eisenberg-Berg (1977) "Changes in Political-Economic Attitudes During Adolescence." *Journal of Genetic Psychology,* Vol. 130, pp. 69–76.

Naumov, A. (1990) "Afraid of the Wrong Things." *The Literary Gazette International,* No. 2, p. 16.

Nelsen, E. A., N. Eisenberg, and J. L. Carroll (1982) "The Structure of Adolescents' Attitudes Toward Law and Crime." *The Journal of Genetic Psychology,* Vol. 140, pp. 47–58.

Niles, W. J. (1983) *The Effects of Moral Education on Delinquents and Predelinquents.* Ph.D. Dissertation, Fordham University.

Niles, W. J. (1986) "Effects of a Moral Development Discussion Group on Delinquent and Predelinquent Boys." *Journal of Counseling Psychology,* Vol. 33, No. 1, pp. 45–51.

Nove, A. (1989) *Glasnost' in Action.* Boston: Unwin Hyman.

204 Bibliography

Olcott, M. B. (1990) "Youth and Nationality in the USSR." *Journal of Soviet Nationalities*, Vol. 1, No. 1, pp. 128–39.

Oleszczuk, T. A. (1988) *Political Justice in the USSR: Dissent and Repression in Lithuaina, 1969–1987*. New York: Columbia University Press.

Ovchinskii, V. S. (1989) "Criminal Tendencies in the Youth Environment." *Soviet Sociology*, Vol. 27, No. 4, pp. 88–91.

Palonsky, S. B. and M. G. Jacobson (1982) "The Measurement of Law-Related Attitudes." *Journal of Social Studies Research*, Vol. 6, No. 1, pp. 22–8.

Park, J. C. (1970) *Chicago Suburban and Inner-City Student Opinion and Achievement Related to Law in American Society*. Ph.D. Dissertation, Northwestern University.

Patterson, D. W. and A. Doak (1980) "Constitutional Changes and the Russian Philosophy of Justice." *International Journal of Comparative and Applied Criminal Justice*, Vol. 4, No. 1, pp. 29–35.

Piaget, J. (1932) *The Moral Judgement of the Child*. New York: Kegan, Paul, Trench, Trubner.

Pilon, R. (1992) "Individual Rights, Democracy, and Constitutional Order: On the Foundations of Legitimacy." *The Cato Journal*, Vol. 11, No. 3, pp. 373–90.

Podrabinek, A. (1980) *Punitive Medicine*. Ann Arbor, MI: Karoma Publishers.

Pomeranz, W. (2012) "Twenty Years of Russian Legal Reform." *Demokratizatsiya: The Journal of Post-Soviet Democratization*. No. 2, pp. 141–7.

Portune, R. G. (1965) *An Analysis of Attitudes of Junior High School Pupils Toward Police Officers Applied to the Preparation of a Work of Juvenile Fiction*. Ph.D. Dissertation, University of Cincinnati.

Prepodavanie istori v sredneishkde (eds.) (1978) "On Improving the Organization of Instruction in the Course 'Fundamental Principles of the Soviet State and Law' in the Eighth Grade of General Education Schools." *Soviet Education*, pp. 70–81.

Quigley, J. (1992) "Soviet Criminal Law." *Criminal Law Forum*, Vol. 3, No. 2, pp. 271–87.

Radosevich, M. J. and M. Krohn (1981) "Cognitive Moral Development and Legal Socialization." *Criminal Justice and Behavior*, Vol. 8, No. 4, pp. 401–24.

Rafky, D. M. and R. W. Sealey (1975) "The Adolescent and the Law: A Survey." *Crime and Delinquency*, Vol. 21, pp. 131–8.

Rand, R. (1991) *Comrade Lawyer*. Boulder, CO: Westview Press.

Rawls, J. (1971) *A Theory of Justice*. Cambridge, MA: Harvard University Press.

"Resolution of the USSR Supreme Soviet: On Decisively Stepping Up the Fight Against Crime" (1989) *The Current Digest of the Soviet Press*, Vol. 40, No. 34, p. 34.

Rest, J. R. (1979) *Development in Judging Moral Issues*. Minneapolis: University of Minnesota Press.

Rhodes, M. (1993) "Political Attitudes in Russia." *RFE/RL Research Report*, January 15, Vol. 2, No. 3, pp. 42–4.

Richards, D. A. J. (1981) "Rights, Utility, and Crime." In M. Tonry and N. Morris (eds.) *Crime and Justice*, Vol. 3. Chicago: University of Chicago Press.

Rieber, R. W. and M. Green (1990) "The Psychopathy of Everyday Life: Antisocial Behavior and Social Distress." In R. W. Rieber (ed.) *The Individual, Communication, and Society*. New York: Cambridge University Press, pp. 48–89.

Rigby, T. H. (1983) "A Conceptual Approach to Authority, Power and Policy in the Soviet Union." In T. H. Rigby, A. Brown, and P. Reddaway (eds.) *Authority, Power and Policy in the USSR*. London: Macmillan, pp. 9–31.

Riordan, J. (ed.) (1989) *Soviet Youth Culture*. Bloomington, IN: Indiana University Press.

Bibliography 205

Riordan, J., C. Williams and I. Ilyinsky (1995) *Young People in Post-Communist Russia*. London: Dartmouth Publishing Co.

Rosner, L. S. (1986) *The Soviet Way of Crime*. South Hadley, MA: Bergin & Garvey Publishers, Inc.

Rukavishnikov, V. O. (ed.) (1990) *The Pre-Election Situation: Voters' Opinions*. Moscow: Institute of Sociology, USSR Academy of Sciences.

Rumer, B. Z. (1990) *Soviet Central Asia*. Boston, MA: Unwin Hyman.

Sagi, A. and Z. Eisikovits (1981) "Juvenile Delinquency and Moral Development." *Criminal Justice and Behavior*, Vol. 8, No. 1, pp. 79–93.

Saltzstein, H. and S. Osgood (1975) "The Development of Children's Reasoning About Group Interdependence and Obligation." *The Journal of Psychology*, Vol. 90, pp. 147–55.

Sanjian, A. S. (1991) "Prostitution, the Press, and Agenda-Building in the Soviet Policy Process." In A. Jones et al. (eds.) *Soviet Social Problems*. Boulder, CO: Westview Press, pp. 270–95.

Savitski, V. (1990) "Democratization in the USSR: Toward the Freedom of the Individual through Law and Courts." *Criminal Law Forum*, Vol. 2, No. 1, pp. 85–110.

Schmemann, S. (1992a) "Yeltsin's Team Seems in Retreat as Its Economic Reform Falters." *The New York Times*, August 2.

Schmemann, S. (1992b) "Russia, History and the Struggle Not to Repeat It." *The New York Times*. November 29.

Segal, B. M. (1990) *The Drunken Society*. New York: Hippocrene Books, Inc.

Serio, J. (1992a) *USSR Crime Statistics and Summaries: 1989 and 1990*. Chicago, IL: Office of International Criminal Justice.

Serio, J. (1992b) "Organized Crime in the Soviet Union and Beyond." Unpublished paper.

Shcheckochikhin, Y. (1990) "Where The Mafia Reigns." *The Literary Gazette International*, No. 2, pp. 18–19.

Shelley, L. (1990a) "The Second Economy in the Soviet Union." In M. Los (ed.) *The Second Economy in Marxist States*. London: Macmillan, pp. 11–26.

Shelley, L. (1990b) "Policing Soviet Society: The Evolution of State Control." *Law & Social Inquiry*, Vol. 15, No. 3, pp. 479–520.

Shelley, L. (1991) "Crime in the Soviet Union." In A. Jones et al. (eds.) *Soviet Social Problems*. Boulder, CO: Westview Press.

Shelley, L. (1993) "The Soviet Police and the Rule of Law." In D. Weisburd et al. (eds.) *Police Innovation and Control of Police*. New York: Springer-Verlag.

Shipler, D. K. (1983) *Russia: Broken Idols, Solemn Dreams*. New York: Times Books.

Shipler, D. K. (1990) "A Reporter At Large—Between Dictatorship and Anarchy." *The New Yorker*, June 25, pp. 42–70.

Shlapentokh, V. (1989) *Public and Private Life of the Soviet People*. New York: Oxford University Press.

Shubkin, V. N. (1992) "Youth and Society." *Russian Education and Society*, Vol. 34, No. 7, pp. 6–55.

Siegal, M. (1984) "Diminished Responsibility as a Mitigating Circumstance in Juvenile Offenders' Legal Judgments." *Journal of Adolescence*, Vol. 7, pp. 233–43.

Simis, K. (1982) *USSR: The Corrupt Society*. New York: Simon and Schuster.

Smith, G. B. (1992a) *Soviet Politics: Struggling With Change*. New York: St. Martin's Press.

Smith, G. B. (1992b) "Perestroika and the Procuracy: The Changing Role of the Prosecutor's Office in the former USSR." BJS Discussion Paper. Washington, D.C.: U.S. Department of Justice, Bureau of Justice Statistics, February.

206 Bibliography

Smith, H. (1990) *The New Russians*. New York: Random House.

Solomon, P. H., Jr. (1978) "Specialists in Policymaking: Criminal Policy, 1938–1970." In K. W. Ryavec (ed.) *Soviet Society and the Communist Party*. Massachusetts: University of Massachusetts Press, pp. 153–209.

Solomon, P. H., Jr. (1988–89) "The Role of Defence Counsel in the USSR." *Criminal Law Quarterly*, Vol. 31, pp. 76–93.

Solomon, P. H., Jr. (1990) "Gorbachev's Legal Revolution." *Canadian Business Law Journal*, Vol. 17, No. 2, pp. 184–94.

Solomon, P. H., Jr. (1992a) "Soviet Politicians and Criminal Prosecutions: The Logic of Party Interventions." In J. B. Millar (ed.) *Cracks in the Monolith*. Armonk, NY: M. E. Sharpe, pp. 3–32.

Solomon, P. H., Jr. (1992b) "Legality in Soviet Political Culture: A Perspective on Gorbachev's Reforms." In N. Lampert and G. T. Ritterspom (eds.) *Stalinism: Its Nature and Aftermath*. Armonk, NY: M. E. Sharpe, pp. 260–87.

Solomon, P. H., Jr. (1992c) "Reforming Criminal Law Under Gorbachev: Crime, Punishment, and the Rights of the Accused." In D. Barry (ed.) *Toward the Rule of Law in Russia?* Armonk, NY: M.E. Sharpe, pp. 235–55.

Solzhenitsyn, A. I. (1973) *The Gulag Archipelago*. New York: Harper & Row.

Statesteckeske Dane a Prestupnoste v Strane (Statistical Data and Crime in the Country) (1989) Soviet Ministry of Internal Affairs, Moscow, USSR.

Sukharev, A. (1978) "The Legalistic Education of The Younger Generation." *Soviet Education*, August, pp. 6–21.

Sykes, G. M. and D. Matza (1957) "Techniques of Neutralization: A Theory of Delinquency." *American Sociological Review*, Vol. 22, pp. 665–70.

Tapp, J. L. (1970) "A Child's Garden of Law and Order." *Psychology Today*, December.

Tapp, J. L. (1987a) "The Jury as a Socializing Experience: A Socio-Cognitive View." In R. W. Rieber (ed.) *Advances in Forensic Psychology and Psychiatry: Volume 2*. Norwood, NJ: Ablex Publishing Corp.

Tapp, J. L. (1987b) "Legal Socialization Across Age, Culture, and Context: Psychological Considerations for Children and Adults in the Criminal and Legal Justice Systems." Unpublished paper presented at Rutgers, September.

Tapp, J. L. and L. Kohlberg (1971) "Developing Senses of Law and Legal Justice." *Journal of Social Issues*, Vol. 27, No. 2, pp. 65–91.

Tapp, J. L. and L. Kohlberg (1992) *The Current Digest of the Post-Soviet Press* (Izvestia). April 29 and July 29.

Tapp, J. L. and F. Levine (1974) "Legal Socialization: Strategies for an Ethical Legality." Reprinted from *Stanford Law Review*, Vol. 27, No. 1, by the Board of Trustees of the Leland Stanford Junior University.

Tapp, J. L. and F. Levine (eds.) (1977) *Law, Justice and the Individual in Society*. New York: Holt, Rinehart, & Winston.

Thornburgh, R. (1990) "The Soviet Union and the Rule of Law." *Foreign Affairs*, pp. 13–27.

Thorson, C. (1992) "Toward the Rule of Law: Russia." *RFE/RL Research Report*, Vol. 1, No. 27, pp. 41–9.

Timofeyev, L. (1992) *Russia's Secret Rulers*. New York: Alfred A. Knopf.

Torney, J. V. (1977) "Socialization of Attitudes Toward the Legal System." In J. L. Tapp and F. L. Levine (eds.) *Law, Justice and the Individual in Society*. New York: Holt, Rinehart, & Winston.

Bibliography 207

Treml, V. G. (1991) "Drinking and Alcohol Abuse in the USSR in the 1980s." In A. Jones et al. (eds.) *Soviet Social Problems*. Boulder, CO: Westview Press, pp. 119–36.

Tsurkov, A. (1989) "And from the Sky . . . Snowflakes are Falling Upon Us: The Pamyat Movement in the USSR." In *Nationalism in the USSR*. Amsterdam: Second World Center, pp. 65–7.

Tyler, T. R. (1990) *Why People Obey The Law*. New Haven, CT: Yale University Press.

Tyler, T. R. (2006) *Why People Obey the Law* (2nd edn). New Haven, CT: Yale University Press.

Tyler, T. R. and K. Rasinski (1991) "Procedural Justice, Institutional Legitimacy, and the Acceptance of Unpopular U.S. Supreme Court Decisions: A Reply to Gibson." *Law & Society Review*, Vol. 25, No. 3, pp. 621–30.

Unger, R. M. (1976) *Law in Modern Society*. New York: The Free Press.

Uniform Crime Reports (UCR) (1981–90) Crime in the United States, Federal Bureau of Investigation, US Department of Justice, Washington, D.C.

Vaksberg, A. (1991) *The Soviet Mafia*. New York: St. Martin's Press.

Van den Berg, G. P. (1985) *The Soviet System of Justice: Figures and Policy*. Boston, MA: Martinus Nijhoff Publishers.

Wall, S. and M. Furlong (1985) "Comprehension of Miranda Rights by Urban Adolescents with Law-Related Education." *Psychological Reports*, Vol. 56, pp. 359–72.

Whyte, M. K. (1977) "Child Socialization in the Soviet Union and China." *Studies in Comparative Communism*, Vol. 10, No. 3, pp. 235–59.

Wilson, J. Q. (1993) *The Moral Sense*. New York: The Free Press.

Wilson, R. W. (1981) "Political Socialization and Moral Development." *World Politics*, Vol. 33, No. 3 pp. 153–77.

Wishnevsky, J. (1993) "Russian Constitutional Court: A Third Branch of Government?" *RFE/RL Research Report*, Vol. 2, No. 7, pp. 1–8.

World Affairs (1989) "The Soviet Union on the Brink: Part Two." *World Affairs*, Vol. 152, No. 2.

Yakovlev, A. M. (1979) "Criminological Foundation of the Criminal Process." In M. C. Bassiouni and V. M. Savitski (eds.) *The Criminal Justice System of the USSR*. Springfield, IL: Charles C. Thomas, Publisher, pp. 101–29.

Yakovlev, A. M. (1987) "Criminalization and Stereotypes of Public Consciousness." Translated by S. P. Dunn and E. Dunn. Unpublished abstract presented at Rutgers, September.

Yakovlev, A. M. (1988) "Legal Consciousness as a Subject of Specific Social Research." Unpublished paper.

Yakovlev, A. M. (1990) "Constitutional Socialist Democracy: Dream or Reality?" *Columbia Journal of Transnational Law*, Vol. 28, No. 1, pp. 117–32.

Yakovlev, A. M. (1992a) Cited in Fred Hiatt, "Communist Past Is Put on Trial; Party's Role Is at Center of Court Case in Moscow." Washington Post Foreign Service, July 8.

Yakovlev, A. M. (1992b) *The Bear that Wouldn't Dance: Failed Attempts to Reform the Constitution of the Former Soviet Union*. Manitoba, Canada: Legal Research Institute of the University of Manitoba.

Yakovlev, A. M. (1996) *Striving for Law in a Lawless Land*. Armonk, NY: M. E. Sharpe.

Z (1990) "To the Stalin Mausoleum." *Daedalus*, Vol. 119, No. 1, pp. 295–344.

Zaslayskaia, T. (1987) "The Role of Sociology in Accelerating the Development of Soviet Society." *Soviet Sociology*, pp. 7–25.

208 Bibliography

Zeldes, I. (1980) "Juvenile Delinquency in the USSR: A Criminological Survey." *International Journal of Comparative and Applied Criminal Justice*, Vol. 4, pp. 15–28.

Zeldes, I. (1981) *The Problems of Crime in the USSR*. Springfield, IL: Charles C. Thomas, Publisher.

Ziv, A., A. Shani, and S. Nebenhaus (1975) "Adolescents Educated in Israel and in the Soviet Union: Differences in Moral Judgment." *Journal of Cross-Cultural Psychology*, Vol. 6, No. 1, pp. 108–21.

INDEX

accusatorial system 56
Adler, Nanci 57–8
adolescent personality 76
alcohol abuse 83–4
Alexander II (Tsar) 64
anomie 88, 179
antiparasite laws 54
Antonian, I.U. 77
Arshayskii, A.I. 73, 75
attitudes toward law: authority figures
160; efficacy of the law 156–7;
fairness of the law 155, 157; law
operatives 157; moral validity of
the law 155; own law-abidingness
158; Soviet gender differences in
112–13; wrongfulness of behaviors
156–9
authority figures 148; attitudes of
Russians toward 11, 159–60, 174–5;
attitudes of U.S. and Soviet youth
toward 129–31, 174–5; interaction
with 3–5

Babaev, M.M. 77
baby boom 70
Belikova, G. 31
Bentler, P.M. 36
Berdyaev, Nikolai 16
Berman, Harold 49, 54, 170
black market 22, 30–1, 92–3
Blacks 183
Blasi, Augusto 38, 146

Bronfenbrenner, Urie 43, 47n1, 122,
175, 186
Brown, Don W. 36
Butler, William 71

Cambodia 15
capital punishment 65
Cary, Charles 43
Center for Humanization of the Penal
System 28
Center for Strategic and Global Studies
95
Center for the Study of Public Opinion
28, 189
Chechnya 97
child prostitution 84
China 15
clans 95
Clawson, Robert 43
Clinton, Bill 8
Cloward, Richard 77
Cohn, Ellen 14, 34, 39–41, 100, 145,
155, 164
COL (culture of lawfulness) 4–6, 10
collectivism 16
colored markets 91–2
Communist Party of the Soviet Union
(CPSU) 10, 20, 48, 59, 61, 77–8
conniving to survive 6, 12
Connor, Walter 75–6, 81
constitution: United States 17, 180; of
the USSR 53–4, 59

210 Index

corruption 6, 29–31
counsel for the defense 54–6, 62
counterrevolutionaries 52
Cressey, Donald 97
crime 25–31
crime by analogy 49–50
crime rates 26, 68–71, 73
Criminal Code of the RSFSR 49, 52–3
cross-cultural research 41, 101–10

Dallas Morning News 184
defense lawyers 53–6, 61–2
delinquency 70, 84–5; causes of 74–7
    (alcohol and drug abuse 83–4;
    educational problems 80–1; hypocrisy
    in USSR 77; prostitution 83–4;
    urbanization 82) explanation of 161–3;
    scope of 71–3
delinquency index 153–4, 162
delinquent label 152
deviance 176–9, 185
Deviance in Soviet Society (Connor) 75–6
divorce rate 82
Dobson, Richard 31, 77–9
drug abuse 83–4
drunkards 52
due process 101
Durkheim, Emile 88, 99, 186

educational problems 80–2
efficacy of the law: attitudes of Russians
    toward 156–7, 171; attitudes of U.S.
    and Soviet youth toward 134, 171

Fagan, J. 3–4
fairness of the law: attitudes of Russians
    toward 155, 157, 171; attitudes of U.S.
    and Soviet youth toward 134, 169,
    171; Soviet gender differences in
    attitude about 115
family breakdown 82
Fituni, Leonid 95–6
Fletcher, George P. 51–2, 54, 66
Forschner, B.E. 74–5
France 56
Frankl, Viktor 89
Fundamental Principles of Criminal
    Legislation 54

Gabiani, A. 83
gender differences: in attitudes toward
    authority figures 160; in attitudes
    toward law operatives 156; in attitudes

toward the law 112–13; in efficacy of
    the law 156; in justice and fairness of
    system 115, 156; in knowledge of the
    law 112; in law-abidingness 116–17; in
    legal reasoning levels 113–15, 164,
    185–8; in moral validity of the law
    155; in own law-abidingness 158; in
    wrongfulness of behaviors 156–9
Germany 15, 56
Gilligan, Carol 119
glasnost 9, 20–2, 26, 59, 74, 93, 111
Gluzman, Semyon 19, 57–8
Godson, Roy 4–5
Gorbachev, Mikhail 18, 20–1, 26, 30, 59,
    67, 83, 93, 111, 167, 180–1
Green, Maurice 89, 179
guilt 120–2

Hagan, John 187
Hahn, Jeffrey 43
Hazard, John 21, 63
Hendley, Kathryn 11–12
Hesli, Vicki 186, 188
Hess, R.D. 41, 145
higher education 80
Hirschi, Travis 38
homeless children 70
hooligans 52
Huba, G.J. 36
hypocrisy 6, 78, 86

Il'inskii, I.M. 12, 76–7
Industrial Revolution 70
innocence, presumption of 53–6
Internalization of Legal Values Inventory
    (ILVI) 103–10, 190–5
Italy 15
Ivanov, L.O. 42
Izvestia 73

Jacobson, Michael 36
Jews 53
judges: independence of 10–11, 61;
    Soviet-era 50, 60
juvenile corrections colonies 102, 109
Juviler, P. 74–5

Keller, William 43
KGB 57
Khrushchev, Nikita 53
knowledge of law: comparison of U.S.
    and Soviet youth 117–18; Soviet
    gender differences in 112

Kogan, Victor 50, 53
Kohlberg, Lawrence 2, 16, 33, 37–8, 119, 164, 186
Kohn, Melvin 104
Komsomol 43, 76–7, 80
Kornai, Janos 183
Kutsev, G.F. 78

Lampert, Nicholas 62–3
law 48–9
law-abidingness 146; creation of sense of 3; Soviet gender differences in 116–17
law operatives: attitudes of Russians toward 157, 171; attitudes of U.S. and Soviet youth toward 134, 171
Law-Related Education Evaluation Project 35–6, 192
legal consciousness, dimensions of 45
legal context 39
legal development 167–9
legal indoctrination 182
legal knowledge 34–7, 168–9
legal nihilism 4, 9–12, 52
legal reasoning 38–40, 99, 141; and behavior 152–4; comparison of U.S. and Soviet youth 118; and delinquency 184; higher-order 2–3; level I 142; level II 142–5; level III 145; of Russian youth today 144–54; Soviet gender differences in 113–15, 185–8; status variables 149–52
legal socialization 14–18, 44–7; attitude and status correlates of 123–39; comparative levels 169; cross-cultural and comparative studies of 40–1, 101–10; definition of 32; and juvenile delinquency 37–40; at macro level 18–20; in Russia 41–4, 164; theoretical perspectives of 32–4; through legal knowledge 34–7; update on research 2–6; U.S.-Soviet contextual differences in 180–8
Lempert, David 62–3
Lenin, V.I. 6, 21
Levada Center 11
Levine, F.J. 35, 37–8
Lipman, Masha 6–7
Liubery 80
Lubin, Nancy 87, 90

Mafia (Soviet) 17, 28–9, 92–8, 166
Makarenko, Anton 16

Malia, Martin ("Z") 21–2
Markowitz, Alan 36
Mastering Legal Values (MLV) questionnaire 103–9, 190–5
materialism 84
Matza, David 28
McKay, Henry 77
media, independence of 10
Medvedev, Dmitri 9–11
Mexico 5–6
Mickiewicz, Ellen 24
Miller, Arthur 186, 188
Ministry of Internal Affairs 57–8, 71, 74, 83, 93
Minturn, L. 145
moral authority, centers of 5
moral development 34, 37–8
The Moral Sense (Wilson) 184
moral validity of the law 146; attitudes of Russians toward 155, 171–4; attitudes of U.S. and Soviet youth toward 136, 171–4
moral weightlessness 86–90
Morash, Merry Ann 185
Moscow News 27
murder rates 27

naglost 98
The New Yorker 181
New York Times 27–9, 43, 88
Nikiforov, Alexander 195
nomenklatura 94

Ohlin, Lloyd 77
Olcott, Martha 12, 23
Oleszczuk, Thomas 57
opportunity theory of delinquency 77
organized crime 17, 29, 92–8, 167; *see also* Mafia
own law-abidingness: attitudes of Russians toward 159, 175–6; attitudes of U.S. and Soviet youth toward 138–9, 175–6

Palonsky, Stuart 36
Pamyat 23
parasitism 53
parents: attitudes of Russian youth toward 159, 175; attitudes of U.S. and Soviet youth toward 129–30
peers: attitudes of Russian youth toward 159, 175; attitudes of U.S. and Soviet youth toward 120, 131

212 Index

peoples' assessors 50, 64–5
peoples' courts 63–4
perestroika 9, 20, 22
Piaget, J. 33
Piquero, A. R. 3–4
police power 120
Pomeranz, William 9
power-control theory 187–8
power to punish 119–21
Pravda 27, 84–5
preliminary investigation 55
presumption of innocence 53–6
pretrial detention 63
procedural justice 3–4
procuracy 58
property offenses 73
prostitution 84
psychiatric detention 57–8
public opinion 22
punishment 65
Putin, Vladimir 8–10, 12

Quigley, John 54

racketeers 95
Rafky, David 36, 103
Rawls, John 25
Receiving and Distribution Center
    (Moscow) 106–7
Rechsstaat 20
reforms 20, 30, 59; counsel for the
    defense 61–2; criminal punishment
    64–5; judicial independence 60–1;
    pretrial detention 62–3; trial by jury
    62–4
registered crimes 68
reported crimes 68
reporting (crime) system 71–2
Rieber, Robert 31, 179
Rigby, T.H. 19, 170
right to counsel 53–6, 62
Riordan, Jim 77–8
Rosner, Lydia 86, 177
rule by law 8–9
rule of law 5–8, 20–5, 44, 46, 56, 66;
    Soviet rejection of 50–1, 53, 60, 170;
    young people's understanding of 114,
    136, 174
Russia: nationalities of 165n1; post-Soviet
    6–13, 20
Russian Constitutional Court 61, 166
Russian Orthodox Church 10

Russian Revolution 57, 64, 70
Russians 23–5

Sakharov, Andrei 33, 53
Sanjian, A.S. 84
Savitski, Valeri 52
Sealey, Ronald 36, 103
Segal, Boris 43, 44, 177
self-regulation 3, 11
separation of powers 10
Serbsky Institute of Psychiatry 57
Serio, Joseph 98
shadow economy 30–1
Shaw, Clifford 77
Shelley, Louise 17, 26, 87, 90
Shipler, David 86, 176, 181
Shlapentokh, Vladimir 30
Shliapochnikov, A.S. 77
Shokin, A. 31
Shubkin, V.N. 79
Simis, Konstantine 87, 177
Smith, Gordon B. 17, 49, 54–6, 90,
    170
Snezhnevsky, Andrei V. 57
social control theory 38
social dangerousness 52–4
social institutions 75–6
Solomon, Peter H., Jr. 28, 50–1, 55
Solzhenitsyn, Aleksandr 22, 53
Soviet Congress of People's Deputies 181
Soviet Interview Project 51
Soviet Union: breakup of 1, 6–7;
    colored markets in 91–2; crime rates
    in 26, 69–70, 72–3; hypocrisy in 6, 78,
    86; legal system in 48–9 (crime by
    analogy 49–50; political abuse of
    psychiatry 57–8; presumption of
    innocence/right to counsel 53–6;
    procuracy 58; reform of 59–65;
    social dangerousness 52–4; telephone
    law 10, 50, 52); nationalities of
    165n1
Stalin, Joseph 6, 15–16, 53, 65
Sutherland, Edwin 97
Sykes, Gresham 28

Tapp, June Louin 2, 34–5, 37–8, 40–1,
    103, 119, 145, 194
Tapp–Levine Rule Law Interview 103,
    186, 191
teachers: attitudes of Russian youth
    toward 159, 161–2, 174; attitudes of

U.S. and Soviet youth toward 121, 128, 148, 174
telephone law 10, 50, 52, 61
Thorson, Carla 61
Timofeyev, Lev 86
trial by jury 63–4
Tyler, Tom 3–4

unemployment 23
Uniform Crime Reports 72
United States: corruption in 29; due process in 27; liberalism of 16–17
university system 81
urbanization 82
USSR *see* Soviet Union

Vaksberg, Arkady 87
Van den Berg, G.P. 65
Vilks, A.I. 73, 75
violent crimes 27

Washington Post 184
White, Susan 14, 34, 39–41, 100, 145, 155, 164
Whyte, Martin 43
Wilson, James Q. 183–4
women: crime rates of 73; *see also* gender differences
World War II 70
wrongfulness of behaviors: attitudes of Russians toward 156–9; attitudes of U.S. and Soviet youth toward 136, 138

Yakovlev, Alexander 12–13, 40, 44, 76, 90–2, 103, 176, 194
Yeltsin, Boris 8, 20, 30, 60–1, 167

"Z" *see* Malia, Martin
Zaslayskaia, T. 75
Zeldes, Ilya 70, 77